The Life and
Zen Haiku Poetry
of Santoka Taneda

The Life and
Zen Haiku Poetry
of Santoka Taneda

Japan's Most Beloved Modern Haiku Poet

Sumita Oyama
Translated with an Introduction by
William Scott Wilson
Illustrations by Gary Miller Haskins

TUTTLE Publishing
Tokyo │ Rutland, Vermont │ Singapore

Contents

This translation is dedicated to Robin D. Gill.

Sumita Oyama (1899–1994) was born in Okayama Prefecture, Japan. He practiced haiku and Zen for over sixty years. He was a prolific writer, publishing many books on the haiku poet Santoka Taneda. Oyama was a good friend and benefactor of Santoka, and studied free haiku under the poet Seisensui Ogiwara.

William Scott Wilson has published more than twenty books that have been translated into more than twenty foreign languages. His first book, a translation of *Hagakure*, an eighteenth century treatise on samurai philosophy, was featured in the film *Ghost Dog*, directed by Jim Jarmusch. He was awarded a Commendation from the Foreign Ministry of Japan in 2005 and inducted into the Order of the Rising Sun in 2015.

Prologue

The fifty-sixth hexagram of the ancient Chinese divination text, the *I Ching*, is *Lu*, defined as "journey," "travel" or "traveler." It is composed of two trigrams: "fire" and "mountain." The lower trigram, "mountain," is explained as signifying good, stopping, or looking backward. Its virtue is stopping in peace. The upper trigram, fire, is defined as "separation," or possibly "nightingale." Its virtue is bright wisdom. Thus, fire over the mountain.

Exactly when or why Santoka took his pen name, which is literally "Fire on the Head of the Mountain" (山頭火), is unclear, but it was a prescient choice, as he would spend most of his life after the age of forty traveling, saying goodbye to his friends, looking back on his character, and composing haiku, much like the elusive nightingale, which is sometimes heard but rarely seen.

According to the *I Ching*, if the traveler is steadfast, he will meet with good fortune; and with timing and faith, he will become great. Certainly, Santoka's personal life was a mess, but through perseverance and faith in his only ability—to write poetry—this lonely traveler lit up the Japanese literary sky like a fire over a mountain.

Preface

Those who do not know the meaning of weeds, do not know the mind of nature. Weeds grasp their own essence and express its truth.

Santoka's diary, August 8, 1940

This book portrays the life of the haiku poet and Zen priest Santoka, a man who could well identify with weeds: unruly, unkempt, taking sustenance from wherever he could find it, and inexorably expressing his own truth with the small irregular blossoms of what might be called "free haiku." Like a weed, he was inimical to restraint—in both his life and poetry, which he accounted for as indivisible. "We have to explain ourselves, not control ourselves," he wrote.

As a responsible human being, Santoka was hopeless. Having left his wife and child, he suddenly became a Buddhist priest. Unable to stay in the confines of a temple, he hit the road. When not on the road or staying over at someone's house, he lived in small huts paid for by his friends and apprentices. One of these "hermitages" was finally so broken down that his biographer punned that it might have been called the home of a *haijin* (廃人) or abandoned person, rather than that of a *haijin* (俳人), or haiku poet. He was sometimes found so drunk that he could only make it back to his hermitage with the help of a friendly neighbor. By his own admission, he was incapable of really doing anything other than wandering on his own two feet and writing his own verses. These two, with his Buddhist vows and a hopeless love of sake, made up the karma he was determined to follow through.

I first became interested in Santoka's eccentric, generally technique-less poetry during the late 1960s, reading through R. H. Blyth's *History of Haiku*, while living in a small village in Mino, Japan, in a thatched hut not much better, I think, than Santoka's Gochu-an hermitage. Built around the year 1700, it was a typical tradition-al peasant's house with walls of clay and straw, and a roof of thick miscanthus thatch. With low mountains almost up to the front yard and a small Buddhist temple across the nearby stream, it seemed the perfect place to absorb the material I was reading. During the rainy season, as I daily rearranged the pots collecting the rainwater drip-ping through the thatch, Santoka's haiku were never far from mind.

> *My rainhat's*
> *leaking*
> *too?*

Not long afterward, I discovered a copy of Sumita Oyama's *Haijin Santoka no shogai* (Life of the Haiku Poet Santoka)[1]—the work trans-lated here—in a Nagoya bookstore, a beautifully written volume that not only covered the poet's wandering and sometimes chaotic life, but also included many more of his haiku than available in Blyth's collection. It is, in this translator's opinion, a fascinating look into a beloved poet's character, as well as a minor classic of Japanese liter-ature. Eventually I was able to find Oyama's four-volume *Santoka no chosakushu* (Collection of the Literary Work of Santoka),[2] which included Santoka's *Isso-an nikki* (Diary of the One-Grass Hut),[3] also translated in the appendix to this book. This short, three-month dia-ry contains the poet's views on everything from writing verse to cook-ing rice, his anxieties about his inability to live an ordered life, and a number of wonderful short anecdotes concerning his last days. To-gether, these two works give a fuller image of this mostly wandering shabby man—once a literary prodigy in college—walking through the fields and back roads of Japan, looking under hedges for some shy wild flower, and always finding, as was his wont, himself.

Sumita Oyama (1899–1994) was one of Santoka's greatest friends and benefactors. A minor government official, an educator and a serious student of Zen Buddhism, he was also a prodigious author, writing books and articles on Far Eastern philosophy, on literary fig-ures such as Basho, Ryokan and Toson Shimazaki, and, a miscellany of his own country in his book *Nihon no aji* (A Taste of Japan).[4] He lived the latter part of his life in Matsuyama on the island of Shikoku, not far from Santoka's last hermitage, the One-Grass Hut.

There are always a number of people who have given their help, either editorially or spiritually, consciously or unconsciously, in any one work. For this one volume, it must be stated first that the translation itself would have never been possible without the extraordinary generosity of my late friend, Takashi Ichikawa, who provided me at his own cost with many of the works in the original listed in the bibliography. He was a benefactor and mentor beyond compare. A special thanks to Ms Yasuko Imai, who also helped with providing me with books hard to obtain. I would also like to thank those friends who have encouraged and spiritually supported me over the years, and especially concerning this project: Kate Barnes, Gary Haskins, Jim Brems, John Siscoe, Jack Whistler, Dr. Daniel Medvedov, Dr. Justin Newman, Tom Levidiotis, Bill Durham Roshi, Professor Steven Heine, and especially my wife, Emily, who has patiently proofread this and other of my manuscripts over the years. To my late professors, Noburu Hiraga and Richard McKinnon, I owe a deep bow of thanks for all they tried to teach me concerning every aspect of Japanese language and culture. I also owe a special debt of gratitude to Sean Michael Wilson, Barry Lancet, Prof. Masako Kubota, Nanae Tamura, Terufusa Fujioka, Yasuhiro Ota, and Tsurugi Takata for helping me find the places so important to Santoka in Kyushu and Shikoku; and to my editor at Tuttle Publishing, Cathy Layne, who has patiently seen this project through to the end. Finally, I am profoundly grateful to Masakaze Oyama, who kindly gave us the rights to translate and publish his father's book in this English translation.

—William Scott Wilson

Translator's Notes
1. 俳人山頭火の生涯.
2. 山頭火著作集.
3. 一草庵日記.
4. 日本の味.

Introduction
by William Scott Wilson

Santoka was born on December 3, 1882, in present-day Hachioji, Yamaguchi Prefecture, at the extreme southwest of Honshu, the largest island of the Japanese archipelago, at a time when Japan was still in the early stages of transition from its traditionalist past to its position as an energetic modern state. He was the first son of Takejiro Takeda (twenty-seven years old at that time) and his wife Fusa (twenty-three). Takejiro owned a considerable amount of land at this point in his life, and by all accounts was an amiable, expansive, and generous man who liked to dabble in local politics. He did not drink, but was quick to spend money and had a special love for the company of geishas. Fusa was known to be loving but high-strung. Three years later a daughter was born, and in another two years, a second son. The family would seem to have been doing well, but on March 3, 1892, Fusa threw herself into the old family well while her husband was out on a pleasure trip with one of his mistresses. In what was one of the greatest traumas of his life, the eleven-year-old Santoka was present as the body of his mother was brought up from the well. He never got over this event, and in all of his later years on the road when he carried all of his belongings in two small rattan suitcases, his mother's mortuary tablet was always with him, put up in a place of honor in whatever small hut he stayed. The following year, his younger brother was given in adoption to a wealthy family in a nearby village.

Santoka was an excellent student and was literary-minded from his early teens, even publishing a slender magazine with some other students at the age of fifteen. In 1903, at the age of twenty-one, he entered the literature department of the prestigious Waseda University, where he was hailed as a gifted poet. After two years, however, he withdrew from school and eventually returned home, officially a victim of "neurasthenia." Another likely cause, not so official, but publicly known, was his father's incompetent balancing of the family funds and his numerous mistresses. This was the end of Santoka's formal education.

In 1907, Takejiro made the misstep of acquiring the Yamato Sake Brewery in a nearby village; and, as a moral duty, Santoka was bound to help his father in the family business. It would not be an excellent choice for an open-hearted and open-handed philanderer, and a son whose only thoughts were of poetry. Two years later, Takejiro seems to have pressured Santoka into starting a family by having him marry a Miss Sato Sakino from Wada Village in the same prefecture. There is a photograph of the young couple taken soon after their marriage which shows Sakino as a beautiful young woman, dressed in a simple striped kimono, hair pulled back into the oval bun that was fashionable at that time, and with a look that seems to be focused inward, perhaps already considering the disasters that lay ahead and how they might be dealt with. She was later to state that there were four disasters to Santoka's life: the suicide of his mother, his having a wife and child, and his love affair with sake. She did not elaborate on number four. Their son, Takeshi, was born in August of the following year.

In the meantime, Santoka was busy with literature. The year after his son was born, now at the age of thirty, he published a translation of Turgenev and some of his own haiku in the magazine, *Seinen*,[1] and in the autumn of that year, traveled to the city of Iwakuni to associate with other poets who lived there. It was at this point that he took the literary name "Santoka," forever dropping his given name, Shoichi. In 1913, he became a student of the well-known haiku poet, Seisensui Ogiwara, a man two years younger than himself, who, along with other poets of the time, encouraged haiku writers to free themselves of the seventeen-syllable format and the required season word. Two of Seisensui's poems:

> *Returning*
> *   with mushrooms from the woods behind;*
> *sun shining on tatami.*

> *Snow*
> *   falling on the water, falling*
> *inside the water.*

Santoka's poems now began appearing in the magazine *So'un*[2] and the poets he met through this avant-garde publication would be his friends and supporters for the rest of his life.

In the spring of 1916, two major events occurred for Santoka. In March, he became one of the haiku editors for *So'un*, an elevation that brought him broader contact with various poets and created the necessity of looking at poems more critically. At the same time, it indicated to the others the esteem in which his abilities were held by the senior editors. He did not have much time to savor this happy situation because the following month, the family sake business went bankrupt. This was due in large part to the sake being allowed to sour in the vats for two years running while Takejiro spent more money on mistresses and Santoka attended to his poetry. This disaster sent Takejiro fleeing to another town, and sent Santoka and his wife and child to Kumamoto on the island of Kyushu, where he had a number of literary friends who might help him through this unfortunate time. By May, he and Sakino had opened a combination used-book store and frame shop, which he called the Garakuta, literally meaning "junk," but using the kanji characters for "many elegant amusements" (雅楽多). Two years later, his younger brother hanged himself on Mount Atago during the first days of summer at the age of thirty-five.

By October of 1919, the inability to sit still that was to push Santoka on for the rest of his life was beginning to show, and he left his wife and child in Kumamoto and traveled to Tokyo. With the help of friends, he found lodging there and employment in a cement testing company, a job that he quit at the first opportunity. In less than a year he changed residences three times, and on November 11, 1920, divorced Sakino (at the request of her family), removing her from his family register. This changed their actual relationship very little, for Sakino—and eventually their son—would continue to help Santoka out with finances, food or clothing. She continued to run the Garakuta and brought up their son on her own.

Santoka continued to live in Tokyo for another three years until he was literally shaken out. For two years he worked as a Tokyo city employee, in the end making a decent salary and keeping his job, even though his father died during that time.

At the end of 1922, Santoka quit his job at the Tokyo City Hall, but continued on with his bohemian life there. Where he was exactly on September 1, 1923, is unclear, but when the dust finally settled on the Great Kanto Earthquake which killed over 130,000 people in Tokyo that day, Santoka was among the survivors. Taking flight from the fires and confusion that followed the devastating tremors, he was, oddly, mistaken for a member of the Communist Party and imprisoned. By the end of September, the police recognized their mistake, and Santoka returned to Kumamoto as fast as he could.

Symbolic expression is impossible without stepping into the symbolic world.

Diary, August 18, 1940

Just around the time of his forty-third birthday, Santoka undertook one of the deciding acts of his life: a drunken standoff between himself and a streetcar. The streetcar screeched to a halt, a crowd formed, but a complete stranger whisked the confused man off to a Zen temple, from which he never really returned home. In 1925 he had his head shaved, and became a Zen Buddhist priest.

Santoka was soon put in charge of an unoccupied temple, the Zuisenji—popularly called the Mitori Kannon—in the village of Ueki in Kumamoto Prefecture. Here his responsibilities were to beg in the nearby villages, establish a Sunday school and night school (according to the needs of the families supporting the temple), and provide the boys and girls of the village with religious instruction. By all accounts, he made great efforts to do so.

But by April of 1926, Santoka was no longer able to endure the solitary temple life in the mountains and forests. In the introduction to his second collection of poems called *Somokuto* (The Pagoda of Grasses and Trees),[3] he writes, "Shouldering my insolvable doubts, I left on a trip of wandering and begging." But there is some question as to what this actually meant. To his friends, Santoka told the story of a beautiful widow who appeared with her pillow at his temple one night, insisting that they "exchange vows." Santoka declared that he had remained silent and simply sat in zazen, and that the widow had returned sadly down the mountain. His friends, however, doubted this story and thought that he had likely had a liaison with her for a while. Unfortunately, he burned all of his journals from this period, so there is little else to go on, but it would not be inconsistent with the rest of his life if he had simply gotten tired of living a life isolated from friends.

And so at the age of forty-five, Santoka embarked on a journey of begging, writing haiku, conversing with Buddhist priests, and traveling about with no real fixed home for more than seven years. And if he did not follow the first dictum of the well-known "rules

of poetical pilgrimage" (行脚提) ascribed to Basho[4]—"Do not sleep more than one night in the same lodging"—to the letter, he certainly followed it in spirit. During this time he traveled extensively through Kyushu, Shikoku and southwestern Honshu, stopping at inns when he could afford it, at friends' homes when he could not, at temples, at hot springs, in train stations or, if everything else failed, out in the open. Twice during this period, he stopped for extended stays at the Garakuta, once for more than a few months while suffering from chronic prolapse of the anus. Sakino, as always, fed him, repaired his clothes, and helped him on his way.

Although it must be said that Santoka relied heavily on his friends' generosity, as a Zen priest his fundamental source of income was from traditional begging from door to door, to which he dedicated a number of hours each day. This was a precarious way of making a living, and for Santoka it was met with various degrees of success.

For example, one cold morning Santoka was begging and received unexpectedly generous gifts. Carried away by his good luck, he started intoning the Heart Sutra in front of a large house when suddenly an old lady came out and yelled, "It's bad luck to see a Buddhist priest in the morning!" and threw a bucket of water on him. He noted later that he was soaked right down to his loin cloth and shivered the rest of the day, but never got mad.

On another occasion, when he was begging in northern Kyushu, the weather suddenly turned cold. It started to snow, and people put their heavy rain shutters down so he was unable to beg. Going on to some fishing villages, at dusk he found himself on a street full of brothels, and to his delight found that the prostitutes there were quite generous with alms. Once again carried away, he hired some of the women and spent the night drinking sake and singing, only to wake up the following morning with his companions sound asleep on either side. Chagrined that he had broken the Buddhist precepts once again, he grabbed his robes and went running out into the cold.

> *I walk on,*
> > *the cold wind continually*
> > *scolding me.*

Again, once in late autumn when the rice had already been cut, Santoka was begging in a farming area of Miyazaki Prefecture, stopped in front of a large thatched farmhouse, and began intoning a scripture. An old lady came out of the kitchen to see what was going on, and filled his begging bowl with strong potato wine from a jar she carried. Santoka naturally drank his fill and soon fell asleep. He later woke up with a cricket chirping in his ear, and found that he hadn't gotten far from the farmhouse, but had passed out on the path between the rice paddies. He found out later that the old lady had put a straw mattress over him to keep him from the cold.

> *Drunk,*
> > *I was sleeping*
> > *with a cricket!*

Sometime during the summer of 1932, Santoka must have begun to feel the need for a more settled life. About a year and a half earlier he had stayed temporarily in a room on the second floor of a friend's house in Kumamoto where he had been able to concentrate on writing and had even produced a literary magazine on a small mimeograph machine he worked himself. But now he was looking for a place of his own. In late August of that year, one of his poet friends in the town of Ogori, near the southwestern tip of Honshu, showed him a deserted house at the edge of the nearby village of Yaashi. A few days later they went to inspect it again, and on September 7, Santoka made the decision that would begin another period of his life—not completely off the road, but with a place to come home to—and declared that he would stay. His friends immediately started in on the repairs and reconstruction, and on September 20, Santoka took up residence in the hermitage he would call the Go-chu-an, (其中庵), The Hermitage among Them.

Santoka had a special affection for the Kannon Sutra, or the Sutra of Avalokitesvara, which forms the twenty-fifth chapter of the Lotus Sutra (also called The Chapter on the Universal Gate). In this chapter it is explained how the bodhisattva Avalokitesvara (Kanzeon in Japanese), or the Hearer of the World's Sounds, has the power to help anyone, no matter their status or degree of sinfulness or purity, if that person will only think on the bodhisattva's name with all of his or her heart. One section in particular seems to have captured Santoka's imagination:

> If the three-thousand-great-thousand-fold world were filled with hateful robbers, and there were a chief merchant who was leading a number of other merchants carrying costly jewels over a dangerous road; and if there were one among them who called out, "Good sons! Do not be afraid! If with one heart you will only intone the name of the bodhisattva Avalokitesvara, this bodhisattva will be able to remove your fear, and will do so for all sentient beings . . .

It was from the line, "If there were one among them who called out . . ." (其中一人作是唱言) that Santoka saw himself (the one among them) and saw what his new hermitage would be for him: a source of infinitesimal succor. And so it would be for the next six years.

The hermitage was set at the foot of some small hills; peaceful but not lonely: he could see the lights of his neighbor's house across the vegetable fields through the leaves of the trees, but could not hear their voices. Camellias and persimmon trees were all about, fruit was just beginning to ripen on the latter, and spider lilies were beginning to bloom. Inside, the house had a clay-floored kitchen, two four-and-a-half-mat rooms, one three-mat room and a bathroom (toilet). Along the southern doors to the interior four-and-a-half-mat room was a verandah where he could sun himself from autumn through winter. Not too far from the kitchen were some Chinese date trees,[5] and just below them, a small shallow well about three to four feet (one meter) deep. The water was not quite clear and a little white, but tasted good and was enough for one person to live on.

On the day Santoka moved in, he borrowed a cart from a sake shop and carried over his belongings. The shelf above the clothes closet immediately became the Buddhist altar, and here he put his mother's mortuary tablet, a wooden carving of Kannon, the Buddhist bodhisattva of compassion, and a small bowl he had picked up along the road which he now filled with ashes and used as a censer.

Santoka immediately began to enjoy his new life: he became familiar with the land, worked hard on writing verses, and never missed his three o'clock worship. On the east side of the house there was an area for a garden, and he cultivated a small field and planted vegetables, borrowing a hoe from friends and receiving seeds from the nearby agricultural school. When he had become a Buddhist monk, he had received the name Koho (耕畝), literally "to cultivate furrows," and this might be thought to have symbolized his need to cultivate his mind and pull out the weeds. Now he was cultivating the earth as well, and found that one activity fit the other.

Along with becoming more familiar with the land, having one settled place to live opened a number of new activities to Santoka, all of which would be reflected in his writing. First, perhaps, was a new intimacy with cooking. Again, we turn to his poetry:

> *Meek of heart,*
> *   the rice*
> *bubbled away.*

> *Eating it with all my heart;*
> *   my meal*
> *of rice.*

> *I humbly received it,*
> *   it was enough,*
> *and put down my chopsticks.*

Besides rice, Santoka's taste in food ran to the very simple—usually fresh vegetables and fruit. One vegetable mentioned often in his journals, however, was *chisha*, a kind of lettuce that is described as having a simpler taste than Western varieties, which he liked dressed with vinegar and miso.

Another advantage of having his own place was that now others—his friends and disciples for the most part—had a place where they could come to visit him, and, despite the complaints of loneliness that fill his journals, he often *did* have visitors when not out on the road himself. Santoka attached great value to these visits; he was a man who by his own account did not believe in tomorrow, so he considered each visit the chance of a lifetime. This is the philosophy of the Way of Tea, which considers each occasion for tea as "One lifetime, one meeting" (一期一会). In this way, Santoka happily greeted his fifty-second birthday as the master of the Gochu-an.

Even before the New Year, Santoka had begun to travel a bit, but did not go far. These were mostly begging trips, visiting old friends and attending festivals, but he also stayed at home working on his poetry, and even sent out the fourth, fifth and sixth editions of the poetry anthology, *Sanbaku.*[6]

On March 18, 1933, Santoka was visited for the first time by Sumita Oyama, the man who would become his biographer as well as one of his best friends. They had communicated by postcard a little before this time, and now Oyama made the trip from Hiroshima to meet this eccentric man.

Sumita recorded some of his first impressions of Santoka on this evening, such as this one, after they had finished eating:

He stepped down into the kitchen and washed up the utensils. He had a warped bucket in which it appeared that he had saved the water used for washing the rice rather than throwing it out. In that he washed the chawan bowls and the rest. Having

washed, dried and turned the utensils upside down on the shelf,
he now took the bucket of water in which the rice and every-
thing else had been washed, and dampened a rag for the inside
of the hermitage. He then briskly wiped down the verandah, the
pillars and the doorsill. This done, he picked up the bucket, went
out the back door, and poured the water over the vegetables.
In the Zen sect there are strict regulations concerning water, as
exemplified by the phrases "At the Eiheiji, a half ladle of water,"
and "At the spring of the Soto sect, a drop of water." With one
bucket of water, Santoka washed the rice, the chawan, wiped
up with a damp cloth, and provided nourishment for the vege-
tables. Ultimately he put it to use four times.

Later, they were joined by another friend and drank a large bottle
of sake; it is easy to imagine that many visits by friends were expe-
rienced in just this way. Santoka had a reputation as a great talker,
which must have given the insects and other small animals outside
a good bit to listen to as poets and friends conversed into the night.

About three months later, Santoka was reading the *Hekiganroku*
(*The Blue Cliff Record*),[7] a book of Zen koans, and was struck by
Unmon's phrase, "Every day is a good day" (日々是好日). He de-
cided it was time to write down the "Three Regulations of the Go-
chu-an." This he did, and posted them on the wall for his guests:

1. *Those who like hot or sweet foods had better bring some*
   with them.
2. *You're free to dance and sing, but such activities should be*
   as gentle as the spring breezes and the autumn waters.
3. *No arrogance, putting on airs, or melancholy allowed. You*
   should have the mind of "the one among them."

Reading through Santoka's journals, one feels that Regulation #3
was actually for his own daily attention.

Once again, it did not take long for Santoka's wanderlust to push
him out onto the road, and the next number of years were charac-
terized by journeys, returns to the Gochu-an to receive guests and

recuperate, drinking and writing. Although he tended to keep his wandering to Shikoku and Kyushu, this next year (1934) he traveled on to Nagoya and Kyoto, once getting completely lost in the deep snows of the Kiso Road and being hospitalized for a week.

His writing had always been prodigious. In July 1932 he had published his first poetry collection, *Hachinoko* (The Begging Bowl).[8] In November 1934, his second collection, *Somokuto* (The Pagoda of Grasses and Trees), appeared. Now, in February of 1935, *Sangyo suigyo* (Traveling the Mountains, Traveling the Rivers),[9] was published, and he was getting national attention. Less than six months later, on August 7, he tried to commit suicide. What led to this, or what really happened is vague. His journal on August 6 reads, "If it's clear, fine; if it rains, fine. Anything and everything is fine." Understandably, there are no entries for the next three days, but on August 10 we read:

My second birthday. Bright again with an evening glow. The oneness of life and death; the union of nature and the self.

It finally happened; I fainted. Fortunately or unfortunately, it was raining, so I got hit by the rain and naturally regained consciousness. I slipped off the verandah and fell on my face in the middle of the weeds, and so got my face, legs and arms scratched up. I'm pretty close to being insensitive to pain, but I couldn't even move for a few days, and drank only water. I was constantly and painfully aware that you reap just what you sow, and wandered between life and death.

This is the passage I wrote to a good friend:

To put it properly, I didn't faint; it was an attempted suicide. I lied in my letters to S-san and K-san. Please forgive me. Even I, before committing suicide, would like to clear up at least part of the debts I owe by myself, and I was unable to ask anyone to send money. At any rate, both life and death have passed away. I got intoxicated on an overdose of Calmotin, struggled in my unconsciousness, and threw up. That was coming right to the edge of the precipice and having an unprecedented resurrection. I was looking death square in the face.

And then he simply continued on, noting little more than that he grew a goatee a week later as a commemoration of returning to life. His friends came in to check in on him, but he was almost immediately back to his usual wandering routine.

With the coming year he was constantly on the road, and was visiting friends in Hachiman when his fourth collection of poetry, *Zasso fukei* (The Landscape of Sundry Weeds),[10] was published in February. From there he went on to Osaka, Kyoto and Nagoya, and then farther north to Kamakura. He slowly continued on, and June 26 found him in Hiraizumi in Iwate Prefecture, the farthest point

north he was ever to go, all the while staying with friends or at hot springs or temples, or sleeping out in the open. On July 4, he walked into the Eiheiji, the Zen temple in Echizen founded by Dogen in the thirteenth century, and stayed for three days of prayer and meditation. His diaries indicate that he did a good bit of self-reflection while he was there, but by the fourth day he was ready for a drink in nearby Fukui, and on the following day took the night train back to Osaka. He was back home by the last week of the month.

It is at about this point in the diaries we find Santoka more and more at Yuda, a hot spring not too far a walk from the Gochu-an.

Santoka loved to bathe and he loved to drink, and this was a convenient place for both. While he continued to take short trips back and forth from his hermitage, a pattern was beginning, and he spent a week there in May of the following year, drinking, bathing, and complaining to himself about being old and ugly. Friends, poets and professors continued to visit him at his hermitage, and in late August, his collection of verses, *Kaki no ha* (Persimmon Leaves)[11] was published. In September, desperate for cash, he landed a job at a lumber store, but finding himself unfit for employment, quit after four days and went to drink with friends in Shimonoseki and Moji. He continued his trips to Yuda until on November 1 he took a room and stayed drunk for five days, in the end locked up by the police for going on a spree with no money to pay for it. Brought to the prosecutor's office a few days later, he promised to pay back his debts, and was released. His son, Takeshi, now filling in for Sakino, wired him the money and the debt was paid. Two weeks later, he was back with money from a royalty check, but with new discipline: one bath, one drink, go home. With even more money from Takeshi a month later, he stayed four days, but only for the healing baths.

Now fifty-six, Santoka ushered in the New Year with the same pattern: trips to Yuda, short begging journeys, seeking out friends, but all the while writing some haiku nearly every day. As he wrote in his essay, "Dokushin" (Reflecting):[12]

> I am *troubled by day to day life. I send off yesterday or greet today with either a full stomach or an empty one. It will probably be the same tomorrow . . . no, probably right up until the day I die. Still, I write verses every day and night. I never neglect writing poems even if I don't eat or drink. To put it another way, I can write poetry even on an empty stomach. My poetic consciousness bubbles over like flowing water. To me, to be alive is to write poetry. Writing poetry is nothing other than being alive.*

But his irregular lifestyle and constant worries must have taken their toll. By the middle of May he was distressed more than usual about his sake-drinking, and by the nineteenth of that month he was spitting up blood. Nonetheless, he carried on, and that summer came up with the idea of "composing haiku for food" (俳諧乞食) on the streets of Yuda, a plan that was apparently less than successful. Continuing to wander for another three months, he finally returned to Yuda for a bath, stopped at a drinking establishment on the way home, got drunk and fell down. Two nights later he was literally falling-down drunk again in the same place, and was questioned twice by police while trying to find his way home. By the end of November it was obvious: a place at Yuda would be far more convenient than the Gochu-an. He abandoned the latter on the twenty-eighth of the month and, putting all his belongings into a bicycle-drawn cart, walked the seven miles (twelve kilometers) to a four-mat tatami room abutting an alleyway. This new "hermitage" he called the Furai-kyo (風來居) or, "The Home that Came with the Wind."

Compared to the spacious Gochu-an, the Furai-kyo was quite cramped, and when he cooked, he had to push an earthenware charcoal brazier out into the alleyway. For scenery, instead of camellia and persimmon trees, he looked out through a cracked window on the south side of the room at a hedge, behind which were the priests' quarters of the Ryusenji temple. There Santoka put up a little desk on which he placed the empty shell of a sea urchin. In this he always placed a single flower from the fields.

In the middle of December, Santoka went to congratulate his son on the latter's appointment to responsibilities in Manchuria. It was the last time for father and son to meet. He then went home to greet the New Year from his room in the Furai-kyo.

The year (1939) started auspiciously with the publication of his sixth collection of poetry, *Kokan* (Alone in the Cold).[13] Soon thereafter he was on the road again, taking a ship to the mouth of the Osaka River, meeting with Abbot Yuro Komeda—a poet of Chinese and Japanese verse—on to Nagoya, climbing Mount Akiba, passing through the mountainous area of Kiso-Fukushima, and on and on until returning to the Furai-kyo in late spring. As usual, nothing had changed: he was still poor, there was nothing to eat, and he was unable to sleep. One day in May he reports crying into his rice after not having had any for three days. At the beginning of fall, he wrote:

> *Drinking sake,*
> *shedding tears;*
> *what a stupid autumn.*

The following day, he had so few resources that he tried to sell his
old *haori*, a sort of jacket, at a hockshop, but the thing was so rag-
gedy that it was turned down. For five days he fasted, drank water,
read books, and "considered his shameless way of living" until sent
money by Sakino. Then one night he watched the evening clouds
drift into the wind, and concluded,

> It is enough for Santoka to be Santoka; for Santoka to survive
> as Santoka. That is the true way.

On September 26, he walked around the town of Yuda, in his heart
taking leave of the poetry and drinking friends who had managed his
debts there, and on the following day slipped out of the Furai-kyo
in the early dawn, starting out on what would be his last extended
journey.

Santoka spent the next three months for the most part visiting the
holy temples on the island of Shikoku, begging, staying with friends,

or sleeping out in the open; he visited the graves of a number of poets and participated in Zen meditation groups. But by the middle of December, he knew it was time to stop. He was now fifty-eight years old, his health had not been good for years, despite his declarations of being "too healthy," and he was, perhaps, simply tired out. As it had always been in his life, it was with the help of friends that he secured a sort of shed on the compound of the Miyukidera, a temple not far from the city of Matsuyama on the island of Shikoku, and it was his friends who remodeled it into a place where he could live. By the end of the year, Santoka had moved into what would be his last place of refuge, the hermitage later to be named the Isso-an, "The One-Grass Hut" (一草庵).

The Isso-an was well-situated for Santoka: it was within walking or bus distance of Matsuyama so that he could be in contact with friends; Matsuyama itself was a boat terminal to Hiroshima where he could visit his great friend, Sumita Oyama; and, perhaps best of all, it was quite close to the hot springs at Dogo. It was also large enough for poetry meetings, and the Persimmon Club, a local group of haiku poets, met there under his tutelage a number of times. Santoka did his usual traveling about, and friends came to visit.

At the end of April, a project that he had talked over with Oyama—a publication of a selection of his life's work—was completed, and the volume *Somokuto* (The Pagoda of Grasses and Trees), was published. Through the spring and early summer he visited with friends in southwestern Japan, and in July entertained the Persimmon Club yet again. On the last day of that month, however, he was hopelessly drunk, lost his purse, and had to be helped by the police. As always, he seemed to recover quickly and continued to make short trips, in August and September visiting the graves of the haiku poets, Hekigodo (see page 37) and Shiki. On September 25, returning from a zazen meeting, Oyama dropped in on the Isso-an. This was the last time Oyama was to see Santoka.

The autumn rains now came down cold and steady, keeping him inside the hermitage for a few days. The Matsuyama Obon Festival was on the fifth, sixth and seventh of October, and the festival at the shrine for the war dead[14] would continue on until the tenth. Santoka

watched the approach of the festivals with some reflection, noting that they would hardly be festivals for him if he had no money for a little sake. On October 2, he suddenly decided that he needed to be treated to some sake by a friend, and so borrowed some money, took the train to Imabari and succeeded in getting quite drunk. It was on his late-night return from this trip that a dog dropped a large piece of mochi rice cake on his doorstep, and he ate a good bit of it for his dinner despite being completely toothless by this time. For the next few days he walked from friend's house to friend's house and managed to get something to drink every day. Finally, on the morning of the last day of the festival, he was given a sacred wine offering from an elderly neighbor, Mrs. Ito, and got happily drunk before noon. Then he made the rounds to his poet friends, informing them of a meeting of the Persimmon Club that night. Finally that evening the wife of the priest at the Goseiji temple passed by the hermitage, felt that something was wrong, and peeked inside to take a look. Santoka lay collapsed in the entranceway. The priest's wife made him as comfortable as possible and left. Later, the men of the poetry party arrived and, finding Santoka asleep, carried on without him until later that night. The following morning, the priest's wife again visited the hermitage, but found that he had passed away during the night. He was fifty-nine years old.

The following day, Santoka's remains were cremated and funeral rites were performed. A few days later, his son, Takeshi, arrived from Manchuria and took the ashes to Sumita Oyama's house in Hiroshima. That night, a small group went to the Buttsuji temple, and a service was held with the chanting of sutras. The next morning, October 18, Takeshi took Santoka's ashes on to the Taneda family cemetery in Hofu, where they were finally laid to rest.

Santoka's Poetry and Influences

"Composing verse is nothing other than life" (句作即生活). With this paraphrase of the Heart Sutra, Santoka summarized his life in five kanji characters. Composing haiku was something he couldn't stop; as he said, it seemed to come bubbling up out of him just like water flowing from a spring. Haiku *was* his life. And, while the constant wandering and drinking were inseparable from his life as well, a few notes might be made on Santoka and poetry alone.

Santoka lived at a time when Japan was in a state of great transition, moving from hundreds of years as an isolated country to the status of a modern nation intricately involved with the rest of the world. All of the traditional arts were being questioned, some tossed overboard wholesale, and haiku was not immune to change. In the first decades of the twentieth century, poets like Hekigodo, Seisensui,

and particularly Hosai (see page 34) moved to make haiku more expressive of the poet's emotions, and free of traditional forms such as the 5-7-5 syllable format and the seasonal word. These were poets who believed in "free verse, or *jiyuritsu* (自由律). To them, a haiku was more a matter of content than of style; what unfolded immediately before the poet became the poetry; there was no room for the "lie" of décor or self-conscious technique. Santoka's verse was like this, particularly in the sense that it included no fiction; and according to his friends, completely reflected his surroundings. Further, in his life of constant wandering, he knew nothing about tomorrow and so could only believe in and consider the present.

> *Shitting outdoors;*
> *leaves falling,*
> *falling.*

Santoka summed up his wishes into two: that he die a quick and uncomplicated death, and that he write poetry that was truly his own. While he had little control over the first wish, he stuck adamantly to the second. His life could be nothing other than his own, and neither could the verse that expressed that life. On January 1, 1936, he wrote in his diary:

Basho is Basho, Ryokan is Ryokan.[15] Even if one wanted to become Basho, he would be unable to do so; and one couldn't even start to imitate Ryokan. I am just myself. Santoka is Santoka. I don't think about becoming Basho, and I wouldn't be able to do so anyway. For a person who is not Ryokan to dress up like him only defiles him and at the same time it harms oneself. It'll be fine if I can become Santoka; giving myself life as my self's very self—that is my way.

Nevertheless, he did not write in a personal vacuum, and enthusiastically read other haiku poets, ancient and contemporary. Among the latter, his favorites are on the following pages:

Seigetsu Inoue (ca.1822–1887)

Seigetsu suddenly appeared in the Ina Valley, a center of learning since ancient times, a little after the age of thirty, and little is known about his life before that. He was rumored to have been from a samurai family, or perhaps a family of sword sharpeners, or possibly a family of sake dealers. Why he left home is unknown, but he seemed to have been highly educated and an expert at calligraphy. When Seigetsu first arrived in the Ina Valley he was able to make the rounds of the homes of poets and scholars, discussing haiku and teaching Confucianism. Eventually, however, he became not much more than an entertaining beggar, clad in dirty flea-infested robes. As he walked about, children would yell and throw stones at him, but he never became angry. Seigetsu washed his old garments in the river, taking out the fleas and lining them up on large stones. Dogs barked at him and threatened him in the street, but his attitude never changed, and the dogs would eventually give up and go away. Money was of little use to him, but if his gourd was filled with sake, he was always happy and grateful. He was said to be unrestrained, with a sort of transcendental attitude of no twisted feelings or resentments.

From around 1885, Seigetsu became sick and weaker in body. In December 1886, he was found collapsed in a rice field between the mountains, and covered with filth. He was carried out on a rain shutter and taken to a villager's home. He was unable to speak, and only able to lie down. On March 10 of the following year, he passed away at the age of sixty-six. Two hours before his passing, a brush and paper were put before him, and he was asked to write a death poem. He wrote:

> *Somewhere in the mist*
> *I hear*
> *the call of a crane.*[16]

Then, given a little bit of shochu, he closed his eyes and left the world.

His collected works include some one thousand seven hundred verses. Here are some more of them:

> An October peach
>   the insects have not eaten;
>   the narrow path to the hot spring.

> No short cut
>   to the sake shop sign:
>   year's end.

> A mushroom!
>   While looking for kindling;
>   the luck of a fox.

> Even the beggar
>   throws away his bowl;
>   mountains full of flowers.

> First sky of the year,
>   in my heart,
>   a day of ladling sake!

In April of 1934, Santoka tried to visit Seigetsu's grave, but became lost in the mountain snows, contracted pneumonia and spent a week in the hospital. In May of 1939, he once again made the trip to the Ina Valley, and was guided to the grave site. This was a rough-stone monument surrounded by a cypress fence. Santoka poured sake on the monument, on which was inscribed:

> Fallen on the rush mat,
>   people show me
>   the hazy weather of spring.

Hosai Ozaki (1885–1926)

Hosai began writing haiku at the age of fourteen, but entered law school at Tokyo Imperial University at the age of twenty in hopes of a stable career. Within a year or two, he had proposed to a young lady and been rebuffed by her older brother, had developed a serious drinking problem, and changed his given name from Hideo to Hosai (which means "letting go"). Graduating from law school, he went to work for an insurance company and, at age twenty-six married a nineteen-year- old girl, Kaoru. Hosai was well-respected at work and received a number of promotions, but became deeply pessimistic, and turned more and more towards alcohol. By his mid-thirties, he left his job after being demoted due to his worsening problems with alcohol, was hired by another insurance company in Seoul, Korea, and came down with pleurisy. Later dismissed from his company in Korea, he moved on to Manchuria, where he worked for the Manchurian Railroad. There, his tuberculosis took a turn for the worse, and he returned to Japan to enter a sanatorium.

For the next number of years, Hosai moved between being a patient at the sanatorium and a lay monk working as a temple sexton in Kobe, Fukui, Kyoto, and finally on the island of Shodoshima, usually expelled from the latter job due to drunkenness. At the age of forty, Hosai established himself in a small hut connected to the Saikoji temple on the small island of Azukishima, and was cared for by a fisherman's wife employed by his friends-in-haiku. The following year, in 1926, he became increasingly ill. By the beginning of March, he had lost his appetite and began a rapid decline. On April 7, at about eight in the evening, he passed away in the arms of local fishermen.

Hosai had continuously written and published haiku, sometimes for the magazine *So'un*, thanks in part to his former fellow student Seisensui, the man who became Santoka's teacher. One of Hosai's most famous poems was

> *Right under*
> *a big sky,*
> *I do not wear a hat.*

In Hosai's essay "Shima ni kuru made" [Coming to the Island],[17] he describes his hermitage at the Saikoji temple and expresses his deep gratitude to Seisensui and the head priest of the temple for letting him live there. He was apparently devoted to reciting the Kannon Sutra, the twenty-fifth chapter of the Lotus Sutra, and kept it on the desk in front of him. He ends the essay with the confessional that begins the small handbook of the Kannon Sutra:

All the bad karma I have created since times long passed
Is due to my beginningless greed, anger and stupidity.
These have been born from my body, speech and mind,
And I now repent all of them.

Some of Hosai's haiku:

Just come to this place today,
already intimate
with the dogs.

Writing haiku
with the smell of pickles
on my hands.

Husband and wife
sneezing
and laughing.

Having nothing to put it in,
I receive it
with both hands.

The flies
have taken a liking
to this bald head.

Stole in and bit me, then
sneaked out:
the mosquito.

The road
of myself alone,
coming to an end.

On the night of 21 October, 1939, Santoka was guided to Hosai's grave marker by a haiku friend and the priest of the Saikoji temple. Santoka records that the moon shone dimly on the grave marker, over which he poured sake. He then lit cigarettes, planted them on the ground in front of the marker, and read a section of the book of Zen koans, the *Mumonkan*.[18]

Hekigodo Kawahigashi (1873–1937)

Hekigodo, the son of a samurai of the feudal domain in Matsuyama, was perhaps the most well-heeled of the haiku poets admired by Santoka. He was a mountain climber, a calligrapher, practiced Noh dancing, and traveled around Japan and to Europe, North America, China and Mongolia. As a young student he was taught how to play baseball by the famous poet and writer, Shiki, to whom he remained devoted all his life. Hekigodo was an early advocate of "free haiku," which abandoned the 5-7-5 syllable format and the use of a season word, although later in life he returned to the study of traditional haiku forms.

Hekigodo worked for newspapers off and on throughout his life, married at age twenty-eight, but spent much of his time traveling, mountain climbing and writing travelogues and haiku. In the last days of January 1937, he contracted intestinal typhoid, was taken to a hospital, but passed away on February 5. Santoka visited Hekigodo's grave just one month before he himself passed away. He entered little in his journal, only noting that he visited Shiki's grave and the army cemetery in Asahiyama on the same day, and that he must continue to "thoroughly examine himself to the very end."

The following are typical of Hekigodo's haiku:

> *Knee to knee*
> > *the moon shines in;*
> *how cool!*

> *Boiling daikon:*
> > *dinner together*
> *with the children.*

> *Finding lodging in the rain;*
> > *when the rain clears,*
> > *dragonflies!*

This road:
    all we can depend on;
    the withered moor.

Faraway fireworks
    making a noise, then
    nothing.

Seisensui Ogiwara (1884–1976)

Seisensui was born in Tokyo, the younger son of a general goods retailer. Expelled from one junior high school for publishing a student newspaper criticizing the school's educational methods and administration, he entered another school, quit drinking and smoking, and began to take his studies seriously. Accepted to Tokyo Imperial University, he majored in linguistics and began writing haiku. Along with Hekigodo, he advocated letting go of the season word and 5-7-5 syllable format of traditional haiku, and used modern media, including lectures and literary criticism on national radio to promote his style.

Seisensui's wife and daughter perished in the Great Kanto Earthquake of 1923, after which he took up residence at a chapel in the compound of the Buddhist temple Tofukuji in Kyoto. During this period, he traveled around the country, then remarried in 1929. His house in Tokyo was destroyed during World War II, and he moved to Kamakura in 1944, where he died at the great age of ninety-two.

Seisensui was a popular teacher of haiku, and his students included Hosai and Santoka. He loved to travel, and especially liked hot springs, but like Hekigodo, he enjoyed being at home with his family and neighbors. His more than two hundred works included collections of haiku, which tended to be simple and homely, essays and travelogues.

Some of his many haiku include:

How lonely!
    This whole day,
    not one wonderful thing.

The skylark,
> *sings in the sky, sings on earth,*
> *sings flying away.*

A cold night;
> *with my own shadow,*
> *writing about myself.*

Returning to my house,
>> *and there I have*
> *my own bowl.*

I believe in the Buddha
>> *and the Truth*
> *and the green of the barley.*

～～

Santoka himself wrote as a weed expresses itself in its growth and bloom. In grasping his own essence, he wrote to explain, it was necessary to find and improve himself every day. He illustrated this in his essay, "Michi" [The Way]:[19]

This happened when I was in Hyuga, begging for alms. It was a clear autumn afternoon, and I had a simple meal at a sake shop on the outskirts of town. My own inclination is to feel satisfied even on an empty stomach, and bit by bit, I was feeling better. When I set out in the direction of my inn, there was a man standing directly in front of me, bowing in my direction. He was middle-aged, thin and pale, and had a nervous look on his face.

"Are you a priest of the Zen sect? How can I find my way?" he asked.

"The Way is right in front of you," I said. "Just go straight ahead."

Perhaps I was having a Zen interview tried out on me right there in the road, but nonetheless he seemed to be satisfied

with my prompt reply, and went straight down the road in front of him. I think it can be said that it's the same for the Way of making verses—that is, making verses through the Way. The material for poetry exists anywhere and at any time. In the way you grasp it, or in other words, in the way you see nature, your own character is revealed and your own life realized. In the same way, the character of your verses will be established and their quality made apparent.

"The ordinary mind, this is the Way." This is what the Buddhist priest Chao-chou[20] declared. And all the ancient Buddhas declared "When offered tea, drink; when offered rice, eat." This is the same as "The mountains are not mountains; the rivers are not rivers," being clarified by "The mountains are just mountains; the rivers, just rivers." Mountains are just fine as mountains, rivers just fine as rivers. One blade of grass is one blade of grass, and this is the Buddha. Praised be this Blade of Grass Buddha!

The Way is not to be looked for in the extraordinary, but rather to be put into practice in the ordinary . . .

So to improve your verse is to improve your humanity, and the radiance of the man is the radiance of his verse. Distancing yourself from the human is not the Way, and distancing yourself from the Way is not human. The Way is right in front of us. Let's go straight ahead, straight on ahead.

Kodo Sawaki and Santoka's Way

Santoka was ordained as a priest of the Zen sect at the age of forty-one by Gian Mochizuki, then abbot of the Soto Zen temple, the Ho'onji . Although it is traditionally accepted that his conversion was made more or less on the spot after the showdown with the trolley car, he had been interested in Zen Buddhism for some time. When in college, Santoka found a book in the library explaining the Buddhist concept that if a person commits suicide, someone in the family must become a priest so that the deceased person's spirit may eventually become enlightened. Whether this and his mother's and brother's suicides had any influence on his decision is unclear, but Santoka was assiduous in commemorating each anniversary of his mother's death day by reading the sutras in front of the mortuary tablet he kept constantly with him.

Other than Abbot Gian Mochizuki, the greatest personal influence on Santoka's view of Buddhism and how it would apply to his everyday living was Kodo Sawaki (1880–1965). Kodo was an extraordinarily eccentric and independent priest, even in the annals of Zen. Born the son of a rickshaw maker, Kodo lost both of his parents and an adoptive uncle by the age of seven. He was subsequently adopted again by a lantern maker and gambler, who used the young boy as a lookout for the police. He was, however, taught Chinese literature and non-attachment to money by a friend's father. At the age of twelve, Kodo became interested in Buddhism, was recommended to study Zen by a priest of the Pure Land sect, and spent the next number of years traveling from temple to temple, mostly without money and on foot.

At the age of twenty, Kodo was drafted, spent six years fighting in the Russo-Japanese War, and was seriously wounded. After convalescing in Japan, he was sent back to China until the end of the war. On his return, he studied Yogacara Buddhism with a Pure Land priest, but eventually turned to concentrate on Dogen, the founder of Zen in Japan. In the next number of years, Kodo again traveled from temple to temple, at one point living alone in a small temple, concentrating on zazen and subsisting on rice and pickles.

In 1916, Kodo became a priest at the Daiji-ji temple in Kuma-
moto, and it was at this time that Santoka likely started attending
his lectures. When the Daiji-ji burned down in 1922, Kodo moved
to a small house loaned to him by a friend in Kumamoto, and con-
tinued lecturing. Thereafter, he continued traveling around Japan
lecturing, eventually becoming a lecturer at Komazawa University
in Tokyo. Kodo continued to travel, lecture on Zen and lead medi-
tation groups until 1963, when he retired at the age of eighty-three
to the Antaiji temple in Kyoto. There he died in 1965.

In their eccentricity, general homelessness, and independence,
there are strong similarities between Santoka and Kodo Sawaki, and
the latter's influence on the restless poet cannot be discounted. Some
of Kodo's sayings may well apply to how Santoka would approach
his own life and literary style:

> *Everyone is homeless. It is a mistake to think that you have a
> fixed home.*
>
> *To be born a human being is a rare thing, something to be
> grateful for. But being born as a human being is worthless if
> you spend your life in a mental hospital. It is worthless if you
> worry about not having money. It is worthless if you worry and
> become neurotic because you cannot get a prestigious job. It is*

worthless if you weep because you lost your girlfriend.

You can't exchange farts with anyone, right? Everyone has to live his own life. Who is good-looking? Who is smart? You or I? There's no need to compare yourself with others.

When a person is alone, he's not so bad. When a group is formed, paralysis occurs, and people become so confused that they cannot judge what is right or wrong.

When a large crowd claps their hands, you clap your hands, too; when they laugh, you also laugh, "Ha, ha." You should stop that kind of living, be dignified, stand your ground, be your true self, be awakened and say, "This is me."

Taking a shit. Eating rice. Living. Dying. The passing of the four seasons. All these are expressions of the Buddha's light.

Don't speak hesitantly. Just this existence; just now; just this instant. There is no other path than putting all of your spirit into this place, right here.

As for one's fate, no matter what fate, no matter who, no matter where, no matter when, work it out for yourself.

In one of his lectures on the Zen beggar priest Kojiki Tousui, Kodo quoted this poem:

> *Thus is life, thus is composure.*
> *Shabby clothes, a broken bowl, quiet leisure.*
> *When hungry, eat; when thirsty, drink;*
> > *self-knowledge alone.*
> *Never judge the good and evil of the world.*

The Soto school of the Zen sect was founded in the thirteenth century by the Japanese priest Dogen, who emphasized the practice of "just sitting" or *shikantaza*, meaning meditating free of thoughts and directing the mind to no object or content. Dogen held that this was far more important than meditating on one of the many Zen koans associated more with the Rinzai school. Although Santoka was incapable of staying still in one location for a long time, he did practice sitting meditation, both indoors and out, and apparently achieved some degree of success at it. Oyama notes that one time when he showed up unexpectedly with sake and tofu at Santoka's hermitage, the two talked late into the night, and when it came time to sleep, Santoka had only one thin summer coverlet in the house. Oyama crawled under this and an old robe, and even a loincloth, and did his best to sleep. When a cold wind came through the cracks in the hermitage, he awoke and looked up to see Santoka sitting in zazen, protecting him from the draft as much as possible with his own body. This he did all night.

Santoka did his reading in Zen, and along with studying the various sutras, he was fond of reading through the classical koans found in the Zen texts the *Hekiganroku* and the *Mumonkan*.

In his diaries, however, it is with the five basic Buddhist precepts that he seemed to struggle the hardest, and felt his failure in living the most deeply.

If we look at the precepts in reverse order, starting with the fifth, which admonishes against the use of intoxicants, Santoka was hopeless from the very beginning. Throughout his journals he was alternately aghast at his weakness for sake, and resigned to the fact that it was an integral part of his life. Sake was his karma, he said, writing that "walking, drinking, composing—these are Santoka's three affairs." Nevertheless, he was keenly and openly aware of the mess it made of his life, and his entries are full of self-recriminations and condemnations over his drunkenness, usually after getting falling-down drunk (and usually followed in a day or two with a note about having a cup or two in a little sake shop somewhere along the road). In one of his diaries he wrote:

> Sake is a Buddha; it is also a demon. As a Buddha, it's a hateful Buddha; as a demon, it's a lovable demon.

Still, it was not that he drank all the time, but that when he drank it was hard for him to stop.

The Fourth Precept is the prohibition against promiscuous sexual relations, and it has already been noted that Santoka fell off this track from time to time. But his liaisons did not seem to be many, and the diaries would make him appear almost boyish about matters of sex. Once, while traveling in Kyushu, for example, he could hardly get over the fact that a young prostitute had winked at him. Later, he reports of having an erotic dream, and is deeply ashamed. By 1935, however, that part of his life was perhaps less and less a problem for him, and on August 16 of that year he writes, "I no longer have any sexual desire. I only have the desire to eat. To taste is to live."

The Third Precept—that against lying—was more complicated for Santoka. With his continual lack of funds or any kind of sustenance, one suspects that he had to talk fast from time to time just in order to survive. He saw lying in a broader sense. He wrote dejectedly about the "lie" of walking around in a priest's robes, while not being able to follow the precepts even for a day. It was his conundrum to live his life honestly as Santoka, and to do this without deceiving others or himself.

The Second Precept is against stealing, or taking what has not been given to you, and Santoka extended this to the concept of waste. He was acutely aware that, as a beggar, everything he had received had been by someone else's grace. He knew that from top to bottom, everything he had was borrowed. His clothes, his cloak, his clogs—even his Rikyu cap,[21] which had belonged to Abbot Shun. Only his glasses were his.

We have already seen how he dealt with water, a commodity that others might consider to be the easiest to come by, but Santoka would not treat anything wastefully, and rather would put each and every thing to good use. He ate and lived by receiving alms, and felt strongly that not using something to its fullest was at its best a lack of gratitude, and at its worst a form of theft. This attitude was reflected in the great guilt he felt when unable to pay back loans, and manifested positively in the way he kept his hermitages. Despite his reputation as a continual drunk, his rooms were always kept fastidiously neat and methodical. Books were always returned, and his friends commented on his complete honesty.

The first and most basic precept of Buddhism proscribes the taking of life—of any being, large or small. Santoka was most like the poets Issa and Ryokan in his love and respect for all forms of life, and this approach to all sentient beings runs through the body of both his poetry and his prose. Even his poems concerning the soldiers going to and returning from China are filled with compassion and pathos, and the reader must remember the sad, jingoistic period this was. Santoka was one of those who "wouldn't hurt a flea," and when he did mindlessly kill mosquitoes or cockroaches, he was always quick to feel remorse.

Killing bugs—by this my own egoism is found out.

In the End

In the end, Santoka cannot be reduced to a Buddhist priest, a wanderer, a writer, or even a poet. As he said himself, it was enough for Santoka to be Santoka. One can see him buttonholing a patron in a bar, or playing with the neighbor's dog, or relaxing at the hot springs he loved so much, walking around, big boned, with sake-whitened skin, talking with people, one front tooth left in his wide-open mouth, laughing and mumbling on.

> *The private parts*
> *of men and women, too;*
> *the flowing water.*

It is said that everyone liked to see Santoka coming, even though they knew it was going to cost them. But in the final months, it had perhaps started to cost them too much. According to his friend, Satoru Watanabe, with Santoka's final move to Shikoku, he leaned on his friends for food and lodging more and more, sometimes wetting the bed and soiling the tatami at night. When the Isso-an hermitage was provided for him, these same friends continued to pick up his drinking and oyster-bar tabs. He would also periodically come to friends' work places asking for money, sometimes coming by drunk and "as red as a boiled octopus," unable to understand that these were serious places of employment. When he wasn't drunkenly importuning his friends, he could be found passed out drunk at the side of the road, exposing the lower half of his body, often before noon.

Yet, they all knew his inner virtues, and it was they who cleaned his body after death, and trimmed his goatee with his old scissors, burying them next to the Isso-an under the stone monument inscribed with his verse,

> *In my begging bowl,*
> *too,*
> *hailstones.*

It remains to be noted that Santoka, who lived so long at the margin of society, became a sort of beloved national resource in the years following his death. Although his poetry had always been read in literary circles, his works soon began to be published in newspaper series and books, and programs on his life were aired on the radio and even in television dramas. Look today on amazon.co.jp, and there are pages of entries of his books on his life, poetry and travels.

In following through this biography and the translations of the man's life in his own verse, it is hoped that the reader will be led to understand why.

—William Scott Wilson

Translator's Notes

1. 青年. Youth in English.
2. 層雲. Lit. Stratus Clouds in English.
3. 草木塔.
4. Matsuo Basho (1644–1694), widely considered the master of haiku.
5. *Ziziphus jujuba.*
6. 三八九. Lit. Three-Eight-Nine in English.
7. 碧巌録.
8. 鉢の子.
9. 山業水行.
10. 雑草風景.
11. 柿の葉.
12. 独慎.
13. 孤寒.
14. Shrines for the war dead, called "gokoku" shrines (護国神社, literally "shrines to protect the nation") were of particular significance during this time in Japanese history. Santoka was going to pay his respects to the Japanese casualties in Manchuria and China.
15. Ryokan (1758–1831). Poet, calligrapher and Zen Buddhist monk, famous for his simplicity and childlike manner.
16. "The call of the crane" also means the command of one's lord.
17. 島に来るまで.
18. *Mumonkan* (無門関): *The Gateless Gate*, a thirteenth century book of Zen koans written in China.
19. 道.
20. Chao-chou (778–897). One one of the greatest Zen (Ch'an) masters of China. There are a number of koans concerning him.
21. The type of cap worn by tea ceremony master Sen no Rikyu (1522–1591).

About the Translation

A further word should be said about Santoka's style of haiku and the way I have chosen to translate it. As noted above, haiku during Santoka's time was being reconsidered and experimented with, and while the traditional 5-7-5 syllable format was not entirely tossed overboard, it was not considered altogether necessary either. I have not checked every verse in this selection, but have found that Santoka's poems generally ranged anywhere from a total of eight syllables to twenty-eight. They were—and are—still considered "haiku," but form was given far less importance than what the poem evoked, and I have tried to make that idea the guiding principle of the English versions presented here. Translating even traditional haiku into seventeen syllables of English, I think, is ill-advised at best—the form that is the genius of one language is certainly not that of another—and so I have made no effort to count out and dutifully include each consonant and vowel of the original. I have, however, kept to the traditional three-line presentation of haiku, even with the shortest verses. This decision is not completely arbitrary. I have seen a number of translations that have dealt with these poems as though they were epigrams, printing them out in a single line. So presented, they appear visually as what we Westerners are used to thinking of as either philosophical pensées, or clever sayings. They are neither. At the same time, a single-line presentation seems to miss the in-and-out-and-in breathing rhythm that makes up the pattern of even the shortest of these verses. This can be seen in the very first poem quoted in the preface:

My rainhat's
leaking,
too?

The "too" in this verse is its very focus, a feeling that would be lost if the poem were given as a cute one-liner. The poetry in the original Japanese has been included not for aesthetic reasons alone; as calligraphy is often considered the central art form of the Far East, the inclusion of the original—albeit in printed form—may also give some hint of its visual beauty. Certainly, a translation is never really done or "perfect," and those readers who have a knowledge of the Japanese will likely want to see the original poem. With it before them, they can freely come to their own conclusions concerning the merits of this translator's efforts, and may be moved to try their own.

Transliterations and audio recordings of Santoka's haiku in this book can be found at **tuttlepublishing.com/the-life-and-zen-haiku-poetry-of-santoka-taneda** to offer non-Japanese speaking readers a chance to recite the poems out loud, and hear how they might have sounded at the haiku parties Santoka so loved.

Other notes about the translation

- Notes at the end of every chapter explain references that may be unfamiliar to the reader. Every effort has been made to define people and places mentioned, however, as much of the text is based on Santoka's informal diary entries, this is not always possible.

- With the help of my editor I've done my best to render romanized forms of archaic readings of Japanese script accurately; this was particularly difficult for proper nouns.

- Most of Santoka's original Japanese work is in the public domain, available through online sites such as **aozora.gr.jp**. The Japanese script titles of each of his works mentioned in this book have been given along with their translated titles in English, so that readers wishing to find the original Japanese works can do so.

- The authorship of some entries in *Diary of the One-Grass Hut* has been disputed. I have only included the entries that were also included by Sumita Oyama in his volume *Santoka Chosakushu*.

- Names of Japanese people in the book are given in the order first name followed by family name, for example, Sumita Oyama.

- Japanese script renditions of haiku poems in the text are read from right to left, top to bottom.

CHAPTER 1

The House Where
He Was Born

No traces left
    of the house where I was born;
fireflies.

うまれた家は
あとかたもない
ほうたる

That wall of about seven or eight ken[1] and those ridgepoles of the two-story house on the west side are all that remain of the O-Taneda period. Everything else was built after that. Well, how big was their mansion? More than eight hundred tsubo,[2] I guess you'd say. Nowadays, fourteen or fifteen households can live on that space, as you can see, and mine is one of them. At any rate, being a big landholder, his main house had a high roof of grass thatch, and tiled eaves stuck out in the four directions all around it. A lot of tall trees were planted there, and Shoichi and I used to walk around together picking the cicadas off of them. I was three years older than him, and now I'm seventy-six, but I can still clearly remember what the O-Taneda mansion looked like in those prosperous days, you know. It was really enormous. It must have been at least ten cho[3]—from here to Sandajiri Station. So the O-Taneda folks could walk to the station without stepping on other people's land. You can come out over this way a bit. Let's see—you came here from somewhere around Matsuyama in Iyo, didn't you?

Yes, that's right. His mother was a very beautiful woman, but when Shoichi was eleven, she jumped into a well and killed herself. I'm sure that well was right around here, but they de-molished it and filled it up with earth right away. Just then, Shoichi and I were playing like we were actors in a shed-like building—there must have been five or six of us. Everybody ran towards the well screaming, and we ran after them, too. But they told us that a cat had fallen in, and that children should get away, so they wouldn't let us get close.

As for Shoichi, he was a beautiful little boy, and there wasn't anyone who'd say he was bad. I think he wasn't so good in school at first, but from about the time he got into middle school, he started to do very well, and was always at the top. But he and I started to walk different roads from about that time, so after that I didn't know anything about him at all. I didn't even know that he wrote haiku and took the name Santoka.

The clear black eyes of old man Kawamoto sparkled amiably as he talked and kindly guided me around the traces of the house where Santoka had been born. Even after Yanagi-sensei and I had said our thanks and gone out onto the road, he stood under the eaves for a while seeing off our retreating figures. The osmanthus was pungently fragrant, and the streets of Hofu were quiet. To be specific, the place was Yashiki #130, Hachioji, Nishi-Sawayoshi, Hofu City.

Santoka's real name was Shoichi Taneda, and he was born De-cember 3, 1883, the eldest son of Takejiro, residing in the village of Nishi-Sawayoshi, Sawa-gun, Yamaguchi Prefecture. Hofu is a famous shrine town known for the Tenmangu shrine. His father Takejiro was a good-natured landowner, whose large frame made you think of the samurai Saigo.[4] He had large eyes and was large-hearted as well. At first he was an assistant official at the city hall, but as the political leader of a group of friends, he tried his hand at politics. He did not drink much sake, but had a weakness for women, and kept two or three mistresses. He was good-natured, but seemed to be poor at the management of his finances.

On March 6, when Santoka was eleven years old, his mother

Fusa committed suicide by throwing herself into an old well there at their house. At the time, his father was off on an excursion with one of his mistresses. Santoka's mother, a pitiable woman, hastened to her death at the young age of thirty-three, leaving five beloved children behind, and perhaps the death of his mother was one of the reasons Santoka entered religion later on in life. After the death of his mother, his father indulged himself in women all the more, so with his little sister and brother, Santoka was put in the care of his grandmother, who loved the children very much. In the postscript to the collection of his poetry, *Kokan* [Alone in the Cold] he wrote:

My grandmother lived for quite a long time, but because of that long life, she suffered miserably time and time again. My grandmother always muttered to herself, "Ah, karma . . . ah, karma." Recently, I've also come to think that when I compose poetry (and likewise, when I drink sake, as embarrassing as that is) it is a matter of karma.

In 1897, Shoichi graduated from Matsuzaki Ordinary Higher Elementary School in Hofu, and entered the Shuyo Gakusha, a three-year middle school. His school record was that of first rank and, together with his classmates Iida and Inomata, he published a literary club magazine. From the Shuyo Gakusha, he enrolled in the Yamaguchi Prefectural Middle School, and began to write haiku from about this time. In Sandajiri there was the Gray Starling Poetry Club, which he often attended. Yoshio Yanagi-sensei, a senior at Bocho's World of Haiku at Kurumazaka in Sandajiri, was often there with Santoka. In 1902, he graduated from Yamaguchi Middle School (its seventh graduating class) and began a preparatory course for entering Waseda University. He proceeded to the Department of Literature the following year.

It would seem that he began drinking a lot of sake at about this time. His genius for literature had already been recognized on campus, and he called himself either Mimei Ogawa or Santoka Taneda. In February of 1905, however, Santoka fell ill, withdrew from the university, and returned to his hometown. He himself said this was due to an acute nervous breakdown, but it may also have been that his father's chaotic lifestyle had steadily reduced the household's economy until he could not send funds sufficient even to cover tuition.

In September of 1909, Takejiro liquidated the ancestral Taneda family holdings and moved to the nearby neighborhood of Utan in the village of Daido. As a last strategy, he acquired the Yamano Sake Brewery (currently the Omori Brewery) under Shoichi's name, and father and son went into the sake business. But more and more, the father indulged himself in women as the son indulged himself in sake. In the midst of all this, in the same year, Santoka's father forced him to get married. Takejiro no doubt thought that he could control his twenty-eight year old son, who was now given to walking around drinking, by making him take a wife. The bride was Sakino, the eldest daughter of Mitsunosuke Sato of Wada Village in Sawa-gun. Santoka had no interest in this marriage. He put up a resistance, saying that as he was going to become a Zen priest he would not need a wife, and did not even attend the marriage arrangement interview. For the first ten days of the marriage he led the reserved life of a newly-wed, but then he once again left the house and walked around drinking. To make matters worse, the sake in the sake vaults went bad for the second year in a row: a hard blow for the business. It was about this time that the literary magazine *Kyodo*[5] was launched.

Santoka first started writing "free haiku"[6] about 1911, soon after Seisensui Ogiwara inaugurated this new trend. About this time, his own ideas matched those of his friend Hakusen Kubo who lived out on Sago Island. Santoka connected with the literary magazine *So'un*, and composed a great number of verses.

In 1916, when Santoka was thirty-five years old, the Taneda sake brewery finally went under, due to the negligence of both father and son. Leaving debts and causing a considerable amount of inconvenience to his relatives, Takejiro ran off to another village with one of his mistresses, under the cover of night, as we say. Santoka fled with wife and child to faraway Kumamoto. In Kumamoto at that time, his haiku-poet friends Jitoson Kanezaki and Ruohei Tomoeda were living in the Godaka and Yakusen districts respectively. Shohei Hayashi and Sokyaku Nishiki and others who published the coterie magazine, *Shirakawa kyui shinshigai*[7] were also there. It was with the help of these men that Santoka went to Kumamoto, and the same coterie greeted him with warm friendship.

Also with the aid of these men Santoka at first tried to operate a secondhand bookstore, and received a great number of books from the haiku teacher Seisensui and from Hakusen. That, however, did not go well, and in the end he opened a picture frame shop which he called the Garakuta[8] on a small street in town. At this shop, he and his wife also sold ornamental Western clothing, portraits of famous people both Japanese and foreign, and things like picture postcards from cultural exhibitions. The shop was often left to Sakino's care, and in the end, Santoka's character did not allow him to become the master of this shop any more than it gave him the capability of sitting at the ledger of a sake business.

Here are some of the stories from that time. One day Santoka put a photograph of Emperor Meiji in a frame and went to sell it at an elementary school outside of town. As he was unable to pass through the gate, he was walking back and forth in front of the school. Just then he noticed a literary associate, and they went off to a drinking establishment where they enjoyed themselves until late at night. Another time, leaving his wife to watch the shop, he took the little bit of money that had accumulated and went off to drink once more. Out on a spree by himself, he lacked enough money to pay the bill; and when the shop sent a man home with him to collect, he went to a friend's house rather than his own, and had the friend pay for him. Though he engaged in this behavior day after day, strangely enough he was held in affection by people in Kumamoto. Perhaps sake brought out some kind of grace in him. When Santoka had drunk a good bit, his old friend Kenkichi Miyamoto paid off the man who followed him back from the shop. Kenkichi held no grudge against Santoka, and in fact often happily went out with him to have a good time. Santoka's wife was still young and beautiful enough to stand out from other women on the streets of Kumamoto, and Kenkichi remarked that he wondered why Santoka was unable to love her.

Santoka couldn't settle down in Kumamoto, and again went off to Tokyo. In November of 1920 he became a temporary employee of the Tokyo City Office and worked for two years at the Hitotsubashi Library. This was likely the time he became acquainted with men like Yushi Shigemori and Yoshimi Kudo.[9] The Great Kanto Earthquake struck in 1923, and Santoka was aided by Shigemori. Both men were taken into police custody and incarcerated, but in the confusion of the earthquake, Santoka was able to return to Kumamoto.

Translator's Notes

1. One *ken*: About 6 feet (1.8 meters).
2. One *tsubo*: 36 square feet (3.3 square meters)
3. One *cho*: 119 yards (109 meters)
4. Saigo Takamori (1827–1877): One of the great military leaders during the Meiji Restoration.
5. 郷土.
6. Haiku free of a number of traditional restrictions, among them the traditional 5-7-5 syllable format.
7. 白川及新市街.
8. *Garakuta*: Generally this word means something like "junk" in Japanese, but Santoka wrote it with the kanji characters 雅楽多, meaning elegant, pleasure, many; or, "many pleasurable things."
9. The text provides no notes on these two, and I have been unable to locate them in Japanese biographical dictionaries or online.

CHAPTER 2

Renouncing the World and Becoming a Priest

One day in 1924, a drunken Santoka stood like a temple guardian statue before an oncoming trolley in front of the Kumamoto Public Hall. The trolley safely made a sudden stop, but the passengers were tumbled head over teakettle, and a great number of people gathered to view the commotion. It is a mystery as to whether Santoka was trying to commit suicide—his younger brother Jiro had committed suicide before this time—or was just ravingly drunk. Finally, the police came along as well, and he was surrounded by a crowd of people. Just at that moment, a man by the name of Koba appeared, and with a "Come along now," took Santoka by the arm. Pulling him quickly along the trolley line, he accompanied him to a place commonly called the Sentaibutsu, which in fact is a Zen temple formally known as the Ho'onji .

The abbot Gian Mochizuki smiled and permitted the confused drunk entrance. He neither asked Santoka who he was nor where he came from, nor did he give him any little speeches, but smilingly served him regular meals.

Santoka had, on several occasions, attended meetings given by Kodo Sawaki Roshi [see page 41], who was at that time creating a Zen revival in Kumamoto. With Gian Mochizuki's tolerant treatment and his immersion into the peaceful and simple atmosphere of the Zen temple, the thoughts in his heart took warmth and his interest in Zen deepened. Not only this, but in some fundamental way, he steadied his *will* to enter the path of Zen.

Becoming a priest's student, Santoka was diligent day and night in his Buddhist studies, participated in zazen, and seemed to be driven by his pursuits one day after the next. With this one opportunity brought about by the strange event on the trolley line, he left the tormented and dissipated first half of his life in the past, made the good priest his teacher, and considered this to be the first step of a new life. Once, his wife Sakino came to visit Santoka in the midst of his training. There he was without socks on a cold day, his feet chapped and cracked, briskly sweeping the temple.

This Santoka, who in the past had never even once put away his own bedding, seemed to be a completely different person. He did not return home, but stayed at the Ho'onji temple and continued his Buddhist discipline. This Santoka, whose mouth had once sung songs enticed by geisha, now intoned Buddhist ritual texts, the Heart Sutra, and Dogen's Shushogi chant.

Thus, in February of 1925, Santoka finally had his stiff black hair shaved off by the abbot Gian, renounced the world, and became a Buddhist priest. His Buddhist name was Koho,[1] and he was now forty-four years old.

In August of this year, the poet Hosai Ozaki [see page 34], also a contributing member of the magazine *So'un*, entered the Nango-an hermitage in Mamejima. It was about this time that Hosai's poetry made great improvements and adorned the magazine every month.

The wife Santoka had left at home took care of their only child, Ken, who was then fifteen years old, and the family business, doing her best on the road of life. From the time she had married Santoka—a scholar, but irredeemably selfish and a sake drinker to boot—there had never been a single day when her heart was at peace; it had been nothing but worries and distress. Santoka thought this was pitiful and felt apologetic in his way, and gave her the Bible he had brought with him. This Bible became a factor in Sakino's attending the Methodist church. Hers was a life that a woman without faith could not live, and the minister did his best to guide this lonely woman.

In the autumn of 1951, in order to understand Santoka's "Kumamoto Period," I stayed in Kumamoto three or four days and met a number of different people. One day I attended a round-table discussion on a "Retrospect of Santoka" sponsored by the Kumamoto

Daily News. Among the people at this symposium, there were a number of his old friends who had walked around composing haiku and drinking sake with Santoka during this anguished period.

"Yeah, I went drinking with Santoka. When he couldn't pay the bill, a man from the place where we were drinking came to my house to ask me to pay up."

"That must have really put you out."

"No, no. It was our pleasure, not a bother. Enjoying yourself with Santoka somehow always gave you a good feeling. Maybe you could say that sake was good for him—that he was a man who had been blessed by sake."

"What about women?"

"Disliked women; loved sake. He wasn't the kind of man made for love. At drinking parties, he was a happy man if he just drank without eating much."

"In one of his journals he wrote that the drunker he got, the better the expression of his words. First they dropped melodiously, then tottered, then raved, then rumbled like thunder and lightning, then crumbled apart, then became something like mud."[2]

"He was an interesting guy. When he got drunk, he wanted to stand up and pee. No matter where he was, he stood up and let it go at full volume. We've stood along next to him and done it plenty of times. His shop, the Garakuta, on Shimodori Street, burned down in the war with all the other disasters. I immediately went to check on what was left of it, and was so full of emotion remembering the past that I just stood there alone and peed into the moldering ruins. It reminded me of Santoka."

Gian Mochizuki, the abbot who helped Santoka become a priest, lived at this time in the Daiji-ji, a large temple in Kawajiri-machi, so I visited Sakino and asked her to guide me there. It was a day when tea flowers were blooming white in the temple grounds and an autumn breeze was whistling through the area. Looking to the east, the plume of smoke from the Mount Aso volcano rose faintly in the distance. The white-eyebrowed old roshi looked as though he were calling up a dream from the distant past.

Ah, ah, Santoka-san. It must be thirteen years now since he passed away. I made him a priest because he was so single-minded about his seeking. After that, I gave him the name Koho. Ah, so it was you who put out this book, The Haiku Poet, Santoka. Well, well. If Santoka entered the road he loved and became a first-rate Japanese poet after that, then he did well. Well, then, let's go to the main hall now and recite a sutra for him.

Putting down his book, the old roshi picked up some incense and stood up. At that moment I looked at his rough and gnarled hands. The Zen master Hyakujo had said, "A day without work is a day without eating," and had done farm labor every day. This old roshi, now nearing his eighties, was a man who seemed to enjoy his daily work, too: when we came to visit, he was making preparations for the rice harvest. I looked keenly at those hands. These were the very hands that held the razor that cut off the hair of the troubled Santoka.

The bus from Kumamoto to Yamaga runs to the northeast on a single road through Kunihara. After just forty minutes, I got off at a town called Ueki, visited Mrs. Toshiko Hasuda, and paid my respects at the grave of her husband Zenmei.[3] After another ten minutes on the bus, I arrived in Mitori. Three of us got off there, turned to the left from the business street, and soon ascended a slope. Stone steps continued upward beneath the drooping branches of a large pine. Climbing the stone steps to the top, we found the Mitori Kannon temple standing desolately in the autumn wind. There was a sort of wide garden in the front, and the leaves of a persimmon tree were falling down by ones and twos.

This was the temple where, on March 5, 1925, Santoka came to live alone as the resident priest, thanks to the kindness of the abbot Gian Mochizuki. Verses that Santoka wrote here come to mind right away:

All the pines,
their branches drooping:
Namu Kanzeon.[4]

松はみな
枝垂れて
南無観世音

Morning and evening,
striking the bell
in the autumn wind.

松風に
明け暮れの
鐘撞いて

Sweeping along the hedge,
its flowers blooming
after a long time.

ひさしぶりに
掃く垣根の花が
咲いている

Having indulged himself in literature and sake, Santoka had been shot through with confusion after confusion, and hardship after hardship. In renouncing the world, he transcended the line of death and—for the first time in his life living as a temple's resident priest on a peaceful mountain—if he was lonely, well then, he was lonely; if he was thankful, well then, he was thankful. He now entered a completely different kind of life.

Santoka looked back on the road that he had walked for the forty-four years of his past as though it were a dream. He now discovered his solitary way in a totally changed form. The man who had downed one cup of sake after another, now placed his palms together and intoned "*Namu Kanzeon.*"[4] He lived as a solitary man, restrained this solitary man and, although it was small, struck the bell that hung from the eaves morning and evening, and served the Buddha.

When Santoka was alive, he kindly spoke to me about the Mitori Kannon temple, and I remembered his words as my hands touched the thick trunks of the pines.

It's a little temple at the top of some high stone steps. I became more settled down and grown up, and the people in the village treated me kindly. I could read books and didn't have to worry about something to eat. I might have continued to live there much longer, but after just a year, being as immature as I am, I took off on an aimless wandering journey.

There was no well, so I had some difficulty with water. But, you see, the people in the village filled up two bucketfuls every day, alternating one person with another. That wasn't a lot for one person to use, but I bowed my head to their kindnesses.

There's a phrase, "A half-ladle of water at the Eiheiji," [5] but for the first time in my forty-four years of living, I knew what it is to waste water. And I was one who washed down sake as though it were water!

Since then, I haven't used a drop of water uselessly . . . no, it seems as though I just can't. When I'm walking around town begging and see a young housewife open up a water spigot and let the water run, I quickly turn it off. No matter how beautifully her face may be made up with white powder and all, I would see her as an ugly woman and pass on by.

But the most troubling thing at the Mitori temple was when the old folks in the village would climb up the stone steps and ask me to pray for a sick child. Those people would be so kind as to say that if only I would pray just a little, they would bring me a large measure of rice in thanks, whether the illness abated or not. But I couldn't do that. When a good-for-nothing like me reads the Kannon Sutra, there's no reason for an illness to be cured, is there.

There were also people like old ladies who would come and ask me to write letters and postcards for them, and I could do something like that. During festivals, or the Buddhist services during the Equinox Week, or seasonal celebrations, they brought me mountains of mochi rice cake and dumplings. Of course, they didn't bring me these things because of some virtue of mine. They offered them to the bodhisattva Kannon, and I was rude enough to take them as sort of hand-me-downs.

When I said that I was going to leave the temple, the people in the village would not hear of it. They asked if they hadn't done something to displease me, and I was at a loss. In the end, I wasn't doing anything but writing a few haiku and ringing the bell morning and evenings, and I was pained by the fact that I was being taken care of and receiving offerings from the believers in the village. At the same time, I thought it was horrible for a degenerate priest without the proper qualifications to be hiding and living under the shadow of Kannon. I was without those qualifications, and thought that if I didn't do more training, I would never settle down.

Santoka's wife, who had heard the same wind through the pines long ago and was now already sixty-three years old, talked about some of the events of that time. Even though she had been his wife, this was the first time she had visited the remains of where Santoka had lived in his hermitage.

When it seemed he couldn't stand it any longer, he would go to Kumamoto and drink. But even then, well, it must have been something to live alone in this lonely place.

According to a letter from Santoka to his friend Rokubei Kimura on April 14, 1925, from Kumamoto:

I retreated from the Mitori in a state of confusion. I plan on doing formal training at the Eiheiji, the head temple in Echizen. I'll probably depart about the end of May. Starting today, I'll be doing some formal Buddhist begging in Amakusa. At the end of the month I'll return to Kumamoto and help out at the head temple.

Because all the things a wandering monk would carry—robe, needle, bamboo hat—had been kindly prepared for him by Gian, he did not make an appearance at the head temple, but started buoyantly out on a wandering aimless journey. I think that here, too, was a great fork in the road of fate.

Abandoning the Mitori Kannon temple, Santoka let himself go like drifting clouds or flowing water, and went on a journey of religious mendicancy. This wandering journey continued from April of 1925 to September of 1932. This was, truly, nonstop drifting. From September of 1930 he wrote the detailed diaries *Gyokoki* [Records of Begging] and *Gochu nikki* [Gochu Diary],[6] but for the six years up until then it is unclear where or in what direction he walked along. I can conjecture from what he told me when he was alive and from some of his other writings, however, that Santoka first made a pilgrimage to the temples of Kyushu, then crossed over to the island of Shikoku and made the pilgrimage to the eighty-eight temples there.

Though this was a pilgrimage, it was also a journey left to aimless wandering. This could have developed after getting used to a good bit of travel, or by at first following a planned itinerary. Either way, it was an easy walk from one amulet-granting temple to the next. At each temple on these pilgrimages in the Kyushu area and Shikoku, a section of a sutra was stamped in a register Santoka carried, marking his visit there. Later, when he was living at the Gochu-an hermitage in Ogori, he gave the register to me and said, "I don't need this anymore. I'm giving it to you." I had no idea what he was thinking or what I was going to do with it, but took it anyway. Why would he have given it to me?

One day at the Gochu-an, I was talking about my mother. She had gotten old, so once a month I would travel from Hiroshima to my home village in the countryside of Okayama to visit her. I told Santoka that going to the Buttsuji temple,[7] going to visit my mother, and meeting him from time to time at the Gochu-an were my three biggest pleasures in the midst of a busy life as a government official. Santoka's eyes moistened and he seemed extremely moved.

Thereupon, I received the sutra register from Santoka, went to my old hometown, and put the register in my mother's care. My mother had also had the experience of making the Shikoku pilgrimage. Overjoyed, she put great store in the register and placed it in her Buddhist altar. In the summer of 1943 when my mother passed away at the age of eighty-two, I placed the register in her coffin. I thought in my heart then that Santoka would be kind enough to travel in that other world with my mother.

In April of 1926, I shouldered my insolvable doubts, and left on a trip of wandering and begging.

Pushing through,
ever pushing through;
the blue-green mountains.

分け入っても
分け入っても
青い山

On June 17, 1926, Santoka left Kumamoto and went to Hamamachi. After passing through Umamihara and Takachiho, on the twenty-second he came to Takinoshita in Miyazaki Prefecture, which runs along a river called the Gokasegawa, and stayed. The verses he wrote between those dates were about the proliferation of green leaves, the new green of the leaves deepening with the beginning of summer, and the green in the mountains deepening every day. He made his journey passing over mountains, pushing through mountains, and pushing through again. Day after day of endlessly continuing mountains.

What was he looking for? Deeper and deeper into the mountains, his surroundings became only more and more green. No matter how many times he called out, there was never an answer. In silence, the mountains in the distance consisted of limitless blue layers. Sometimes he took off his bamboo hat and gazed at those mountains; or sometimes his figure might be seen sitting alone on a rock gazing upward. The following verse was written on a *tanzaku* poem card.[8] When someone requested a poem, Santoka happily wrote it down and left it behind. It is a representative work of Santoka the traveler.

いとどに濡れて
これは道しるべの石

Soaked to the skin!
Here's the stone guidepost
showing the way.

A passing shower goes through, and with wet straw hat and wet robes, Santoka has become a wet monk. Walking along the mountain road in the rain—isn't that a soaking wet lonely guidepost over there? Ah, signpost, have you been drenched by this rain, too?

炎天をいただいて
乞い歩く

Out begging for alms.
My gift:
the scorching sun.

While on this journey, before he knew it, the scorching sun of the dog days of summer seemed to continue one after another. Santoka walked along under this scorching sun, holding his begging bowl and reciting the sutras, going from eave to eave and from house to house. This must be the humblest position a human being can reach. Some people may have seen him as simple beggar, and this was not a false impression. For this "not one thing"[9] Santoka, if he did not beg as he walked, he would not eat.

But Santoka was not begging and traveling in order to eat. By begging, one attempts to diminish one's own attachments and to remove one's selfish opinions and pride. This is called Buddhist self-discipline. Thus, one cannot talk of heat or cold. Raising one's voice under the scorching sun and reciting the sutras, one attempts to extinguish the rambling thoughts in the mind.

風の中
声はりあげて
南無観世音

Raising my voice
  into the wind,
    Namu Kanzeon.

踏みわける
萩よ
すすきよ

Stepping right through them:
  Bush clover!
    Miscanthus!

Summer turned unnoticed into fall. Bush clover bloomed beautifully on the mountain roads where there was no one to see it, and the silver tufts of miscanthus were bent in the autumn wind. Although commonplace, bush clover and miscanthus naturally symbolize the Japanese autumn. Stepping through these beautiful plants, Santoka traveled on with his journey yet again today.

When the autumn began to deepen even more, the mountain roads became filled with fallen leaves. When a gust of wind rushed in from the north, the leaves fluttering down from the trees and spilling over his bamboo hat truly seemed to bury the mountain. In the midst of these falling leaves, Santoka walked along alone without thoughts. When you walk, just walk; this is the Way.

この旅、
果てもない旅の
つくつくぼうし

This journey,
  this journey without end;
    tsukutsukuboshi.[10]

This was a verse he wrote the summer of the following year. In the villages tucked away between the cool mountains, the cry of the cicada resounded inconsolably. As Santoka listened alone to this insect tied emotionally to his old home since times long ago, the loneliness of an endless journey pressed in on him. Where, after all, was he going by walking this road? Santoka, where were you going?

Tasting the water,
*   my heart*
*   afloat.*

へうへうとして
水を味ふ

Walking, being on a journey, the pure water in the valleys is a parent to one's life. Santoka, who especially loved water, would put the bubbling liquid to his mouth, taste it, and drink to absolute satisfaction, forgetting everything but its savor.

The falling moon;
*   a solitary figure*
*   watching.*

落ちかかる月を
観ているに
一人

The solitary traveler leans heavily against the pillar of an old temple and watches the moon sink into the mountain. The autumn is deepening and the moon is waning. He sits alone facing the moon, watching it go. If you would call this loneliness, it was a lonely contemplation of the moon, but Santoka was determined to penetrate his solitude to its core.

While there's still sun,
*   stretching out*
*   my legs.*

投げだしてまだ
陽のある脚

Santoka's legs kindly walked along for him day after day. Stretching those dog-tired legs out on the grass, he sat looking intently at them and himself, the western sun shining on his thighs and calves. Perhaps it was saying, "Go ahead. Walk some more."

Giving a lift
　　to the dragonfly:
　　　my bamboo hat.

笠にとんぼを
とまらせて
あるく

As the summer came to a close, a great number of dragonflies flew about in the mountains and fields. The dragonfly is an insect that takes to people, and one suddenly came and rested on Santoka's bamboo hat. This was somehow pleasing to him, and this was Santoka with his child's heart: making his journey together with the dragonfly, being as careful as he could not to move his bamboo hat so that it would not fly away.

Walking without end;
　　spider lilies[11] blooming
　　　without end.

歩きつづける
彼岸花咲きつづける

This verse was perhaps one he wrote around 1929, when he was in the San'yo area. If it was in September, spider lilies would have been blooming continually, day after day, along the side of the road, in the shade of thickets and by the side of Buddhist temples. While he would have been thinking about how wonderfully the flowers bloomed one after another, he himself would have been walking along step by step, day after day, as he looked at them. Looking at the flowers blooming infinitely, Santoka walked totteringly along the endless road of his journey.

How lonely
    the road
      so straight ahead.

まつぐな道で
さみしい

This is a straightforward expression without embellishment. Persimmons ripened and flowers bloomed along the paths that wound and turned around the ridges of the rice paddies or the foot of the mountains, and one never tires of the old guideposts and stone Jizo bodhisattvas[12] standing at the side of the road. But a large, broad, charmless single road, whether quiet or filled with passing vehicles, was a lonely road for Santoka, a road that gave him cheerless thoughts. This is a feeling that will be understood by anyone who has made journeys on foot.

Silently putting them on:
    today's
      straw sandals.

だまつて
今日の
わらじ穿く

This is a verse written on a morning he departed a cheap lodging house. Santoka exercised body and mind with one koan per day. He would continually walk silently and earnestly for months and days. There were days when, no matter how much effort he put into it, he could not realize physically the true meaning of the teachings of the ancients. "Today I'll walk on and turn this over correctly in my mind!" Thinking this way, he put on his straw sandals, stood up and departed.

Pleasantly drunk,[13]
    falling
      leaves.

ほろほろ酔うて
木の葉ふる

Santoka loved sake. From amongst the money offerings he had collected in the beggar's bag suspended from his neck, he would from time to time pick out a few coins and knock down a cup. This, for him, was a supreme pleasure. In fact, Santoka could not pass by the front of an old sake shop in the countryside without stopping for a drink. The feeling of being "pleasantly" drunk came after a pint or so. Smacking his lips, he would once again walk out into the autumn wind. He himself would be pleasantly drunk, and the leaves would scatter with a light sound as they fell on his bamboo hat. Sake, Santoka, and the falling leaves—the above verse has the three merged into one. Later, when somebody made a request for a poem, he would happily write this verse down:

A cold autumn drizzle:
　　somehow not dying,
　　I carry on.

しぐるるや
死なないでいる

Imperceptibly, the autumn deepened and the late autumn showers began to fall on the mountain roads.

A "traveler"
　　let my name be called;
　　the first autumn shower.
　　　　　　　　—Basho

In Basho's verse we somehow feel that walking along soaked by the autumn shower is one of the fanciful elegances of making a journey. But to Santoka, it was a matter of life and death. He was a mendicant who lived solely by means of the rice he received while begging. When he looked back on the way he had traveled along, soaked by the late autumn showers, he must have thought, "Well then, I've been allowed to live at least up to now!" Whether this was by the Buddha's protection or the compassion of others, Santoka could do nothing but hold gratitude in his heart as he listened keenly to the sound of the rain.

Translator's Notes

1. Koho (耕畝): Lit., "cultivating furrows."
2. The words translated as verbs in this sentence are all mimesis in Japanese. The sequence here is: *horohoro, furafura, gudegude, gorogoro, boroboro* and *dorodoro*. These all suggest certain sounds and states to the Japanese, but unfortunately not to us.
3. Zenmei Hasuda (1905–1945): Great interpreter of classical Japanese literature. Created theories on the nature of words and languages.
4. *Namu Kanzeon*: "Praise to Kanzeon." Kanzeon is another name for the bodhisattva Kannon (Sanskrit, Avalokitesvara; Chinese, Kuan Yin).
5. *Eihei hanshaku no mizu* (永平半杓の水): At the Eiheiji, the main temple of the Soto sect, water was never to be wasted. This phrase was to instruct the monks to use water (and all resources) sparingly, watering the flowers with the water used to wash dishes, for example.
6. The tiles of these books are 行乞記 and 其中日記 respectively.
7. A temple of the Rinzai Zen sect. Founded in 1397 by Haruhira Kobayakawa. Located some distance from Mihara City in Okayama Prefecture.
8. *Tanzaku*: a strip of fancy stiff paper used as a vertical poem card at special events or leave-takings
9. "Not one thing" (無一物). From the Zen phrase from Huineng, the sixth Zen patriarch, "From the beginning, not one thing exists" (本来無一物). Here "not one thing" seems to refer to Santoka's pursuit of Buddhist self-discipline.
10. *Tsukutsukuboshi*: A kind of singing cicada. Literally, a priest who goes "*tsukutsuku,*" as if intoning the sutras.
11. Spider lilies, or Equinox flowers: Scarlet trumpeted spider lilies, *Lycoris radiate*. These flowers bloom at the autumnal equinox, which, like the vernal equinox, is an important Buddhist festival. They are found at the edges of fields, on banks, and around the moat of the Imperial Palace in Tokyo. It is an ancient belief that they are among the flowers found in paradise, and so are often planted in graveyards.
12. Jizo: Lit., "Earth Womb" or "Earth Repository." Jizo is a bodhisattva who travels through the six realms of Buddhist cosmology saving suffering beings, but is especially well known for his compassion towards children, small animals and travelers. His stone statues are ubiquitous in Japan, and mothers will often tie a bib around the necks of these stautes, asking for

his protection of their children. Jizo carries a staff with six iron rings at the top that jingles as he walks so that small animals will not get underfoot. With this staff he also can break through the gates of Hell.

13. The Japanese word is *horo horo*, mimesis implying pleasantly, scatteringly, or melodiously.

CHAPTER 3

The Mountains and Rivers of Kyushu

Santoka continued his wandering journey into the year 1930. On September 14, he stopped at the Miyakawaya, a cheap boarding house in the village of Hitoyoshi in Kumamoto Prefecture. As always, he wrote in his journal. Included in this day's entry:

> *I've left again on a journey. In the end, I'm nothing more than a panhandling priest. Somehow, I can't help being a foolish traveler spending his whole life in perpetual motion. Like floating weeds, I go from this shore to that. Enjoying a pitiable tranquility—I'm sad, yet happy.*
>
> *Water flows on, and clouds move unceasingly. When the wind blows, the leaves fall from the trees.*
>
> *When fish swim, they are like fish; when birds fly, they resemble birds. So, you two legs of mine, just walk as long as you can; go on to the place we're going to.*

He called himself a "panhandling priest," and this was a rather frank confession. As one who tried to devote himself to his own Way, and with an excellent teacher, he went so far as to renounce the world and become a priest. Then, did he not become the resident priest of the Mitori Kannon temple for a while, serving the Buddha day and night, ringing the temple bell, and reciting the sutras?

But then he abruptly left on a wandering journey. If he really had had the will to become a Zen monk, he should have spent any number of years attached to the dojo at the Eiheiji temple following the fundamental Buddhist discipline. It was no doubt unbearable for Santoka, however, just to hear that sake was prohibited. And for a man over forty to take the lowest seat and engage in Buddhist austerities among young monks in their twenties would have been truly difficult. Thus, walking endlessly through Kyushu, Shikoku, the San'yo and the San'in regions, he wandered on for five years without any fixed destination. It was his intention to try and make his daily travels function as Zen self-discipline, but he never reached a realm that was anything like enlightenment. Thanks to alcohol, he sank into a pitiful sleep.

Yes, Santoka dressed himself in a black robe, put a bamboo hat on his head, held a begging bowl in his hands and—standing under the eaves—recited the sutras. But, he wondered, wasn't hiding under a monk's robes and hoping to receive a lot of alms just one example of being nothing more than a swindler? One way of looking at it is that the man who takes on the appearance of a priest is himself nothing more than a beggar.

"I'm a panhandling priest." He himself realized that he was nothing more than that.

Then, as a foolish traveler, he did no more than live his life drifting around and around like floating weeds. He simply went on to wherever he was going, giving himself over to the universe, flowing on like water and moving like detached clouds. He would live as long as he received enough to be able to eat—this would be a day when he could eat; but if he could not eat, he would die a pure and manly death. This was the stance the traveling Santoka took.

The evening crickets crying; [1] *I'm alone.*

かなかないて
ひとりである

Drawing water
　　　from a single sluice,
　　one house's autumn.

一すじの水を
ひき一つ家の秋

Burning my diaries:
　　　is this all that is left?
　　The ashes.

焼き捨てて
日記の灰の
これだけか

These were entries in his diary for September 16.

Yes, there is no mistaking that he was a panhandling priest, but this panhandler was one who wrote haiku. If he did not compose haiku, he could not help feeling lonely. No, he composed haiku *because* he felt lonely.

The day came to an end as he walked along the mountain path that followed the Kuma River. Where would he stay the night? But even as he was thinking about where tonight's lodging might be, there were those cicadas crying incessantly in the branches above his head. Santoka stood there at the day's end of his journey without destination, wrapped in the mournful melody of the cicadas, and closed in on thick and fast by his loneliness. Was this the moment his verse came bubbling to the surface?

At the side of this lonely road stood a solitary house. Water was being drawn off from the river by one little sluice that took it in the direction of the house. Here, too, was human life. The colors of the deep autumnal crimson leaves could still not be seen, but that one stream of water added its features to the scene of the peaceful house.

Santoka's diaries are singular and without precedent as journal literature among Japanese. Yet regrettably, here he burned all of his diaries up to September of 1930. When reading the lines, "Is this all there is of my diaries' ashes?" one feels that he must have burned a great volume and then wondered at the few ashes that remained. If it were for me to say, I would state that if he had not burned these diaries and kindly left them to us, we would have known his footsteps quite clearly and would have nothing to regret.

After this, his single volume of notes filled up, and he sent them to his friend Rokubei Kimura for safekeeping.

Therefore, I think Santoka had a number of different feelings about burning up his diaries at this point. One of the reasons he did so may have been that he had come to despise himself. Another may have been that as he walked around carrying old diaries, he began to think of them as annoying extra baggage on his journey and, not being attached to things, simply burned them up.

> Today while I was begging, I got sad. At one of the houses an old lady tottered out and was kind enough to give me some alms. But looking at her, I was suddenly reminded of my grandmother, and wanted to cry.
>
> Rather than saying that my grandmother was unhappy, you could better say that she was unhappiness itself. And in response to all that I owed her, I did nothing, nothing at all. It seems that I only pained and distressed her. I didn't do anything more than prolong the unhappiness of her long life of ninety-one years.

On September 17, he arrived at the town of Kyomachi in Miyazaki Prefecture. Here there were thermal hot springs. And here was potato shochu liquor. These were both things that Santoka had a liking for—first soaking himself in the hot springs, then sitting down at the shochu shop counter and tasting a cup. You can almost see Santoka's laughing, drinking face. And beyond that, today, he encountered one other thing he loved, and that was tofu. Not only that, but the tofu shop was a companion business to the boarding house. He must have been able to eat this tofu—the tofu he loved so much—to his heart's content.

The hot springs, the shochu and the tofu. What a blessed day it must have been. A journey can be lonely, but even in the midst of loneliness such happiness can exist. This may be nothing more than a low-cost simple "elegance," but Santoka's traveler's heart was warmed by such things, and his body and mind made gloriously happy. And because such things existed, he may have been unable to stop being a "panhandling priest."

This area has the feel of a mountain village. When I go out begging, the children follow along after me.

Wearing his large bamboo hat, Santoka's figure of a Zen priest must have been a rare one, and a large number of children flocked along behind him. Whether this was pleasant or embarrassing for him, Santoka probably continued reciting the sutras and holding out his begging bowl as he went from house to house, periodically looking back at the innocent faces of the children.

The following day, it was not the smiling faces of children that he encountered, but the barking of a large dog that looked as if it would bite him. As might be expected, the plucky Santoka was not unnerved by the situation. Reciting the sutra, his voice never changed, and he continued his begging with perfect composure. This dog was known throughout the village as being quite ferocious, and the villagers were concerned for Santoka. He, however, was so composed that the dog probably grew weary of barking and, lowering its tail, returned home. While on a begging journey, various things can happen on the road, it seems.

In the village of Miyakonojo, people appeared to be quite warm-hearted, and the alms Santoka received exceeded those received in other villages. The feeling there was more free and easy as well, and Santoka stayed three nights at a boarding house called the Enatsuya for forty sen[2] a night. A forty-sen boarding house was a high-class place for Santoka.

One night Santoka went to the Christian church in the town and listened to the sermon by a Shunpei Honma. Honma-san was from the same prefecture as Santoka and, even as a Christian, led a unique existence. So it would appear that Santoka went with considerable expectations. Nevertheless, he wrote:

I was happy to hear the sermon, but cannot say that I was not disillusioned. It was more commonplace than I had anticipated, and he was a bit overly skillful, I suppose. I was disappointed, but sat through it.

The next day while begging, he stood in front of a certain café. Two or three waitresses were occupied and paid him absolutely no notice. Ordinarily he would have given up right away and left, but Santoka began to feel a little mischievous, perhaps to beguile the tedious hours of his journey. In a sort of standoff, he continued to recite the Kannon Sutra with a humorous rhythm. At the point where he had read through just about half of this long sutra, one of the girls came out and went to toss a one-sen coin into his begging bowl. Santoka, however, did not take it, and said, "Thank you, but since it's really the same as if I'd already received it, I'll give it to you as a tip." At this, the girl laughed, as did Santoka. Later, he wrote:

Even though it was just a little disagreeable, how about that as a scene of nonsense?

This was just horseplay, but Santoka was able to feel that kind of latitude in Miyakonojo.

A short while later, an old lady on her way to visit a temple gave Santoka two sen as they passed each other by. But when he looked at the coins carefully, he could see that one of them was a blackened nickel five-sen piece. To receive six sen was a bit too much—the usual amount being five rin[3] or one sen. Santoka called out to stop the old lady, and returned the five-sen piece. The old lady was extremely happy at this, pocketed the coin, and gave him another one sen. Such things happen from time to time, but a roadside scene like this would make anyone smile.

For Santoka, it was a fine thing to receive alms from others. Although one sen is a small amount, it can be charged with the beautiful heart of the Buddha. If it was able to call forth people's Buddha Mind and Buddha Nature to awakening, the begging bowl was no longer a means for him to receive rice and money in order to eat; it was the great work of a bodhisattva done without preaching or anything else. It was far and away more religious than the disillusioning and overly skillful sermon he had heard the night before.

The one-sen coin
    tossed to me;
      what radiance!

投げ与へられた
一銭の光だ

The grasses
    trampled by horses,
      in full bloom.

馬がふみにぢる
草は花ざかり

From Miyakonojo he went on to Miyazaki. Here he visited a number of haiku-poet friends, including Sakuro Sugita, Kosokuba Kuroki, and Togyuji Nakajima, who provided him with various sorts of entertainment. From Miyazaki, he followed the seacoast, begging as he went along, and on September 30, was able to do some sightseeing in Aoshima. He looked at various tropical plants such as the *biroju*[4] and the *hamaomoto.*[5] Loving water as he did, he scooped and tasted the water from the Shima no Ido well on the grounds of the Aoshima shrine. This he thought vary tasty and without any hint of saltwater.

The straw sandals I bought today were excellent. My sensation was that they fit my feet perfectly. This is a pleasure known only to travelers like me. Basho mentioned that a traveler's hopes are for a good lodging and good straw sandals. This has not changed in the past or present.

This he wrote in his journal; and as he thought about Basho's travels, Santoka walked happily along the sea through the fishing villages of southern Miyazaki, where the local accent is a little hard to understand. Nevertheless:

The unending sound of waves;
my hometown
far away.

波音の
たえずして
ふるさと遠し

The sound of waves, far away,
close by; of my remaining days,
how many?

波音遠くなり
近くなり
余命いくばくぞ

If such verses depict a welling loneliness, then, yes, it was a lonely journey. In his hometown, his house had fallen into ruin and people passed away, and there was not one person who would be thinking of someone like Santoka. Strangely enough, however, he could not forget the mountains and rivers of his old hometown. As he walked along with the sound of waves at his left all day long, somehow he could not help thinking about his own destination. Where and in what way would he die? He didn't care as long as he could keep going on to wherever it was that he was going. Day by day he walked on, staring hard at death.

Walking until he was tired out, he was able to get lodging in the village of Ishii, but there was no bath. There can be nothing more lonely than being tired and in a lodging house without a bath. To a single man like Santoka, a bath is a pleasure that warms the entire body at the cheapest price. With his mood somehow deflated, he went out as usual, knocked down three cups of shochu, and fell into a deep sleep.

But what about the taste of the new pickled greens that came with breakfast at this lodging house? It was absolutely the taste of the beginning of autumn, and its savor filled body and mind. In his journal he wrote:

As a Japanese, I feel that those who have been unable to taste a Japanese pickle, miso soup and tofu are ineffably unlucky.

On October 2, Santoka visited the Udo shrine. Passing among the silent old cedars and camphor trees, he went down the road of pure sand that led there. From the sanctuary inside a rocky cave on the shore, he could see huge waves rolling in from the expansive sea just as they had since ancient times. After finishing his devotions, he stayed at a cheap boarding house called the Hamada-ya. This was a nice and extraordinarily peaceful inn, and thus he was able to compose haiku and write picture postcards to his friends. Later, he thought things over to himself:

There is both bad luck and good luck in knowing the taste of sake. Heavy drinking and a love of sake are two different things, but a good number of people who love sake are heavy drinkers. One cup is a cup of unhappiness; one bottle is a bottle of woe.

Getting mellow with one, two or three cups, a person adapts naturally to human life—and this is good fortune. To be drunk and laughing is truly so. But to be drunk and disorderly is due to drinking excessively.

Today while begging, though I received just enough for lodging and food, I went out and begged through Udo again and received more rice and money. That was because I wanted to drink some sake. What a despicable thing—to turn alms right into alcohol and nicotine.

Santoka, who had a mind strongly prone to reflection, was self-critical in this way when it came to sake.

No matter what, no matter how, I absolutely must renounce

and abandon sake on this journey. I must reach that point in
life where it's all right to either have a drink or not have a drink.
The act itself of tasting sake is fine.

In this way, he outfitted himself for Buddhist austerities every day, and stood begging at people's houses; and it was by that alone that he was able to eat and get by. As such, he was nothing more than a mere beggar. But at the least, he was determined to abandon his own self-attachment and see through to the real Santoka. Now within that self-attachment, the element with the strongest root was sake. Without thinking over the problem of sake, acting on it and becoming enlightened, would he really understand the purpose of this pilgrimage?

From Udo, he went south along the coast, crossed two small mountain passes, and arrived at the beautiful and peaceful town of Obi, begging as he passed through. At one house he was thrown a one-*sen* copper coin as though it were quite a troublesome act by a woman who was reading the magazine *Shufu no tomo.*[6] Santoka silently picked up the coin from the ground, returned it to her husband who was there as well, continued reciting the sutra, and then departed. What kind of hardhearted woman could she have been? But if one became angry in such situations, there would be no tossing away of self-attachment.

Not long thereafter, an old lady purposefully chased after him and humbly gave him a donation of one sen. Now, though it was the same one-sen coin, the one woman threw it at him while the other offered it devotedly. In continually coming into contact with the hearts of such people, Santoka continually polished his own.

This was a day when Santoka encountered a number of strange women. He now decided to continue his begging and return to his lodgings, but on his way he passed by a young lady who very respectfully offered him a ten-sen coin. A ten-sen coin? He bowed his head with deep emotion. Perhaps this woman reminded him of his dead mother or father.

As he had received a rather good amount of rice and money, he went to a barber shop and got a haircut for the first time in a long time. His face reflected in the middle of a large mirror, he could see how much his hair had turned white over the years he had spent in travel. The barber was a young man, but conducted himself in a truly polite way and showed no annoyance at all at the grime that covered Santoka.

I sit in weeds
that have become
this fall.

秋となった
雑草にすわる

My body imbued
with the taste of water;
autumn has come.

水の味も身にしむ
秋となる

Leaving the town of Obi, Santoka arrived at Yutsu and begged through the town, spending three nights there. He then continued walking through Odotsu and Kami no Machi. On the road in Odotsu, a middle-aged man stood in front of Santoka and bowed politely. He then asked, "Where is the Way?" [7]

"The Way is beneath your feet," Santoka responded. "Just go straight ahead."

Santoka had drunk a little shochu. He was feeling slightly inebriated, but answered without hesitation.

"The Way is not distant, but is close at hand. Aren't you really on the Way right now?"

Then the man asked him,

"Where is the Mind?"

"The everyday mind—this is the Way,[8] you know. When you encounter tea, drink tea; when you encounter rice, eat rice. If you have parents, be filial to your parents. Be loving to your children. The Mind is neither inside nor out."

The man once again lowered his head, bowed and then left. Santoka walked on with a smile. For him, that had been a good performance.

My priest's robe,
lousy with dirt.
I don't care.

まよ法衣は
垢で朽ちた

I should walk slowly;
I'm upsetting
the bush clover.

ゆつくり歩かう
萩がこぼれる

The village of Shibushi was in Kagoshima Prefecture, and the police there were quite strict. Begging, peddling in an importunate manner, and mendicancy were all controlled according to the letter of the law, so that if you stood under the eaves of a house panhandling, you would be reprimanded. It was all right to simply recite the sutras as you passed through town, but in this way no one would give you alms. Santoka was rebuked any number of times and, since there was nothing to be done, he went to the train station behind the town, read the newspaper, and then went to his inn about eleven o'clock in the morning. This was a cheap boarding house called the Kagoshima-ya, and all of the other boarders at the place were bad characters.

There were three men to one room: a traveling salesman dealing in essence of pine needles, a man whose employment was nondescript and who was a heavy drinker, and Santoka. In the next room was a masseur who was also a pilgrim, and a knife-sharpener. However, five Chinese traveling salesmen were moved into their room, so the masseur and the knife sharpener were moved to Santoka's. In the end, five men stayed in Santoka's room that night. In Santoka's ideal inn there was one person to one room, one lamp and one bath, and then one cup of sake. To have five men in a small room and to be overloaded with their various small talk, reading a book or anything else was impossible. But Santoka, who made travel itself his own little nest, had no problem with being in the middle of such disorderly dubious characters, and expertly spent the night harmoniously with them in the inn.

When the masseur saw Santoka take out his writing brush, he asked him to write two postcards for him. At this, the knife sharpener brought out six postcards of his own and asked Santoka to write up the latest news to his wife and children. Yet even in the midst of such a boarding house scene, Santoka did not forget to write down haiku in his journal after the others had gone to sleep.

After they've all gone to sleep,
     a wonderful
          moonlit night.

みんな
寝てしまつて
よい月夜かな

Moonlight everywhere;
          a night of self-indulgent
     bugs.

月光あまねく
ほしいままなる
虫の夜だ

Stretching out my leg,
          the fellow I touched:
     a man from Shikoku.

伸ばした足に
ふれた隣りは
四国の人

From Shibushi, Santoka begged through Kishigawa and the village of Sueyoshi. He then went back to Miyakonojo.

Anything like mendicancy has been impossible, so I've been lying down reading books. It's been a pleasant day, a carefree day. "Sufficient unto the day is the affliction thereof." These are Christ's words, and I am thankful for them.

Santoka relaxed here the entire day, without attachment, without desire, without thinking of tomorrow, and being thoroughly compassionate to both body and mind.

年とれば
故郷こひしい
つくつくぼうし

As I get older,
    I yearn for my hometown;
tsukutsukuboshi.

一きれの
雲のない空の
さびしさまさる

Not one shred of cloud;
    the sky's increasing
loneliness.

こころ
しづかに
山のおきふし

A heart at peace;
    in the mountain,
waking and sleeping.

家を持たない
秋が
ふかうなつた

Having no house,
    the autumn
has grown late.

On this journey, a romantic traveler like Santoka would no doubt want to leave Shibushi and once again travel the seacoast of the Osumi Peninsula, turn south, and go on until he heard the torrent of the Black Current in the Pacific Ocean. Moreover, the autumn was gradually deepening, and wouldn't it be considered natural that he would turn towards the warm south? Retracing his steps, he entered the mountains from Shibushi and once again found his way back to Miyakonojo. Because the police in Kagoshima had been so exacting, he changed the direction of his journey to an area of full harvest—to an area where he would be free in his own activity. This he related to me at some time or another.

Because his was a wandering journey with no fixed destination, he went either to the west or the east, almost wherever the wind blew him, flowing along like a cloud. Being able to eat, to stay in an inn, allowing himself to down a cup—he traveled on and on in the direction that would permit him to fulfill these smallest desires.

Begging from Miyakonojo to Takaoka, Santoka suddenly became ill, which was rare for him. He left his inn at eight o'clock in the morning and went to go begging as usual. He had an unpleasant feeling, however, and his whole body trembled so that he was unable to walk. He found a small temple alongside of the road, and when he lay down on the wooden floor, four or five children came up to him.

"Honored priest, please rest on this."

As he looked at them drowsily, he saw that they had kindly spread out a mat on the ground. At the children's words, Santoka plopped down on the mat and lay down. Two hours passed like a bad dream. He seemed to have a high fever, but perhaps the earth swallowed it up, for at last he felt better. Seeming to regain his voice, he stood up. He looked around him, but the children had gone off somewhere and could not be seen. At that point, the following three verses came to mind, and he later recorded them in his journal:

大地ひえびえとして
熱のある体を
まかす

Chilly and cold,
entrusting my fevered body
to the earth.

I may die
  just like this,
    sleeping on unknown ground.

このまま死んでしまふ
かも知れない
土にねる

Stretching my fevered body
  out at length;
    the broad earth.

熱あるからだを
ながながと
伸ばす土

Santoka walked a short while and continued his begging from house to house. But at one house, an old lady who seemed to know the sutras well, listened intently to the Shushogi chant that Santoka intoned. Because she was listening with such ardor, there was no way that he could stop halfway. But even so, she threw nothing into his begging bowl at all. He finally finished reciting the Shushogi, and began with the Kannon Sutra, but the old lady only listened silently, neither giving him anything nor telling him to go away. Santoka stood there under the eaves, forgetting about the old lady, forgetting about himself, and just detachedly reading the long Kannon Sutra. When Santoka had chanted it all the way through, the old lady got up and tossed a one-sen piece into his bowl. At that moment he returned to himself and was once again aware of his body. During the thirty or forty minutes he had stood reading the sutras, his frame of mind and physical condition seemed to have improved almost completely. Perhaps this was what is called "invoking the strength of Kannon"; it was certainly wonderful and strange.

Nevertheless, Santoka was prudent and quickly finished the day's begging. Returning to his inn, he took a bath, found a drinking establishment, knocked down a cup, and slept soundly. By the next day, he had completely regained his health.

In a town called Tsuma in Miyazaki Prefecture, Santoka stayed two nights. This was the town to which he had come in 1926 when he had first gone out on a journey of mendicancy. In a room mixed with a number of different travelers, Santoka, as usual, wrote in his journal.

A day of not walking is lonely.
A day of not drinking is lonely.
A day of not writing poetry is lonely.

This would seem to say that while it was lonely being by himself, walking alone, drinking alone and writing alone were not lonely at all.

This, I think, truly says everything straightforwardly about the human being, Santoka. Santoka's life was in walking, drinking sake, and composing verse. The person who abandons his house, deserts his hermitage, and goes out on a one-man journey cannot help but be lonely, but he will not be so if he continues his travels, writes his verses, and drinks his sake. This is what he felt the value of living to be. I am not saying that this is good, bad, great or foolish; but I think it is right to say that it was in this way that Santoka came to know himself well.

In Fukushima, Miyazaki Prefecture, Santoka shared the inn with a singular fellow. This man had let his hair grow out and, as he was making a pilgrimage tour, supported his journey by reading the sutras and receiving alms. For all that, he loved fishing; and after finishing his meal, he gathered the other guests around him and exultantly told fishing stories with great pride, enveloping everyone in the smoke of his tales.

Sure enough, the following day he put off his Buddhist disciplines and went out to the river to fish. Moreover, he carried not even a one-sen piece in his purse. Borrowing a little money for bait from the people in the inn, off he went to fish, and in the evening came back—

just like in his stories—with a really big catch. He carefully prepared and cooked the fish himself, and then had everyone eat—Santoka also receiving the man's beneficence. An easygoing man, indeed.

The following day Santoka, along with the fisherman pilgrim and an elderly shakuhachi player, went off to town to look for some income; and each returned having received enough to pay for lodging and rice. But the next day it rained and they all idled about, shut together in the small room. The famed fisherman borrowed five sen for bait and went out in the rain to fish. Santoka relaxed, composing verse and writing in his journal. By evening the fisherman returned, having caught about thirty fish. Santoka once again received a donation of some of the catch, and enjoyed an evening drink of sake. Santoka offered a cup of this evening sake to the elderly shakuhachi player. The old man truly rejoiced at such an unexpected thing, and enjoyed his drink with a smiling face. Because of this, Santoka was now left without even one rin. This was a gathering of indigent, lonely and peculiar eccentrics, but even so, it was its own small society. Santoka called them World Masters, and he, of course, was one of them.

Such World Masters have their own vocabulary. When the day's take was meager and they had not received even enough for their room at the inn, for example, it was called *onryo*.[9] Breakfast was called *jigokuhan*, or the Hell Meal. Considering that after breakfast they would have to go out to some yet undetermined work, the meal must have been irritating and unpleasant. In the evening, however, the meal was said to be the *gokurakuhan*, or Paradise Meal, because they could enjoy themselves talking and dining at their leisure. The subjects of the World Masters' conversations were mostly fixed, no matter where they were. These would be: if the inns were good or bad, if the takings were plentiful or few, and if the weather was good or inclement. Also included were the pleasures of the World Master: sleeping, eating, drinking, and buying or selling when times were good.

Santoka lived in the midst of such good-for-nothings, but even though at a glance he resembled them in form, he was always thinking seriously about literature, the refinement of haiku, and the practice of religion.

In the village of Takanbe he was struck by how inexpensive things were. White rice that looked like silver was eighteen sen for one *sho*.[10] This was the price of a box of cigarettes. One bunch of greens was one or two rin. A splendid daikon radish was five rin. As Santoka begged, he wondered with the air of an administrator if the farmers could get along like this. On his way, he spied some of the yuzu citrus fruits he loved so much, bought one for one sen, and returned to his inn. At the inn he bought some miso before anything else for two sen, and made yuzu miso.

The next day he begged in the town of Tsuno. Forgetting the past and not thinking of the future, Santoka walked and lived only for his day-to-day life; but suddenly he was thunderstruck on the road: he had thought of his mother. He had also thought of his younger brother and his father. Both his mother and his younger brother had committed suicide. His father had fled his hometown and died a lonely man in another place. Santoka had not even been able to go to his funeral. What a tragedy for blood relatives! He himself had become a priest like this, wearing robes and reading the sutras every day, and this, of course, was a matter of his own religious awakening. At first he had had the feeling that he wanted to pray for such people's happiness in the next world. But now Santoka was on a journey, looking just like the so-called World Masters with whom he was associating, and simply consoling himself in the weariness of his travel with cups of sake. Wasn't this it? Now he was assailed by thoughts of self-condemnation:

Ah, Santoka! Have you no thoughts of shame about the priest's robes you wear?

On October 28, Santoka begged through the town of Mimitsu in Miyazaki. This day, for the first time, he was smitten by the late autumn showers in the mountains. It had been warm in southern Kyushu up to now, and he had worn an unlined robe. Now, however, he was no longer able to go along dressed like that, and changed to a lined garment. Soaked by the late autumn rains but continuing to beg in a truly unattached way, he received a sufficient amount of rice and money. Strangely enough, he gained a certain selflessness, and begged without particularly thinking about receiving. In this way, the result of his mendicancy was all the better. He walked as far as Tomitaka, quickly found an inn, and was able to write some verses:

Rotting away,
     every day coming apart at the seams:
my priestly robes.

朽ちてまいにち
綻びる旅の
法衣だ

Today's box lunch,
     too,
       sitting on weeds.

けふの
べんたうも
草の上にて

The sound of waves,
     wet with rain
     and dark.

波の音
しぐれて
暗し

The box lunch
     I'm eating, too,
     wet with rain.

食べている
おべんたうも
しぐれて

Showers off and on,
     everybody's
      wet.

しぐるるや
みんな
ぬれている

さんしぐれの
山越えて
また山

Late autumn rains, hey! [11]
　Crossing over the mountains,
　more mountains still.

墓がならんで
そこまで波が
おしよせる

The waves push in
　just so far;
　the line of graves.

The autumn rains continued to fall the following day. There was nothing he could do but relax in his comfortless single room at the inn. Whether from exhaustion due to the long journey or from not taking good care of himself, he was having some digestion problems and feeling out of sorts. When he rested without doing anything specific, a keen self-reflection came upon him. He wrote in his journal:

Today, all day, no getting angry.
Today, all day, no telling lies.
Today, all day, no wastefulness of things.

He had placed these three vows in his heart previously, and recently he rarely got angry. This was thanks to his Buddhist discipline and begging. Not telling lies was somewhat difficult. He did not want to tell lies with either his body or his mouth. Next, not to treat things carelessly, but to use each thing mindfully, was the hardest of all. He himself, who ate by receiving and lived by receiving, had to put things to good use more than others. The cold drizzling autumn rain called up in Santoka a day-long mood of reflecting on himself like this.

As might be expected, by November the autumn deepened even

in southern Kyushu. The weather was uncertain: sometimes drizzling with the late autumn rains, sometimes clearing up, and sometimes remaining cloudy. Although he had a slight fever, it would not do to stay in the inn forever. He was not a traveler who was going just so far; and if he stopped his body, his mind would shut down as well. Not only that, but there was no money to pay for lodging. Santoka was resolved to go from Mimitsu to Nobeoka, and thus decided to walk out and beg.

Going, going,
    right up to collapse;
the roadside weeds.

道の草
倒れるまでの
ゆきゆき

Slightly fevered,
    I hurry
through the wind.

急ぐ
熱がある風の中を
少し

Thankfully, however, while he walked on for ten miles [seventeen kilometers], reciting the sutras and begging, his fever went away and he began to feel better. He quickly found an inn in Nobeoka, took a bath and, refreshed, knocked down a cup of sake. After that he fell into a deep sleep.

The sky so high,
    I happily receive
my box lunch.

空たかく
べんたう
いただく

光あまねく
御飯
しろし

Light everywhere;

my rice,

white.

These are verses he wrote when he ate his box lunch by the side of the road. When the sky is clear in Miyazaki, it is truly blue, clear and high. Autumn indeed, one would think.

Under that huge sky, Santoka ate his box lunch which had nothing more than a dried plum for garnish. But how white that rice must have been! Was not each and every grain sparkling and bright?

This was a lonely and solitary journey, without destination. Life tomorrow could not be relied upon, and he could do no more than walk until he collapsed. But in this way he could thoroughly taste his white rice in the beautiful light of the sun under the huge sky; and with gratitude for just such a condition, he was able to feel true happiness.

At the inn in Nobeoka, he lodged by chance with a man whose hometown was Suo. This fellow had lodged with him two or three years before in a country inn in Tottori Prefecture, and now the two of them—shabby travelers who had drifted here and there—met again here by a turn of fate.

"The world seems big, but it's small, you know . . ."

Even the lilt of the Suo dialect stirred up memories for Santoka, and the two lined up their pillows and talked about this and that.

On November 3, the sky was clear and cloudless, and there was a good feeling to the day. Santoka got up early and departed. He crossed the Mikuni Pass and went as far as the town of Mie in Oita Prefecture, walking twenty-five miles [forty kilometers] of mountain road. On the way, the bush clover was blooming, the silver tufts of miscanthus were shining, and it was a truly Japanese autumn.

At the pass he sat down at a teahouse and drank a cup while gazing at the vast form of Mount Sobo. The garnish was a dish of pickles. Calmly observing the mountain, he drank his tea. This day he was able to compose a number of good verses.

しぐるるや
道は
一すぢ

Late autumn rains!
The Way
is straight.[12]

山の一つ家も
今日の旗を
立て

The one house on the mountain, too,
today
displaying the flag.

As he walked briskly along the single mountain road, he saw a lone farmhouse. And on that house, the *hi no maru* Japanese flag[13] stuck out from the sloping thatch roof.

枯草に
残る日の
色はかなし

How sad—
the remaining light of the day
in the dried grass.

暮れてなほ
耕す人の
影濃く

The waning day;
the shadow of the man tilling the field
darkens.

軒も
傾いたまま
住んでいる

They live there
with the eaves drooping,
just as they are.

Santoka begged through the town of Mie. He was happy to sense that his countenance in begging was improving, even if this seemed a little conceited. By his cunning, he was able to stay at inns, eat and sleep with the rice and money he received, and continue on his journey. Now for the first time he felt a love and faith in the virtue of his surplice and the heart of mankind. Alone, he placed his palms together in gratitude. For Santoka, it was apostasy not to walk or beg. There was nothing other than to advance along this road one step after another.

While these were feelings he had as he begged, it seems that for the most part he was refused at large houses or houses that seemed to be well-off. Or else he was given a small amount of rice with what seemed to be stingy resentment—so little rice that Santoka felt embarrassed that he was receiving rather than giving. Nevertheless, at places like poor tenement houses at the backside of town, people would of themselves call out for him to stop, and give him bowls filled up with undue amounts. Still, he did not want to concern himself with the large or small quantities of rice, but rather he wanted to become a Santoka who detachedly received whatever was given to him. Every day, day after day, he made himself experience the strict Zen teaching to "kill your selfish desires."

Today, too, Santoka was able to soak in the bath he loved so much. For some reason, he was the only person in this bathhouse and was able to stretch out both body and mind, feel truly at ease, and wipe away his exhaustion. And, with a very sweet water bubbling up around him, he was able to sample its taste to his heart's content.

Santoka then begged from Mie to the town of Takeda, a place he had once drifted to three or four years before. Here he wrote such verses as

腰かける岩を
覚えている

Remembering
the rock,
I take a seat.

飯のうまさも
ひとりかみしめて

The savor of my rice;
alone,
I chew it well.

最後の一粒を
味わふ

I taste
the last
grain.

Walking, traveling, receiving, eating—in this way, tasting one's rice is all the more delicious. One does not waste even a single grain. With some introspection, he wrote in his journal:

The countenance of my begging today was certainly successful.
It depends on whether my heart is moved in the interests of its
limits or not. It also depends on whether I'm close or far from
the mental state of being "the master of wherever I am."[14]

Writing in his journal, he could hear the sound of water. He had heard this sound of water all night long the night before.

夜をこめて
水が流れる秋の宿

Water flowing
into the night;
the autumn inn.

As he tentatively composed this verse, an unclouded moon eventually shined through his window. How pure and clear it must have been! The light of the moon on the sound of the water—an absolutely oriental and Zen scene.

From Takeda he went on to Yunohira, and soaked leisurely in the hot springs.

あかつきの湯が
私一人
あたためてくれる

The bath at dawn
kindly warms me up,
just me alone.

Waking up early, Santoka soaked himself alone in the hot waters in the still feeble light. Ah, the warmth of the hot spring bubbling and gushing forth! It seemed as though perhaps the hot spring here was brimming over for Santoka alone. His aloneness, his poverty, his destination—all of these he forgot completely and, in a daze, enjoyed the taste of the water and gave thanks.

壁をへだてて
湯の中の
男女さざめき合う

In the hot water,
a man and woman laughing out loud:
the other side of the wall.

Then, all of a sudden, he could hear from the bath next to his, the happy chattering of a man and a woman who had spent the last night together. This, too, was one of the scenes of a hot-springs inn. Without being particularly distracted by this, Santoka simply listened to what entered his ears.

ホイトウと呼ばれる
村のしぐれかな

Called a beggar! [15]
   Late autumn rains
in the village.

This verse came to him while walking on a road through fields. Some children looked under his bamboo hat and cried, "It's a beggar!" Well, yes, yes. I'm really nothing but a solitary begging monk. But being called a beggar would, of course, make one feel lonely, and there he was on a road through the fields being pelted by heavy rain.

手ばな
かんでは
山を見ている

Watching the mountain,
   I blow my nose
in my hand.

しっとりぬれて
岩も私も

Slightly damp:
   the rocks,
me, too.

法衣
ふきまくるは
まさに秋風

My priest's robes blown about;
   surely this,
the autumn wind.

The lonely autumn gradually deepened.

Ah, how long would he continue to travel, entering the mountains without dying? Entering the villages without dying? The *Eye of the Law* [16] says:

Step by step, you arrive. (步步到着)

But while Santoka was alive, his "step by step" was simply in going forward. In stepping forward in this moment, he did not think about going beyond the step he had taken just before. Neither did he think about the step he would take next. One step in itself was Santoka's life. With such continuous efforts, he tasted "walking meditation" thoroughly.

> *To taste the thing itself.*
> *An unskillful person penetrates that unskillfulness to the bone.*
> *A foolish person penetrates that foolishness to the bone.*
> *Rather than being added unto, take the character you were born with to the limit.*
> *That is human life.*
> *No, isn't it the* taste *of human life?*

The next day he begged through the hot-springs town of Yunohira, a town of continuing hot-spring inns situated on a slope. The mountains had already gotten cold, and he was wishing for a single layer of padded clothing. As he stood in front of a certain shop, a little girl came out and said,

"I'm sorry. Right now nobody's home. My mother said to tell you that nobody's home."

You can't complain about the honesty of a child, but what can you think about a mother who teaches her child to lie?

Totally becoming
a traveler
of the autumn wind.

秋風の旅人に
なりきっている

Santoka soaked himself in the fine hot spring of a fine inn. And, like everyone else there, scooped up the hot water and drank it. It was absolutely delicious. As it was such good water, he stayed there the entire day, writing in his journal and reading books. In the afternoon, he went down to the stream and washed the grime of travel out of his clothes. While what he had washed dried out on the riverbank, he became absorbed in reading Seisensui's *Tabibito, Basho* [The Traveler, Basho].[17] Suddenly he noticed that it was drizzling here in the mountains, wasn't it. As he was about to hurry down to the riverbank, he saw that the mistress of the inn had run down to collect his clothes and was now coming back. How kind of her, he thought.

In the room next to his, something rare: three Chinese people were staying over, and they were traveling acrobats. The little child had become very much like a Japanese. They sang traditional *kusatsubushi* folk songs from Gunma Prefecture and talked with Santoka.

Late autumn rain;
at someone's kindness
my eyes brim with tears.

しぐるるや
人のなさけに
涙ぐむ

しぐるる旅の
支那さん
いっしょにねている

Sleeping together
    with traveling Chinese;
later autumn rains.

ひとりあたたまって
ひとりでねる

Warming up alone,
    sleeping
      alone.

It was economically difficult for Santoka, who loved hot springs, to stay in Yunohira for two nights, but he did—having both body and mind relax in the hot water. The hot-spring water here was especially useful in treating digestive ailments, and so a great number of people who suffered from such problems came for a "hot water cure." And they did not just bathe themselves in the hot water, but took teapots to the source of the hot spring and drank the water down in great gulps. It seems that many people would drink ten quarts [ten liters] in one day and Santoka drank a good bit as well. Then he cocked his head and mused,

"Ah, if this had been sake . . ."

November 20. Recalling the verse he had written some time ago,

だまって
今日の草鞋
穿く

Silently putting them on:
    today's
      straw sandals.

he sat down at the entrance to the inn and put on his straw sandals. Thinking that they were oddly cold to his feet, he sensed that winter had come.

Santoka walked ten miles [four kilometers] on the road, begging as far as Yufuin. The various trees with their colored leaves were so beautiful that he sometimes forgot to recite the sutras. Just as he noticed that cold clouds had descended from Mount Yufugake, it suddenly began to snow. This was the first snow of the year, and his begging bowl became colder and colder to the touch. Human habitations were few, so there weren't many places to beg; but even so, he had collected about fourteen sen and seven *go*[18] of rice.

How much more than I deserve . . .

There were a great number of hot springs in the place at which he had arrived, and even houses where streams of hot water moved water wheels. Here he stayed at the Chikugo-ya in a place called Yutsubo. This was an inn of reputation, truly accommodating and homey. He quickly immersed himself in the hot waters and thought up the following verses:

Washed, then dried
    just as they were
    on rocks in the riverbed.

洗ふとそのまま
河原の石に
干す

I only wanted to sleep, then after—
    stretching my body out
    in the hot water.

寝たいだけ
寝たからだ
湯に伸ばす

*Meeting the Chinaman
once again,
Good Morning!*

また
逢うた
支那のおじさん
こんにちは

Taking the road west from Yufuin, he passed through the town of Kusu and arrived at the town of Mori. In Kusu he had been treated badly.

"Get out of here, you panhandling monk! You're bad for business!"

"It's bad luck to see some dung-faced monk in the morning. Get going! Get going!"

But thinking that this, too, was the compassion of the Buddha, Santoka fervently recited the Kannon Sutra.

But what of the inhabitants of the town of Mori just across the river? What about *their* fellow-feeling? Didn't they kindly and happily give him alms at almost every house? By the time it was past two o'clock, he had received rice enough to make his neck feel heavy.

Santoka settled down for the moment at a small inn called the Hita-ya just outside of town. Asking the price of lodging, he was told it was thirty sen. Fine, fine. That won't be a problem . . . Borrowing some clogs from the inn, he took a walk with a light heart.

Oddly enough, there were a good number of sake breweries in the area. And he got completely dizzy with a fragrance that went aromatically from his nose right to the top of his head. He made a round of three shops, drinking one cup at each shop, sitting down at the shop front, then sipping from the corner of a one-*go* measuring box.[19] He didn't need any side dishes; this was a good sake that felt like a slow-moving oil.

Now in a perfectly good mood, he went to tour the area of Mount Iwa'ogi, reciting the Shushogi chant as he walked through town. Suddenly, he spied a newspaper and saw that Prime Minister Hamaguchi had been shot. Ah . . .

When suddenly arriving at Impermanence, the king, his min-isters, their familiars, their employees and valuable jewels will be of no help. One can only walk alone to the Yellow Springs,[20] followed by his good and evil karma.

—Shushogi

Was the Prime Minister also walking alone to the Yellow Springs? What an infinity of emotions!

Nothing suggests
they will die before long:
evening fireflies.[21]

やがて
死ぬる気色は
見えず夕蛍

After all,
every last one of us:
spring snow.

さりながら
人はいづれも
春の雪

Santoka looked hard at the "death" that was before him.

My iron begging bowl,
receiving
falling leaves.

鉄鉢、
散くる葉を
うける

Everyone at the inn was kindhearted.

On November 15, autumn had deepened all the more. And the day came at last when he walked down the deep Yaba Ravine as he had longed to. The weather was fine and his straw sandals fit well. He forgot about begging altogether, and just gazed at the mountains.

How he enjoyed looking at the red leaves. Taking off his straw hat, he gazed—totally absorbed—at the mountains.

山を観る
けふいちにちは
笠をかぶらず

Looking at mountains,
today, all day,
not wearing my hat.

けふの
べんたうは
岩のうへにて

Today's box lunch?
On top
of a rock.

藪で
赤いのは
烏瓜

In the thicket,
that red thing?
A snake gourd! [22]

Santoka took a train from the station at Yaba Ravine and got off at Nakatsu. There he was put up at the residence of his friend-in-haiku, Maimai Matsugaki.

また逢へた山
茶花も咲いている

The mountain,
well met again;
tea flowers blooming, too.

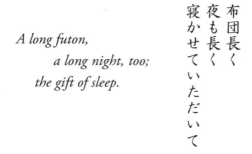

布団長く
夜も長く
寝かせていただいて

A long futon,
    a long night, too;
    the gift of sleep.

The pleasant comfort of sleep is provided when two hearts melt together as one. The autumn nights at cheap boarding houses are long, but wherever you go, the futons are short and cold. Here he was able to stretch out his two traveler's legs to their full length, and fall into a deep sleep.

寝酒
したしく置いて
ありました

A nightcap
    kindly left out
    just for me.

He also came up with verses like these. The friendly consideration of Master Maimai, who knew Santoka well, provided the traveler with a peaceful sleep at last.

In Nakatsu, he visited the old mansion of the writer Yukichi Fukuzawa,[23] which inspired two verses:

土蔵そのそばの
柚子の実も

The godown,[24]
    the fruit of the yuzu tree
    alongside of it, too.

Put in the ground:
miscanthus,
one clump.

すすき一株も
植えてある

It had been some time since Santoka had felt this comfortable in body and mind, and—rare for him—he wrote down some Zen monk-style *gatha* verses in his journal.

Spring breezes, autumn rains;
flowers open, grasses fade.
One's own nature, foolish of itself;
step by step to the Buddha Land.

春風秋雨、
花開草枯
自性自愚、
歩歩仏土

Drunkeness comes, the rock is your pillow;
the valley voice never dies.[25]
In the midst of drinking and at its end;
No-Self, No-Buddha.

酔来枕石、
谷声不滅
酒中酒尽、
無我無仏

Then, a joking verse:

Rather than being quick
to put on the mask
of a distinguished priest,
the panhandling monk
becomes the real thing.

名僧の
メンかぶらうと
あせるより
ホイトウ坊主が
ホイトウなるらん

From Nakatsu, Santoka passed through Unoshima and arrived in Ori in Moji. Asking directions from a young officer at the police station, he was once again put up at the residence of a friend-in-haiku, a Master Genzaburo Kubo. When Santoka arrived, first there was sake, and then, with the combined efforts of husband and wife, a warm reception.

> *Though it's been a long time,*
>   *a soft*
>   *futon.*

なつかしくも
柔らかいフトン
である

> *The futon,*
>   *so fluffy, dreams*
> *of my hometown.*

ふとん
ふうわり
ふるさとの夢

In these two verses, the feeling of a warm dwelling appears effortlessly. Crossing the straits from Moji brought one to Yamaguchi Prefecture. The town of Hofu could be reached in two hours on the train, so dreams of seeing his hometown were not in vain. The following day, he crossed the Kammon Straits so dear to his heart and begged through the city of Shimonoseki.

> *A city whose words*
>   *belong to my hometown,*
>   *I've arrived!*

ふるさとの
言葉となつた街に
来た

Ame ga futchoru—it's raining. *Samui nonta*—it's cold. Hearing these phrases in the Yamaguchi dialect after so long a time, Santoka was aware that he had been on a journey to faraway provinces until now. He had been in trouble when listening to the difficult-to-understand dialects from Kagoshima Prefecture to Miyazaki Prefecture. The first time he had come to Shimonoseki was when he was on an educational trip in middle school. At that time, the city was quite different, and now the faces of his former friends and the face of his old teacher came to mind in stark contrast to his own present figure begging in tattered priest's robes.

After his student days, Santoka had often walked drunkenly through the red-light district. The days when he carried on with the coffeehouse waitresses and geishas were now an old story from far away. Santoka suddenly stopped and looked in at a fish store. There was a young woman there skillfully shelling an abalone. The seas seemed to be heavy and a cold early-winter rain was beginning to beat down from Mount Hiyori. This was truly a Shimonoseki scene.

Soaked,
  mumbling to himself:
a lunatic.

ぬれて
ひとりごと
いうて狂人

That was my face!
  The cold
mirror.

それは
私の顔だった
鏡つめたく

Santoka was reciting a sutra for all he was worth in front of the barber shop. Suddenly he was aware of a strange beggar whose face—with a beard extending from its chin—was being reflected right in front of him! Ah, it was his own face; it was Santoka! Surprised by his own self, here was a large mirror, coldly brilliant. Yes, this was one cold day.

Santoka ducked under a shop curtain made of rope, and then knocked down a cup of cloudy unrefined sake. Still not drunk. Then a cup of shochu. Finally his body started to warm up.

As the day was ending, he went out to the town once again. A young lad who seemed to be alone was standing there despondently. Standing next to the boy, Santoka began to think about the measly thirty sen in his purse. The boy seemed to sidle up to him and for some reason said, "Mister . . ." in a small voice. Santoka was about to ask if the boy had no mother or father, but he stopped and grasped the boy firmly by the shoulder. A cold, cold rain was still falling. Then the boy laughed; he was counting *menko* toy coins[26] with both hands.

Sidling up silently,
*   the look of a traveler:*
the child.

寄り添うて
黙つて旅の
身なし児は

A child on the road
*   playing with menko*
alone.

旅の子供は
ひとりでメンコ
打つている

Beyond the ken of sutras,
*   the cacophony*
of jazz.

お経とどかない
ジャズの騒音

It was rejected, but—
*   the chrysanthemum's*
glory!

ハジカレたが
菊の見事さよ

These verses occurred to him spontaneously on the street, and delineate his true feelings. The poem about the chrysanthemum expresses regret or refusal, but looks squarely at the beauty of the flower. Each verse, one verse at a time: the falling off of body and mind.[27]

The sound of the wind, too,
wasting away
in dissipation?

風の音も
更けている
散財か

Fading away,
the voices,
gambling.

更けて
バクチ
打つ声

Late autumn rains!
Hitting the mark, visiting
your house.

しぐるるや
あんたの家を
訪ねあてた

How evocative of the dark scenes of the streets near the Kammon Straits these verses are! In Shimonoseki he was able to compose verses on such aspects of human life. Santoka loitered around the city for two or three days, then again crossed over the straits and arrived at the city of Hachiman. Here, his friends-in-haiku Kojiro Mitsuyoshi and Seijoshi Iio were instructors of kendo at the Hachiman police station, and possessed the style of ancient warriors. Stoutheartedly, they exchanged cups and talked things over at their own leisure.

Chewing on cuttlefish,
talking over things
long ago.

かみしめては
昔を話す

On this trip he also met up with Gian Mochizuki.

Gian: *Yes, yes, six years must have passed on by since then. You made a complete round begging through Shikoku, Chugoku, and Kyushu, didn't you. Every day turned into a good discipline, I suppose.*

Santoka: *I think I was able to walk a good bit. But it seems that I turned my back on your venerable teachings, and there were plenty of days when I was just a loafer and a fraud. I'm ashamed; and when you get old, of course, you start wanting a settled place to sleep.*

Gian: *That's true, too. There's a saying: Return home and sit quietly (帰家穏座). But Santoka, why don't you stop your begging trips, settle down in a small hermitage, go begging when you feel like it, compose haiku, and work a little in a vegetable garden? That's right! There's a thatched hut that's vacant over in Chino that should be just right. How about going over to take a look at it?*

Santoka visited the hermitage in the village of Chino outside the city of Kumamoto just as his venerable teacher had suggested, but one of the villagers had already moved into it. After that, he visited some old friends and, with various efforts on their parts, finally rented a single room on the second floor of a house in Harutake, inside the city limits. Here, after his long, long journey, Santoka took off his straw hat and put down his staff.

Rain, then clear weather;
I look for a place
to die.

降つたり
照つたり
死に場所を探す

At long last,
　　　finding a bed,
　　dreams, too.

やっと
見つけた
寝床の夢も

The house was next door to a field planted with trees, so the view was nice and the people who owned the house were kind. Santoka was associated with the *Sanbaku-fu* (三八九府)[28] of the T'ang dynasty Chinese abbot Ch'ao Chih, so he named his place the Sanbaku-kyo.[29] This was December 25 of 1930. Then he put out a small mimeographed magazine entitled *Sanbaku* for which he cut out the kanji characters and printed by himself. Auspiciously, the very first person to apply as a subscriber was the abbot who had given Santoka ordination rites, Gian Mochizuki. Other than him, people who knew Santoka from both near and far happily became readers.

After that, for exactly one year, Santoka continued to roam around the city of Kumamoto and put out five issues of *Sanbaku*. Yet, he was unable to settle down even here. One day he got into some chaotic fooling around with some old drinking buddies, just like in the days before he became a priest. Santoka! Is this a good thing? He passed a bitter day and night questioning and answering himself—and then, once again, set out on a journey, the destination of which not even he knew.

Once again I've had to tie on my straw sandals. I am someone who can do nothing but travel continually, journey after journey.

This is what he wrote on postcards to intimate friends in various places, and on December 22, 1931, he put the area of Kumamoto behind him.

The difficulty of one man living his life with his very own undefinable foolishness, easily becomes a lie on a journey of lonely begging. Santoka thought that, no matter how miserable, this was his bed, so he could stretch his arms and legs out peacefully and go to sleep. But in this world, it is impossible to play up to that image. In the end, Santoka, who was selfish and a loafer as well, once again abandoned his temporary residence, and could not help feeling sorry for himself as someone who was only capable of going out on journeys to beg.

Santoka boarded his shabby figure onto the bus bound for Yamaga, but when the bus had passed Naoki and stopped at Mitori, he suddenly had a notion. Getting off the bus, he climbed up the slope and dropped in at the temple. The pine wind blew high through the sky just as it had seven years before. The priest, Kashiwagi, who had come here after Santoka had left, quickly called together the people of the village. Everyone forgot about the busyness of the time of year, and quite intently exchanged sake cups throughout the night, surrounding this rare guest and talking over memories of old times. After they all returned home, the priest prepared a hot bath for Santoka, even though the temple had very little water to spare. Santoka, who loved sake with a hot bath, warmed himself thoroughly and got into bed. But any number of things floated up into his mind—were they dreams or reality?—and he was somehow unable to sleep until the temple bell was rung at dawn.

Santoka walked through Yamaga, Fukushima, and Fukkaichi, and at the end of the day of the twenty-seventh, prayed at the Tenmangu shrine in Dazaifu.[30]

He begged through Dazaifu, soaked by the cold winter rain.

右近の橋
の実の
しぐるるや

The mandarin oranges
of the Minister of the Right;
soaked by the early-winter rains.

大樟も
私も犬も
しぐれつつ

The great camphor tree, me,
and the dog, too:
continually soaked by the rain.

ふるさと恋しい
ぬかるみをあるく

Stepping through the mud,
longing for
my hometown.

On the day before New Year's, he begged through the town of Iizuka. Basho had recited,

年暮れぬ笠きて
わらじはきながら

Wearing my bamboo hat,
tying my straw sandals;
the year comes to an end.

And this was exactly the traveler's figure Santoka now cut.

師走のゆききの
知らない顔ばかり

Coming and going,
the last month of the year,
unknown faces only.

This is what he wrote in the margin of his journal that night at his lodgings, with the words sending off 1931:

First and foremost, I must be circumspect about sake.
Though I think two cups would be sufficient, I should not
allow myself three. I should not drink shochu or gin.

It is fine to sleep "melodiously."[31]
I should constantly intone the Confession of Sins[32] *and not forget the Four Great Vows.*[33]

Seen from behind
as I go:
soaked to the skin?

うしろすがたの
しぐれてゆくか

Santoka spent New Year's of 1932 warmly and cheerfully, embraced by friendship at the house of Rokubei Kimura, a doctor for a coal mining company in the town of Itoda in Fukuoka Prefecture. There was nothing in the world more beautiful than the friendship between Rokubei and Santoka. I think you could say that Santoka was able to continue his journeys because of Rokubei's constant and unchanging support.

On the sixth, he came out to the shore of the northern sea and, from Akama, after praying at the Munekata shrine, he begged through the town of Konominato. There he visited the priest Shun Tashiro, and stayed at the Rinsenji temple. On the eighth, he begged on the outskirts of the town of Ashiya. The weather had turned cold and the wind from the sea mixed the snow with the water spray; it was cold, but how beautiful the area around this plain of pines! Santoka held his begging bowl and stopped at house after house along the road, but because of the stormy weather, at no house would they be kind enough to open the storm shutters and be of any company to him.

Suddenly at that moment, a shower of hail fell. Or rather than "fell," it struck him with a clang, sounding with a clatter on his bamboo hat. It made a noise on the monk's robes he was wearing as well and a metallic clink in his begging bowl. Santoka returned to himself with a start and composed a verse:

In my begging bowl,
too,
the hail.

鉄鉢の中へも
あられ

The fact was that Santoka had slackened in both body and mind due to his being spoiled by the warm, happy friendship at New Year's, followed by the treat of boundless sake courtesy of the priest, Shun. Then his entire body and entire mind were struck by the hail as though he were being set upon. He felt something with a start, took notice of himself, and laughed with a chuckle. He then briskly turned his steps in the direction of the Yuzen Kannon temple, forgetting all about begging for the while.

Continuing his journey westward, westward, along a plain of pines, he arrived at the town of Hamazaki in Saga Prefecture. Looking into his bag, he seemed to have enough money for a haircut. And so, for the first time in a long time, he went to a barber shop and had his head shaved. A winter's sky on a monk's head! Even the barber kindly said,

"Thanks to you, I've been able to shave a monk's head for the first time in quite a while. Usually I just use clippers and scissors, but it's so easy to shave a monk's head. And it gives you a good feeling to shave it, too."

Santoka rubbed his head that was reflected in the large mirror.

"Just as you'd think, a monk's head is fitting for a monk's head."

Whether he said that to the barber or to himself, it was not exactly clear—nor was its meaning—but he put his bamboo hat on top of this head and left.

In the town of Karatsu he begged from nine o'clock in the morning to three in the afternoon, truly forgetting himself, forgetting the cold, and forgetting about receiving anything altogether. There was no wind, and both people and houses were genial and refined. He returned to an inn called the Ume-ya and, checking the contents of his bag, found just over two *sho* of rice, and forty-seven sen in cash. How grateful he was! He did not consider that he received all this by his own efforts, but rather by the compassion of the Buddha.

To the mountains,
  to the sky:
    Makahannyaharamita shingyo.[34]

山へ空へ
摩可船若波羅蜜多
心経

The following day, he prayed at the Kinshoji temple, bowing deeply at the grave of the playwright Sorinshi.[35] This was the family temple of the Ogasawara clan. He then begged through the port of Yobiko, and found the beauty of Matsuura Bay to be irresistible.

Placing two islands
  in the morning
    calm.

朝凪の
島を
二つ
おく

Sentimentally
  losing
    a tooth.

ほろりと
ぬけた歯
ではある

Surrendering its length
  to the sea wind:
    her black hair.

黒髪の長さを
汐風に
まかし

There were many brothels in this town, and the scene of long black hair being unraveled and tangled in the sea wind reminded him of the long ago Sayohime.[36]

On February 3, Santoka begged through the streets of Nagasaki.

This was a settled and calm town and, particularly in the case of the Oura district, you could not imagine this to be any other place than Nagasaki—in the view, in the line of houses, in the stone steps, or in the cheap sweet shops.

Climbing stone steps
in the winter rain.
Santa Maria!
(at the Tenjuto temple)

冬雨の石階を
のぼる
サンタマリア

Winter cloudiness;
the cracks
in the large kettle.
(at the Shufukuji temple)

冬曇の
大釜の
ひび

Completely faded,
my cotton robes;
continual laughter.
(at the Rinzaiji temple)

すっかり
剥げて布衣は
笑ひつづける

On the seventh he was able to stay at the house of Juhenka, a friend-in-haiku, and did some sightseeing in the streets of Nagasaki.

Pierced through
by another's compassion;
stroking the brazier.

人のなさけが
身にしみる火鉢を
なでる

The streets of the town were laid with stone, and a light rain now soaked that stone. Santoka went up, then down, then up again the slopes of the town. That was the feeling of Nagasaki.

He walked through Tara, Kashima and the surrounding villages, and approached Saga.

When he stood in front of a house and read the sutras as usual, an old woman came out and threw not one, but two fifty-sen silver coins into his bowl in an offhand manner, glanced for a moment at his face, and went back into her house. Usually Santoka might receive five rin or one sen at a single house, so he was shocked. Perhaps she had mistaken these for copper coins. If that were so, he thought he would be sorry if he didn't go back and ask, just to make sure. Then he thought that—though he was unworthy—there was nothing else he could do but accept it as an extraordinary donation. Finally, he felt that he had the obligation to use this money as efficiently as possible. So he wrote this in his journal:

> *Rather than forget-me-nots, day lilies.*[37]
> *Perhaps I should take a little break.*

> *Alcohol rather than Calmotin.*[38]
> *Shall I have a little cup?*

How very like Santoka.

When he arrived at the town of Saga, Santoka first rushed to a window at the post office. This was to pick up any mail being held for him. When you are traveling on a solo journey and have no fixed whereabouts, there is no blessing like the general delivery post. With a leap in his heart, he picked up thirteen or fourteen postcards and letters. Moreover, among them, wasn't that in fact the letter of "substantial content" he was expecting? He sat down on the stairs of the waiting room where people were coming and going, opened the letter, and read it greedily. In it were the affections of his friend, news of his acquaintances, and other things to warm his heart; and the "substantial content" was a money order! Furthermore, this was the large amount of fifteen yen from his friend Rokubei.

Santoka slowly walked through the town of Saga. With this turn of events he would be unable to do something like begging, and probably felt disinclined to do so. That came from the secure feeling that he had a "substantial" purse, but he also knew that for a person with this kind of money, begging would be a lie. Begging in preparation for tomorrow's life is begging with deep greed.

The streets he looked upon without a heart of supplication had a rather different taste. There was a signboard over the public bath that read:

> *With just one bath, your mind will expand and your body will be at peace.*

What an excellent phrase, he thought. Then, turning his head around, he saw a noodle shop. Here, on a plaque showing a huge bowl of noodles, it read:

> *He who doesn't work shouldn't eat.*

That's an odd slogan! As a shop for eating and drinking, this kind of place must reflect the temper of Saga, he thought.[39]

Santoka stayed overnight at a cheap boarding house called the Taku-ya and, although the thirty-five sen charge was not expensive, the fact that there were seven people in the same lodgings was inconsistent with that price. There were two monkey trainers, and four children accompanying a couple on a pilgrimage. The inn was fully diffused with ignorance, vulgarity and uneasiness. Unable to stand it, Santoka went out into the streets and, for the first time in a long time, saw a movie—a double feature with *The Story of Saikichi* and *The Three Brave Bombadiers*. War, death, tragedy. He shed tears and returned to his inn, but various things came into his mind and he was unable to sleep well.

The following day he walked the streets and went to a place called Okuma Park, which, I think, was the birthplace of Count Okuma.[40] A pleasing stone monument had been built, and the small pines that had been planted were also beautiful. The fragrance of flowers—

perhaps sweet-smelling daphne—came from some undetermined place. At the scent of these flowers, Santoka sat down on a bench and was led into the memories of something from long ago. It was an event that happened just thirty years before this time. Together with two or three student friends from his college days at Waseda, he had visited the Count's mansion. After having been told a number of stories, they went out into the garden, and he even took a picture with the Count standing among them. After that, they had gone to the customary shop, drunk beer, sung "Northwest of the Capital" in ringing voices, and returned to their lodgings. At that time, Santoka's friends all wore their student uniforms and nice shoes. Only he had worn heavy clogs and a cotton country-style crested *haori* jacket. Now that crested *haori* had changed into the tattered priest's robes he wore as he stood before the remains of the Count's birthplace.

Santoka was unable to stay still. Forgetting himself, he hurried into a Japanese-style restaurant and was of a mind to spend—at a single stroke—the fifteen yen that embodied Rokubei's friendship. At that moment, the words from Rokubei's letter appeared before him.

I suppose that your daily journey must often be hard to bear. This is just a scrap of my monthly salary, but please use it for traveling expenses.[41] From time to time a cup of sake would be fine, but I think that the shochu you like is bad for your health, so please desist from that if you could. Take care of your body, and compose a lot of good haiku. When the verses that flow out of your experiences sometimes appear in the magazine So'un, our hearts are struck with a rush of feelings.

> *Into my begging bowl,*
> *too,*
> *the hail.*

> *Seen from behind*
> *as I go:*
> *soaked to the skin?*

No one but you can create verses like these. Take care of your-self, respect yourself, have a good journey, and write good verses.

These words calmed the speeding colt of Santoka's mind, and embraced him soothingly to a halt. His mind reined in, he went out begging from house to house.

It was mostly "Sorry," "Sorry." His own mind was not composed, so it was natural that his requests for alms were declined. He had taken up the appearance of begging while uncomfortable in the place where he was, and his mind seemed not to be actually in charge of itself. Thus, not a single house gave him a donation.

He continued reciting the sutras in a haphazard voice, when someone said, "Yes!" and a five- or six-year-old child dropped a little rice from his cute fist into Santoka's begging bowl. Then, with a contrite heart, he received lunch at a certain small shop; a real feast laid out on an antiquated dining table.

In Saga, prices were cheap: one cup of sake, eight sen; items in small bowls, five sen; a large helping of udon noodles, five sen; curry and rice, ten sen. Although he was being moderate and restrained, he had a pleasant lunch for the first time in a long time. After finishing his meal, he wrote out twenty postcards there at the dining table, sending news to his friends in all directions.

In the evening he returned to his lodgings, and it was the same confusion and clatter. An old tramp and a young traveler were also there, and his room was more and more disordered. The couple in the room next door was having an argument, and the man was browbeating his wife. The monkey trainer was having a good time, saying that he was not the kind to attack *his* wife like that. One man was shaving his beard, another singing popular songs—it would seem to be nothing other than the scene of the human condition to which he had become so accustomed. Santoka found a corner where he had only the light of a dim lamp by which to write in his travel journal; you could say that this, too, is one of the disciplines of a vagabond, and indeed, this is true. Santoka added the following to the end of his entry, and crawled under his thin coverlet:

Don't get angry.
Don't talk.
Don't be covetous.
Walk slowly.
Walk steadily.

He left Saga and walked two and a half miles [four kilometers] to the east. As it was March 7, the season would soon pass from a time of withered grasses to one when the young green grasses would begin to bud. Santoka lay down on the withered grass and listened to the voice of a skylark high in the sky. After a while, he noticed that a man had lain down next to him.

As they were lying here talking, the man informed Santoka that he had been a cook for a long time in a restaurant in Nagasaki, but had been fired on New Year's. Being out of work, he was returning to his hometown. He did not go on to say why he had been fired, and Santoka again listened to the skylark for a while. Finally, he took his leave of the out-of-work cook, and went on to beg. At this point a bicycle came up behind him and stopped. It was a middle-aged man in a business suit who seemed to be a police detective.

"Are you going somewhere?"

"Yes. I'm going in the direction my feet are pointing."

"Your lodgings last night?"

"The Taku-ya in Saga."

"Would you remove your straw hat and let me take a look at you for a moment?"

"Yes. As you can see: grandly hatless."[42]

"That'll be fine."

"All right?"

This was just like a Zen *mondo* question and answer session. Without turning around, the man hurried off ahead on his bicycle. The skylark was even higher in the sky, and sang out bright and clear. *Peechiku pee pee. Peechiku pee pee.*

Walking on another one *ri*, he crossed the Kamizaki Bridge and was begging through the next hamlet. Just then, a helplessly drunk old man stumbled out of the restaurant in front of him and gave him an order to stop immediately.

"Hey, you panhandling monk! Stop that! Stop chanting your sutras!"

As Santoka was thinking what a strange old man this was, a heavy rain began to fall. This would never do for begging. He stopped, took out his raincoat, and decided to go quickly in the direction of the Niizan Kannon temple. When the weather cleared up on the way, he begged.

"Absolutely not!"

At a certain farmhouse a woman came out and firmly dismissed him. Despite that, her husband soon appeared and said,

"Come on, sit down. Please have a cup of tea before you go."

Today I've met nothing but strange people, from morning till now—it's been a strange day, he thought. The out-of-work cook was a strange man, and the detective was strange, too. The old drunk was a strange fellow, and this husband and wife were a strange pair as well.

Niizan was a peaceful mountain and a sacred place with a murmuring mountain stream. At the Niizan Kannon temple the priest's wife was kind, and he accepted the cup of tea she ladled out for him.

"This is a peaceful, nice place, huh. Your mind can settle down here."

"No, somehow it's too peaceful, you know."

The two of them smiled as they sipped the taste of the coarse tea.

Ureshino is indeed a pleasant place.[43] *With hot baths and tea, it is a good place for the solitary traveler to take off his straw sandals. If I could, I would like to settle down in a place like this.*

This he wrote on a postcard to a friend. Santoka—and perhaps this was so for all solitary travelers—loved hot springs. Sinking those two legs that had continually walked for five or six years into the hot water, he forgot about everything and truly enjoyed himself, stretching his limbs out right from his heart.

He stayed at an inn called the Chikugo-ya. At thirty sen, this was a good inn for composing his mind, and the master of the place was rather affable. It was the first day of the equinoctial week and was bitterly cold, snow falling from time to time. The local people called this "forgetting snow."[44] The weather was cold, but he bathed himself leisurely in the hot springs. Plus, he had a nice inn. Thus, both body and mind were warmed and mellowed, and the fact of the matter was that both had grown weary on this begging trip. The lonely rain and snow of travel had pierced his body through; and perhaps his vitality had been sapped by being soaked by the elements while doing nothing but begging.

He had tossed everything aside, and come on a one-man journey; his only attachment being to hot springs. He would likely not be able to travel forever. The following year he would become fifty—the age when one must know "Heaven's command."[45] If he were blessed with a small hermitage and were able to live the hermitage life, one strongly imagines he would have liked to do so in a place like Ureshino.

That night, strangely enough, he had dreams of his father and younger brother. And finally, for some reason, he dreamed that Japan had lost a war and that its people were living miserably wreaked lives.

During his stay here, Santoka washed all of the things he carried with him, and even cleaned his priest's robes. His frame of mind was also refreshed. That night he went to the Zuikoji—a temple of the Rinzai sect[46]—to hear the sermon for the equinoctial service. He listened intently to the very end, reflecting on the phrase from the Diamond Sutra, "Give birth to the Mind without residing anywhere."[47] This gave him an ineffable pleasure. Also, the abbot clearly explained the poem of the Buddhist priest Takuan Soho:

> *Do not stand still.*
> > *Do not go; do not return.*
> > *Do not sit.*
> *Do not lie down; do not get up.*
> > *You know, and you don't know too.*[48]

He stayed in Ureshino for four nights.

On the way to the town of Hayagi, he saw a tree putting forth buds all at once, and wrote this verse:

My hometown,
far away;
the buds of trees.

木の芽
遠くして
ふるさとは

Santoka arrived at the town of Sasebo, where the streets were full of sailors, and where the sailors were drinking and dancing under the full cherry blossoms. There was a restaurant called the Proletariat Hall and a cheap boarding house called the Easy Hotel, which made it seem very much like a naval port. Santoka begged with composure in the midst of all this. The countenance of his begging was not bad, and so the results were good. When in a country, do as that country does; so he counted out one sen, then two sen among the rice bran in his bowl, and went to see a revue that evening. The flowers were beautiful and the women bewitching. They made him think that, sure enough, "Earthly passions are themselves enlightenment."[49]

Men and women,
their shadows, too,
dancing.

躍る
その影も
をとこをんなと

Cherry blossoms blooming,
cherry blossoms falling;
dance, dance.

踊る踊る
サクラ散つて
サクラ咲いて

That night he wrote four or five postcards to intimate friends.

Food is cheap here, so the old loafer has been saved. A dish of sashimi is five sen; tempura is five sen too; a fish salad is two sen; and boiled bean curds are two sen. So even a drunk like myself can "become a Buddha in this present body"[50] for only thirty sen. Gyate, gyate, boji sowaka.[51] One might think it's disgraceful when a beggar feels like sightseeing or amusement, but it is not good for people to think too much—they become foolish and it becomes necessary to give a good horselaugh. At least sometimes, right?

He spent five nights in Sasebo and continuously begged through the city streets. One day he stood in front of a shop selling wooden clogs, and, as they were cheap, thought about buying a pair. Just then, the shopkeeper's wife said,

"Not today, Pilgrim."

"You're mistaken," Santoka replied. "I was standing here thinking about buying a pair of clogs. You're rather quick to make judgments, aren't you?"

The young wife's face turned bright red. This was something blameless, but at any rate, the "floating world"[52] is like this. That night he went to the Sasebo Public Hall for "An Evening of Lecture and Cinema" at the invitation of the sponsors of the Society for the Support of Troops Wounded in the China Incident. He thought that the words of a certain colonel, "The Japanese people do not understand the most Japanese of Japanese people" were quite witty.

The next morning he was suddenly afflicted with diarrhea and pains in his intestines. He had eaten and drunk something bad. Lying down in his cheap boarding house, he continually drank nothing but water. He was sick on a journey. Basho, too, had become sick on a journey and died. Thinking of death, something cold suddenly penetrated his entire body. If you call it loneliness, it was loneliness. If you call it fear, it was fear. What he felt was something unutterable.

In the afternoon his condition improved a little; and as he got better, he was unable to stay still. He was, after all, a begging priest, he thought, and it would be a kind of apostasy if he did not go out and beg.

He only begged for three hours, but he continually chanted the sutras, forgetting all about his illness. And he thought that, at this point, to collapse at the end of this journey and die by the roadside would be all right. Oddly enough, when lying down, death had been frightening; but when he stood and read the sutras, he forgot about death altogether. The results were eight *go* of rice and seventy-three sen. Returning to his inn, he sat in a corner of his small room with his back to the other guests. Counting his money, he shed tears to himself.

Isn't this a waste of their money? Isn't it so that these days a healthy man might work by the sweat of his brow from morning till night, and his daily allowance would be eighty sen? And for all that, I beg for half a day and receive all this! All of this is the compassion of sentient beings. It is thanks to the Buddha. How can I be without compassion? It's not this worthless Santoka who's doing the receiving. It's the hat I wear, my priest's robes, and my sacred stole that are doing the receiving for me . . .

That night it rained again and the wind came up. The other guests in the inn were a "bamboo" group of three. The word "bamboo" is cheap boarding house slang for playing the shakuhachi. Just as Santoka thought they might let him hear a nice tune, the shakuhachi tumbled down on the floor as though there was an internal quarrel or something going on. It was a troubled group.

One other guest was an old man from the countryside looking for a son who had left home. Santoka could not help but sympathize with the old man's story. This was a problem of the human character, so full of care and vexation. For a parent and child or a man and woman, the Japanese home was difficult.

There is nothing more lonely than living alone.
There is nothing more tranquil than living alone.
The tranquility more than makes up for the loneliness.

He muttered such things to himself on and on, listening intently to the sound of the wind and rain.

Ferried across
      from island to island;
            the cold spring.

春寒い
島から島へ
渡される

At the island of Hirado both mountains and sea were beautiful. The cherry blossoms on the island were blooming and the petals fell gently into his bamboo hat. He walked the streets that had been evangelized by the Christians; and as he begged at places like The Dutch Wall, and the Remains of the English Residence, he was reminded of the past. The inn called the Kimura-ya cost him thirty sen and was peaceful. For the first time in a great while he got a room just for himself. There were no other guests. He was able to enjoy

One person in one room,
One lamp on one desk,
One bath and one cup of sake.

Just when he was finally alone and writing in his journal, a strange woman lumbered into his room. She was, perhaps, the island's prostitute. Santoka, however, was no longer engaged in that sort of thing.

On April 1, he woke up at four o'clock in the morning. One large flea jumped up on to the old tatami. Perhaps the season for lice had passed, and it was now the season for fleas. Santoka, being who he was, thought he had to change his life completely.

Begging through the town, he went as far as Tasuke Bay. He suddenly realized he was in front of the family home of Sago Kohei Kuminaga, one of the Three Brave Bombadiers.[53] He stood stock still, but in his heart recited the sutra for the Buddhist memorial service so the people in the house would not notice. He thought that he would not feel right receiving a single sen from the honored surviving family. In this area there were a great number of camellia flowers, which added even more to the island's already full measure of beauty. The bush warblers were twittering happily. An old man purposefully came out from under the eaves and gave him some warm *kusamochi* rice cakes.[54]

草餅の
ふるさとの
香を
いただく

> *I humbly receive*
> *the fragrance*
> *of the kusamochi's hometown.*

笠へ
ぽつとり
椿だつた

> *Plop!*
> *On my bamboo hat;*
> *it was a camellia.*

Santoka walked from Hirado to Mikuriya, and then another five miles [eight kilometers]; and although he thought it was yet too early to stay someplace, he checked into a cheap boarding house called the Matsubara-ya, which stood in the middle of a grove of pines. Here he was told to go ahead and take a bath, as it was already bubbling over. Five or six stakes had been driven into the ground next to a creek, and within them was held a cauldron with neither covering nor lid, truly a country bath. The place was filled with the air of rusticity, and Santoka chuckled to himself under a blue sky. Slowly, he immersed himself into this country bath in the shade of the pine needles,

まつぱだかを
太陽に
のぞかれる

> *Stark naked,*
> *and peeped at*
> *by the sun.*

and improvised this verse. Electric lamps had yet to be installed in this inn.

In this same lodgings were a traveling candy vendor and a very ugly middle-aged Japanese woman. The candy vendor was rather kind and, with a smile, offered Santoka a large piece of candy. These two, however, rollicked around in bed while the day was still quite bright.

Spring has come to them as well. May their love be blessed . . .

Thinking such things, Santoka walked downstream and washed his shirt and loincloth.

Able to wash
my loincloth:
a warm little stream.

ふんどしは洗へる
ぬくいせせらぎが
あり

The following day he begged another five miles along the road, and wound his way to the town of Imafuku. Thinking about World Masters like the man and woman of the night before, he wrote down a number of things about human life in his journal:

There is no tomorrow for World Masters. There is only today. There are only one day's meals for today and one night's bed for tonight. Eating and drinking until their stomachs are full; considering the bed they sleep in as their home—this is their morality, this is their philosophy. The value of living life as a human being is in the tasting of it. You could say that living itself is tasting. And you could say that the happiness of life as a human being is in becoming one completely. To be a beggar, become a beggar completely. If you don't become beggar in full, you will not be able to taste the happiness of a beggar. For the human being, there is no way to live other than becoming a human being completely. While you have money, you cannot become a beggar. Again, should you even become one in such circumstances?

In the end, I have become "not one thing" or even "not one penny."[55] *The money that S-san and G-san promised to me for*

> *pocket money, I have spent in little sips, and before I knew it,*
> *my pockets were empty altogether. This is good. Quite good.*
> *Tomorrow I will beg for all I'm worth.*

Entering Saga Prefecture, Santoka passed from Karatsu through Fukae, and went as far as Maebara. How peaceful the spring scenery must have been. Horsetails were growing primly right up to the side of the road, and a young woman was letting her cute little girl pick them. Thinking how fine this was, he chanted the sutras as the spring wind continually blew at the sleeves of his robes. Then three white dogs ambled over almost as if to pay obeisance. "A country road is really something in the spring," he thought.

His inn was accommodating and clean. After making do with just a cup of the sake he loved so much, he wrote this news to a friend:

> *Sake is a luxury item. But that it has become a necessity can't*
> *be helped. I am being circumspect about sake but, well, even*
> *though I am, I can't be entirely so, can I. Just as you'd expect,*
> *sake is a sigh of relief. In my youth, it may have been tears, but*
> *now that I've gotten old, it's a sigh of relief. And because it's a*
> *sigh of relief, I let it out in secret, so you should not be worried*
> *about it.*

Passing through the town of Deki, Santoka entered the streets of Fukuoka. Aspects of his begging were even better than before: he begged with good feelings—like the flowing of water or the passing of clouds—receiving one sen and then another. He then knocked down a cup and, with what remained after paying for his board, bought a secondhand book on Daruma Taishi.[56] Then he wrote to a friend:

> *I drank and I walked. I walked and I drank. And now today and*
> *this evening have passed by. And that's it. Life and death, com-*
> *ing and going are in life and death, and coming and going. It's*
> *just as you'd think. Amen![57]*

And just as you'd think, Santoka was unable to live without sake. To be drunk and selfless and living with no thought of time may outwardly resemble being enlightened and selfless and living the boundless and vast, but the two are quite different. One would hope that he could be circumspect and still have the desire to taste sake fully, but . . .

There were a great many friends-in-haiku for Santoka everywhere in northern Kyushu, and they were kind enough to be waiting for his arrival.

"Santoka is coming!"

If such words were exchanged over the telephone, these friends would quickly all gather together at one place, gather around the traveler, listen to the stories of his journeys, and discuss haiku until late into the night. The one thing they could not be without at such times was sake. The sake deepened the sense of heartfelt friendship as well as warming the mind.

Among all such friends-in-haiku, the man who was closest and really like a brother to Santoka was Rokubei Kimura from the town of Itoda. Rokubei was employed as a company doctor at a coal mine in that town. It was he who inserted the money order in the letter in care of general delivery for the wandering Santoka to give some comfort to the loneliness of his begging.

How I long to meet him;
having spotted
Mount Bota.[58]

逢ひたい、
捨炭山が
見えだした

Santoka followed the Onga River upstream, and when he visited Rokubei yet once again, the latter was kind enough to greet him happily in his usual way. Santoka made himself quite comfortable, read various books, listened to the radio, took a walk, and spent an entire day resting. There was a dog by the name of Nero, which wagged its tail and played happily. In the garden, peas and butterbur were growing luxuriantly. The lady of the house knew very well that Santoka's teeth were bad, and so fed him primarily tofu and the bamboo shoots that were in season, boiling them to soften them up.

A package arrived, a rare thing. It was from his wife Sakino. Although Santoka had abandoned his house and his wife and child to go on this long begging journey, Sakino, whom he had left behind, had a strong will to live, doing so by her own hand while bringing up their child, Ken, at the same time. She was counseled by a certain minister who was then the principal of Seinan Seminary, and entered a life of faith. She ran the Garakuta stationery shop on a small street in town.

Santoka opened the package with his heart dancing. And what was this? It contained one lined kimono and two thin shirts. Santoka put his palms together and then picked up the lined kimono. Although it was in fact the first day of May, he was still wearing a winter wadded-cotton kimono and was sweating all the time. Now he received this, sent by the woman he had caused so much pain. He felt conscience-stricken, but gratefully put it on right away.

So then—one bath, one cup. It was reasonable that Rokubei could not drink but four or five cups, but a one-*sho* bottle was entrusted to Santoka. Dinner was first, then Santoka leisurely heated the sake by himself, taking just what he wanted. When the electric lamp was being turned off, Santoka noticed by chance that Rokubei's hair was thinning.

That dear old head,
going
bald.

なつかしい頭が
禿げている

When it was time to depart, Rokubei secretly slipped a ten-yen bill into Santoka's bag and, taking up his customary briefcase, left for his job at the mining hospital, turning to look back again and again.

How heavy,
the baggage that I carried
at departure.

別れて来た荷物の
重いこと

Santoka begged through the city of Shimonoseki and, after staying one night, walked briskly from Haba through Asa, Funaki, Koto, and Kagawa. He decided to take a train from Kagawa to Tokuyama. The road that he could see from the window he remembered as the road he walked on a school trip forty years before. Through the window, he felt as though he were watching a movie of a generation—Daido-san, Sandajiro-san and, who else?

One of his friends in the same class at Yamaguchi Upper School had become a major general in the army; others had become mayors, government representatives and professors. Nevertheless, he himself wore a bamboo hat over a tattered black robe and begged at the side of the road. But that was fine. For he himself would, in the end, write good haiku. He would give birth to the mind of poetry. When he meditated on it in this way, his mind settled down peacefully.

When he arrived at the station in Tokuyama, he went to visit his friend Hakusen Kubo in the town of Sado. Since their time in middle school, the two of them had been companions in the world of haiku and in the world of literature. Hakusen was surprised with this sudden visit, and pleased into the bargain. They had not conversed for over ten years, and now their talk could not be bound. Late into the night, Hakusen suddenly strained his ears and said, "Just now there were plovers! Plovers were crying!"

Taken by the goodwill of husband and wife, Santoka stayed here for a day. Hakusen was practiced at the Way of Tea, and was also quite good at painting in the Japanese style. Santoka delighted in inscribing haiku on paintings Hakusen had done. And while they were doing this, Hakusen's wife, Kyoko, washed and mended Santoka's dirty robes.

Hakusen kept on talking:

They say that your first collection of poetry is finally coming out to the public, isn't that so? Recently, everybody thinks that every one of your poems published in the magazine is great! Your lot in life, after all, is haiku, and nobody can imitate you. Keep on composing your own individual world, please.

Since Hosai Ozaki passed away, we felt our magazine was a bit lonely. So everyone got excited about your published work, which is head and shoulders above the rest. The title—Hachi-noko [The Begging Bowl]—is great! It's just like you. I hope to see it soon.

*My bamboo hat's
leaking,
too?*

笠
も
漏
り
だ
し
た
か

On hot days his bamboo hat provided him with an awning from the sun. On windy days it protected him from the wind. On rainy days it managed not to leak. Crowned with this bamboo hat, this hat as the only thing he could rely on, Santoka walked and begged from April 1926, going along through Kyushu, Chugoku and Shikoku, from village to village in western Japan, meandering over how many mountains and rivers? During this journey he passed the age of fifty, when one should know Heaven's command, and turned fifty-one. It had been an endlessly wandering journey. Wet by passing showers as he walked on, raindrops dripping through the rips in his bamboo hat would go right through his robes, giving him the sensation of being soaked to the skin. It is a desolate rain that seeps through one's bamboo hat, and that reverberated in Santoka's weary mind. He had walked until he was worn out. Now he wanted to call a bed someplace of his own.

On May 24, 1932, Santoka held out his begging bowl as he walked along the sea from village to village in Toyo'ura-gun in Nagato. Just before dusk he arrived at the hot-springs town of Kawatana. There was a Zen temple here called the Myoshoji, and he put up at the Sakura-ya—the Kinoshita Inn—on the right hand side of the stone steps beneath the temple. The master of the inn was not particularly well-spoken, but was a kindly man. Santoka dusted off his purse and managed to find the three-sen entrance fee for the bath. Then, before anything else, he slipped into the hot springs he loved so much. The water was a bit lukewarm and did not have as pleasant a sensation as the bath in Ureshino, but both body and mind quietly calmed down considerably.

In the beginning of summer the days are long, and it is still light after the sun has sunk beneath the horizon. Walking in the foothills behind the village, he found the flowers of the mandarin orange fragrantly sweet. They were now blooming in full measure.

Mandarin orange flowers;
time for their fragrance
in my hometown.

ふるさとは
みかんのはな
のにほふとき

He had one cup of sake, taking it taste by taste, wrote in his travel journal, and then slept soundly. The following day, however, he suddenly developed a fever and couldn't move. He was unable to get up the following day as well.

Lying there idly, he borrowed the books in the inn and did some desultory reading. Then, when he felt better, he took a stroll around the foothills of the mountains behind the inn. The beauty of the pines, the purity of the sand, the shape of the continuing mountain range—this was truly a wonderful place. *And* there were his beloved hot springs. That night, he wrote this in his journal:

Being sick and unable to move for two days has hardened my resolve to come to an anchorage in this place. As for the world or the people in it, I have no understanding of what will happen.

Is this the so-called ripening of karma? Comparing Ureshino and Kawatana, the former is superior in terms of hot springs, but the topography of the latter is impeccable. The hills enclosing the foot of the mountains in Kawatana are my favorite kind of scenery. At any rate, I will make myself a place to die here.

About this time, the volunteers at the magazine *So'un* formed a Santoka Supporters' Association. They published his collected poems and advocated building a small hermitage—if possible—where Santoka could live in peace now that he seemed tired out from all of his walking. Having raised a reasonable amount of contributions, it was decided to put them in the charge of Rokubei Kimura. Santoka, who had found a good place to die, naturally wanted to discuss the matter of settling into a hermitage quickly, and so decided once again to visit the town of Itoda in Tagawa-gun, Fukuoka Prefecture. He had slept for three days, however, and had not been able to beg, so he had not one sen left after paying for his lodging.

Thus, once again, he had to stretch out his heavy legs and make yet another begging journey—going by the way of Yasuoka, Yoshimi and Shimonoseki. In Shimonoseki he visited his friend Jitoson and stayed for one night. Not only was he treated to a good meal, but he was given a contribution as well. In Hachiman he stayed one night with Seijoshi Iio, and felt that his heart had been warmed by the usual acts of friendship. Here, he also received a donation and, taking a train, hurried on straightaway to Itoda.

Summer had come to Mount Bota as well, and evening primroses were blossoming beautifully at the foot of the mountain of coal cinders. As usual, he and Rokubei slept with their pillows side by side. Rokubei thought that it would be good for Santoka to settle into a hermitage at Kawatana, and approved of the matter. But Rokubei understood Santoka's character quite well, and would by no means have handed over the support money (five or six hundred yen) directly to him. He was kind enough to Santoka to decide to send him money according to his need.

Increasingly strengthening his resolve to settle into a hermitage, Santoka embraced this hope, crossed the Kammon Straits, and hurried to Kawatana. On the way, he stopped for a night at the stone baths in Yoshimi. Stone baths are probably more a special feature of the Kansai region, so the local people here think of them as quite interesting. Attacked by fleas, lice, rain and wind, he was not able to sleep well.

Lice attacked me throughout the long night.
The voice of dawn reverberated from within my heart.
The wind of a complete change in my life has started to blow.
No matter what, abandon the self that has existed until
yesterday. Just let it go.

In this way, with clear readiness, he embraced the hope of settling into a hermitage and once again stepped onto the earth of Kawatana. The Kinoshita Inn was bustling with a wedding party, so they helped him to find lodging that night in a cheap boarding house called the Nakamura-ya. It was June 1, the mountains were filled with young green leaves, a policeman was wearing a pure white uniform, and Santoka had a new heart, a new day, and a new life.

Having returned to Kawatana, Santoka met the head priest of the Myoshoji temple through the master of the Kinoshita Inn, and discussed various arrangements for renting land. Kinoshita-san is now eighty years old and in excellent health. When I met this elderly man, he informed me about a number of events during these days.

Before he came to ask for lodging at our inn, he passed by here
seriously reciting the Sandokei, *an important sutra of the Soto*
sect. His bamboo hat was torn up and his robes were old, but
at a glance, his attitude was different. This is not a usual beg-
ging monk or pilgrim, I thought. I was interested in him, and he
stopped for a while. He was an honest man and, although the
contents of his purse were always scanty, he paid the lodging
with a clunk, clunk of the coins. I would sometimes loan him ten
or twenty sen, and he would always pay it back. I usually don't
drink even a drop of sake, but if I had a little and drank with
Santoka, we became much more intimate and friendly, I think.

He really liked this place, Kawatana, it seems. He made various efforts and was quite tenacious, negotiating to rent a corner of the temple grounds. But at that time there was no one living at the Myoshoji temple, nor was there anyone acting as caretaker for the place. So perhaps they thought it would be fine for a traveling priest to stop there if he were healthy, but it would be difficult to manage if he had an extended illness. In the end, he was unable to rent the land and left about the end of August, finally going to Ogori.

Later I heard stories that he died around Matsuyama, and that a number of his poetry collections and books had been published. Also, verse memorial stones were put up in various places, and so it turned out that he was really a great man after all, huh. But we didn't get to have him live here, even though he liked Kawatana that much, and I think that's a shame somehow. Now, as a voice for Kawatana and to erase our offense, we should at least put up a verse memorial stone stating that Santoka wanted to have a hermitage here. Perhaps that would comfort him, don't you think?

Other people sympathetic to this idea also came to my inn and talked to me earnestly about this.

The traces of where one haiku poet walked. Moreover, the traces of where he walked twenty-two long years ago. Even now, something to call up the memory, something to be rummaged out. Then to be loved and respected by the people of the village. Even here, I can't help but to contemplate the way human beings think.

The following day, I visited the Myoshoji temple and talked to the abbot, Reido Okamura, about Santoka. The abbot said:

Ah, I heard about that man later on. The time you're talking about was before I came to this temple, and I think they let a fine man slip through their fingers. Nowadays, even those of us who specialize as Zen priests do not live like Zen priests in certain circumstances, and this is somewhat of an embarrassment. As a haiku poet, I suppose Santoka was one of the finest in Ja-

*pan; but he also penetrated the Way as a Zen priest; he seems
to have been a man who did not pretend to himself and who
knew himself well. Zen, in the end, is knowing your own self,
and so really isn't just in being a priest who lives in a temple.*

   *When I talked to the representative of the congregation
the other day, he also said something to the effect that, if they
could, they'd like at least to erect a verse monument, too.*

The abbot seemed a bit nostalgic.

On June 7, 1932, Santoka wrote this in his journal:

*I, too, seem to be turning steadily from sake to tea. A thatched
hut in the style of the taste of Tea. I am struck by the saying in
the Way of Tea that goes, "Each meeting is once in a lifetime"
(一期一会). But to attain that level is truly not easy. Day by
day I feel that what is left of my life is becoming more and more
precious. These are the natural feelings of the common man, I
suppose. It seems that I'll be able to continue living like this in
this place, so this lodging is a good one with true kindness. And
I've started cooking for myself.*

As Santoka took leave of his long wanderings and was about to
enter the life of keeping a hermitage, his frame of mind gradually
settled down. To grasp three sen and go off for the morning bath was
truly delightful. Morning sake was worth a thousand ryo; a morning
bath, ten thousand. [59] In the midst of a materially poor life, his heart
was rich.

*My cheerless body
dipped
right in.*

さみしいからだ
ずんぶりつけた

A bath
　　for one,
　　overflowing.

ひとりの湯が
こぼれる

The Buddhist temple gate,
　　already
open.
　　(at the Myoshoji temple)

もう山門
あけてある

How long will I live?
　　Building
my hermitage.
　　(at the Myoshoji temple)

いつまで
生きよう
庵を結んで

From branch to branch
　　through the huge camphor:
a green storm.
　　(on a forest of camphor trees)

大楠の
枝から枝へ
青あらし

Hanging branches
　　of the huge camphor, flowers
reaching the ground.
　　(on a forest of camphor trees)

大楠の枝
たれて地に
とどく花

ここの土と
ならうお寺の
ふくろう

Becoming part of the earth,
   right here;
     temple owl.

笠ねけば
松の
しずくで

Taking off my bamboo hat;
   the pine,
     dripping.

さみしい道を
蛇に
よこぎられる

Crossed by a snake;
   the lonely
     road.

つつましく
咲いて
げんのしようこ

Blooming
   modestly,
     the cranesbill.[60]

Translator's Notes

1. In the original, "crying *kana kana*." This cicada is also know as the *kanakana*.

2. 100 sen equaled one yen.

3. 100 rin equaled one sen.

4. *Biroju*: Perhaps a kind of palm, the *Livistona subglobosa Martius*.

5. *Hamaomoto*: A white crinum, *Crinum asiaticum L. var. japonicum Baker*.

6. *Shufu no tomo* (主婦の友, Housewife's Friend), a popular women's magazine published from 1917 to 2008.

7. The Way: in Japanese 道 (*michi*) can be interpreted as the "road," the "path," the "way," or the "Way."

8. An allusion to Case 19 of the *Mumonkan*, the thirteenth century collection of Zen koans: Nansen was asked by Chao-chou, "What is the Way?" Nansen said, "Your everyday mind is the Way."

9. *Onryo*: Oyama gives this only in the katakana syllabary (オンリョウ), and there are several homonyms of this word in the dictionary. The best bet, however, is 怨霊, which itself means both "revengeful ghost," and "loan."

10. One *sho*: 1.6 dry quart (1.8 liters)

11. *Sansa shigure*, the first line of the haiku, possibly refers to part of a folk song from the area of Sendai, accompanied by shamisen and clapping. In this case, *sansa* would be a meaningless word just added for rhythm. On the other hand, *sansa* can also mean "in three different places," and this would change the poem from "late autumn rains, hey!" to "raining in three different places"; not an uncommon sight deep in the mountains.

12. The Japanese word 道 (*michi*) can mean both a "road" or the "Way." The word *hitosuji*, on the final line of the haiku, means not only "straight," but also "with a single purpose."

13. *Hi no maru*: the Japanese flag with the red sun on a field of white.

14. *Zuishosakushu* (隋所作主): from the commentary in Case 47 of the *Mumonkan*, the thirteenth century collection of Zen koans that Santoka studied constantly.

15. *Hoito*: originally meaning the taking charge of a Zen monk's food, it eventually came to mean the monk and the food itself, and later a beggar or panhandler.

16. 法眼: probably the *Shobogenzo* (正法眼蔵), the great treatise on Zen by founder of the Soto school of the Zen sect, Dogen Zenji.

17. 旅人芭蕉.

18. The old measuring unit *go* was used for liquid and solid measurements. 1 *go* is about 6 fluid ounces (180 ml) or 5 ounces (150 g).

19. A favorite way of drinking sake in Japan. The small wooden boxes, open at the top, are made of cedar, which is said to enhance the flavor of the drink. Sometimes a little salt is sprinkled on the edge of the box.

20. The Yellow Springs: the oriental version of Hades.

21. Influenced by the famous haiku poet Basho, who wrote, some 250 years earlier:

Nothing at all suggests
　　they will die before long:
cries of the cicada.

やがて
死ぬけしきも
見えず蝉の声

22. Snake gourd: a kind of cucumber, *Trichosanthus cucumeroides*.

23. Yukichi Fukuzawa (1835–1901): The modernizer of Japanese education. He hoped to make Japan more like America.

24. Godown: a storehouse, usually with whitewashed walls, built next to the main house.

25. The second line of this gatha paraphrases the sixth verse of the Tao Te Ching: "The valley spirit never dies"(谷神不死).

26. *Menko*: a kind of children's toy or game, consisting of coin-shaped objects made of copper, clay or glass, with figures of the Japanese gods Ebisu, Daikoku, or demons or foxes stamped on each side. Played in the fashion of marbles.

27. The falling off of body and mind: 身心脱落. Dogen Zenji's phrase on the process of zazen.

28. Oyama gives no explanation of or any further reference to the *Sanbaku-fu*, which literally translated means "389 prefectures."

29. *Kyo* (居): residence.

30. A shrine commemorating Sugawara no Michizane (845–903), now worshipped as a deity of calligraphy and scholarship. He served the emperor Uda, and eventually attained the title of Minister of the Left. His influence and popularity was envied by other nobles and officials, however, and they accused him of plotting against the following emperor, Daigo. Michizane was then exiled to Dazaifu in remote Chikuzen Province (today part of Fukuoka Prefecture), where he lived for only another two years. During his exile, he was said to often climb Mount Tempai, face faraway Kyoto, and venerate the emperor who had disgraced him.

31. *Horo horo*: mimesis implying pleasantly, scatteringly, or melodiously.

32. The *Zangemon* (懺悔文): a sort of Buddhist confessional verse:

> All the evil karma I have committed from times long past
> Has sprung from beginningless greed, anger and ignorance,
> Born of my body, words and thought.
> I now confess it all.

33. The *Shiguzeigan* (四弘誓願): the four great vows of a bodhisattva: 1) sentient beings are innumerable, but I vow to save them all; 2) worldly desires are without number, but I vow to extinguish them all; 3) the Dharma teachings are inexhaustible, but I vow to study them all; 4) the Buddhist Way is the highest, and I vow to attain it.

34. *Makahannyaharamita shingyo* (羯諦羯諦菩提薩婆訶): The Heart Sutra. The shortest of the Wisdom Sutras, and recited daily by both monks and lay Buddhists.

35. Sorinshi: pseudonym of Chikamatsu Monzaemon (1653–1724). A Buddhist monk in his youth, and later the great writer of puppet and kabuki plays.

36. Sayohime (sixth century): Matsura Sayohime. Wife of Japanese general Otomo no Sadehiko. It is said that she turned to stone waiting on a mountaintop for her husband to return from hostilities in Korea.

37. *Wasurena-gusa* (don't-forget-grass) and *wasure-gusa* (forgetting-grass) respectively in Japanese.

38. Calmotin: medication to enhance sleep.

39. Interestingly enough, on January 17 of this year, Santoka wrote in his journal:

> For me, it's not the [Zen phrase] "One day with no work is one day with no food (一日不作一日不食)," but rather, "if I'm going to eat, I've got to work." Today when I begged in the rain, it was just like that. ("When you don't work, you don't eat" is the truth. "Even if you work, you won't be able to eat" is a lie.)

40. Shigenobu Okuma (1838–1922): former Japanese prime minister and one of the great men of the Meiji Restoration. Founded Waseda University, Santoka's alma mater.

41. The Japanese word for "traveling expenses" is *waraji-sen*: lit. money for straw sandals.

42. Santoka seems to be making a sort of joke here. *Roto* (露頭) means "without a hat." *Dodo* (堂々) means "grand" or "stately." Santoka has answered with a combination of these two: *Rododo* (露堂々).

43. *Ureshino* (嬉野) literally means "pleasant field."

44. *Wasureyuki* (忘れ雪). Possibly indicating the end of the year—the time to forget about all the problems of the last twelve months.

45. A reference to Confucius' dictum "At fifty, I knew Heaven's command."

46. Santoka's lineage was Soto Zen.

47. 応無所住、而生其心

48. たたずむな、行くな戻るな。伊豆割るな、ねるなおきるな。しるもしらぬも。

49. 煩悩即菩提. This is according to the Mahayana principle of non-duality. While appearing to be different, earthly passions and enlightenment are the same.

50. 即身成仏 (*Sokushin jobutsu*): an essential doctrine of the Shingon sect.

51. An abbreviated form of the mantra at the end of the Heart Sutra.

52. The "floating world," means "this transitory world" or mundane life, as opposed to the life of a Buddhist priest

53. No doubt heroes of the Russo Japanese War.

54. *Kusamochi*: rice cakes mixed with mugwort.

55. A play on the words of Huineng, the sixth patriarch of Chinese Zen who said "Fundamentally, not one thing exists" (本来無一物). The last three characters of this phrase (無一物) are used in the Japanese language to mean "not one penny."

56. Daruma Taishi (Bodhidharma): the first Zen patriarch of China (died 528 or 536 A.D.)

57. The repetition here is a common feature of Zen/Taoist-style phrases.

58. Mount Bota is *botayama* in Japanese, which is also the general name for a huge heap of coal waste.

59. The *ryo* was an old gold currency unit.

60. Cranesbill: *geranium nepalense var. thunbergii*. A pink, five-petaled flower.

CHAPTER 4

Light and Darkness
at Kawatana

On the morning of June 10, 1932, Santoka walked through the outskirts of Kawatana Village, cut two or three green rush reeds, and returned to his lodgings. He put these into a long narrow jar he had picked up at some point from a rubbish heap. It was slightly cracked, but was a work with fine self-composure, fitting for whatever kind of flower one put into it. Santoka looked at it intently while drawing on a cigarette butt. The green leaves of the rushes swayed in the morning breeze. The smoke from his cigarette rose and drifted around the room. Alone, he quietly calmed his mind. As he sat there, the young lady of the house was kind enough to inform him that a package had arrived. He quickly descended from the second floor and received it. With a glance at the characters of the address, he immediately understood who the sender was: Sakino of Kumamoto. His heart beating, he opened the package and looked at the contents:

futons (top and bottom; one each)

kimono (one for summer; one lined)

books (seven volumes)

chawan bowl (one)

mortuary tablet (his mother's)

sake cups (two)

paper (an undetermined amount)

hand towel (one)

a stringed loincloth (one)

pen points (five)

envelopes (ten)

sewing needle and thread (an undetermined amount)

What detailed consideration she must have had for him! How perceptive women are! After he had sent a postcard relating that he had discontinued his long wandering journey and had settled into this place, his woman had immediately sent a package in this way. And though I say "his woman," was she not the very woman from whom he cut off relations and divorced a good ten years prior to this?

A single letter was there inside the package. It seemed to be nothing more than a simple invoice and there was nothing of particular interest written down on it. In that same envelope, however, there was enclosed a voucher for a money order for ten yen she had sent him in another letter. "I'm absolutely inexcusable," he thought, but could do nothing more than meekly accept what she had sent.

The mortuary tablet was for his mother, whose suicide was forty years before. It was wrapped in white cotton. He gave a start, then held it reverently in both hands and, without a moment's delay, placed it in the alcove and put his hands together in prayer. For the housewife of the Taneda family, "Awakened Obedient Constant Sincere Woman"[1] was a bit too desolate of a posthumous Buddhist name. When he had been traveling, he wrote this name on a piece of paper, placed it between the pages of a sutra, and walked about carrying it in his pack every day. During that time, his wife had not seen his face even once, but had been kind enough to pray for the repose of her mother-in-law's soul in his place. The truth was, he thought, that she had been kind enough to send this to him because he had stated that he was going to settle down in a hermitage. Arranging the contents of the package, he once again puffed on a cigarette butt. Any number of things came to his mind. Wasn't it about the time that Ken would be graduating from middle school? What a good-for-nothing father he was. But there was no other living Way Ken's father could walk than this one.

When he returned from the hot springs that evening, strangely, his poetic heart bubbled over; forgetting even to turn on the electric light, he was absorbed in writing verses. It would not do for him to be attached to wife and child. Rather than that, he should write verses—if he could only write verses he would be saved. Such were Santoka's thoughts.

Here, for the second time,
    I shave
        my white hair.

ふたたび
ここで
白髪を剃る

Somehow, right here,
        I want to settle down;
    the evening moon.

どうでも
ここに
落着きたい夕月

Offering reverence
        to the mortuary tablet:
    all that is left.

これだけ
残っている
お位牌をおがむ

Santoka muttered the words of this last haiku to himself. The house, the land, the fortune—everything that had been passed down by the Taneda clan since long ago—all had been lost, perished, and gone to ruin without a trace. Both he and his father had ruined themselves. Now before his ruined self, the only thing remaining of all the Taneda property was his mother's mortuary tablet. He would have to protect and venerate this tablet until the day he died.

At some time or another, four kittens were born at this lodging— the tenement house behind the Kinoshita Inn. For the children of the place, these were wonderful toys. They would fumble around with them every day while the mother cat circled with apparent concern. Five or six of the young geisha at the hot springs found out about this, came over all together, and asked for the kittens. The master of the house was delighted, and agreed. Santoka watched this from the second floor and smiled.

"Kittens . . . They came for kittens. Well, well now."

The village had begun its rice-planting. This would surely be a good time for strolling around.

All together,
*   dripping in sweat:*
*   oxen, men.*

いっしょに
ぴっしより汗かいて
牛が人が

The mother cat that had lost her kittens cried incessantly. Even though Santoka had abandoned the world, he was forced to think deeply about the affection between parent and child.

The mother cat
*   looking for her kittens, crying*
*   to the end of time.*

子を探す
親猫の
いつまでも泣く

As he was thinking these things, he saw by chance that there were some beautiful *dokudami* chameleon plants[2] blooming in white around the house.

> *Rounding the house,*
> *flowers*
> *of dokudami.*

家をめぐりて
どくだみの花

One day he received seven postcards from people like the haiku teacher Seisensui and other haiku poets from various places. Correspondence is one of life's greatest pleasures. He read the postcards over and over again, tasting the emotion of friendship. There were, however, no postcards for him to write replies. He had no money, and when he finally found one card he had put away somewhere, he could send it only to Rokubei. He needed money every day for his room and board, but beyond that there were the various negotiations concerning the land for the hermitage at this time, so he was unable to go out begging. Poverty is something towards which one is resolved, but it is also lonely. Someone once offered, "You're poor because you're not productive." This was true. And though Santoka replied, "Instead of that, I'm creative," I still think that poverty was hard to bear.

At this time, Santoka was constantly picking things up along his way—not things people had dropped, but rather things that had been thrown away. He would pick up and use a chipped teapot; empty bottles he would pick up and take home, using them to store vinegar. From time to time he would pick up stones. He loved stones and began to feel that he wanted to live with them. Stones are without comment. They are peaceful.

> *Things to eat,*
> *all gone, too;*
> *this morning's glow.*

食べるもの
もなくなった
今日の朝焼

ここの土とならう
お寺のふくろ

Becoming part of the earth,
right here;
temple owl.

After a lapse of ten days, Santoka went begging on June 19. He got up at four in the morning, first taking a hot bath, then reading the sutras alone. All around was silent. Finishing his morning meal, he went out before six o'clock. Passing through the villages of Tabe and Okaeda, he begged a round trip of forty miles [sixty-four kilometers], returning about three in the afternoon. He was an excellent walker. In Okaeda he was treated to a meal at a prosperous house.

Rice – 1 sho 6 go
Cash – 37 sen

It was an undue income. After such a long, long time he was able to buy one cup of shochu. The taste that he savored while gazing at the evening sky after his bath was so delicious as to soak right through his stomach. But for himself, he was ashamed. He was ashamed of the extravagance of eleven sen for the shochu.

A hundred thousand benefactors and perpetual prosperity.
Even then these offerings are turned into alcohol and nicotine.
There will be some punishment for this.

湧いてあふれる中に
ねている

In the midst of the bubbling,
the overflowing:
sleep.

As a side dish for his evening meal, Santoka bought two flying fish. The cost was five sen.

並べられて
まだ生きている

Arranged side by side,
they are still
alive.

From sake to tea, from left to right, he was someone who liked to make an about-face quickly.

ひとりの
あつい茶を
すする

Alone,
sipping
hot tea.

Santoka went to the town of Kogushi to buy books: *Haiku kyoza* [A Course in Haiku][3] and *Daizokyo kyoza* [A Course in the Great Archive of Sutras].[4] These were food for the mind. When you're poor, your mind is caught up in just trying to eat, and your spirit becomes mean. On June 24, yet another package was delivered. This was sent by his younger sister, Shizu Machida, who lived in the village of Migita, outside the city of Hofu. His heart pounding, he opened it to find an unlined cotton kimono, three bars of *Kao* soap, six cigarettes and, placed inside an envelope, three one-yen bills! Secretly, without anyone in her house aware of it, his younger sister had prepared such things and sent them off to him. Now his tears flowed for her kindness.

It is said that blood is thicker than water, and this is absolutely so. When he was walking on from one journey to the next, he was the Santoka who did not look back. He meekly accepted people's goodwill as exactly that—goodwill—but did not stop his mind there in any way. Even if he stayed over at a cheap boarding house where he was truly treated kindly, or if he received the favor of being able to stay over at the house of a friend-in-haiku where he was given excellent treatment, he did not stop his mind there, but, like flowing water, did not turn back. He simply advanced forward, step by step, continuing on with his journey. So at this time, when he put up his staff in this way at Kawatana, it was strange that various memories of days gone by came to him. Perhaps it was because of his age. Or perhaps it was because this place was close to his old hometown. Turning back to look at the past, his heart was filled with the raw wounds of failure and regret.

Today he walked just one and a half *ri*, on a road going through the middle of fields that were being planted with rice, and begged in the village of Kogushi. After returning to his lodgings, strangely, he was in a deep frame of mind, and admitted as much in three wills he sent to his younger sister, to his son Ken, and to his woman in Kumamoto. Later he visited the Myoshoji temple up the hill, and meditated deeply on the temple garden said to have been created by Sesshu.[5] He thought it to be a splendid garden of flowing rocks which, though created by man, contained little human meddling. The large pines in front of the gate were splendid, as was the huge camphor tree which was filled with berries. After this he took a meandering walk by himself around the hill behind the temple, took some blossoms from some of the trees, and returned home. He put the strong-scented flowers into an arrangement, boiled one of the bamboo shoots he had received from the lady of the house, and then concentrated on a half cup of shochu.

I think that, just as there are no bad men among those who truly love sake, there are no bad men among those who truly love flowers.

He added such things to his journal.

Like the sky during the rainy season, the matter of building a hermitage was totally unsettled, and taking no shape at all. The primary matter of renting land was difficult to bring to fruition. Because of everything that had been done up until now, it was assumed that they were going to build a hermitage; but while it was going on sluggishly like this, the endowment from the supporters' organization was uselessly decreasing and Santoka was becoming more and more forlorn.

For a while he had a continuing mild fever, and for three or four days simply idled about, never leaving the gate.

Three Articles for Self-discipline:
  – Do not flatter yourself.
  – Make what is insufficient sufficient.
  – Bring reality to life.

Always drink good sake.
Even if there is plenty of good sake, do not drink beyond 3 cups.
Good sake is something to enjoy both with yourself and others.

He wrote this in the margin of his journal, taking a hard look at himself. They were all next to impossible to put into practice. But Santoka, who could be called a do-nothing, told himself that he would hold fast to these requests [to himself] at least.

In July the weather became increasingly hot and humid. He stayed indoors both day and night, and whenever he thought of the hermitage construction that was not going forward he had nothing but bad dreams. "My only child, Ken, is his mother's child and no longer mine. But still, there's no mistaking that I'm his father . . ." He had more bad dreams thinking such thoughts over and over again. And in these dreams he did nothing but berate himself.

In this way, he was clearly beginning to settle into a quagmire. One night, rousing himself with a jolt, he took a walk on the hill behind his boarding house, smoking a cigarette. Somehow his mood brightened, and suddenly he came back to his former self. Haiku rose to the surface as if on a stream:

さみしい夜の
あまりもの
食べるなど

A lonely night;
    I eat something
like leftovers.

何で
こんなに
淋しい風ふく

Why does it blow,
    like this?
The lonely wind.

*As for haiku, insofar as it is true haiku, it is poetry of the soul.[6]
To put aside the manifestation of the mind is not the essence
of haiku. The sun shines, flowers bloom, insects sing, water
flows—thus there will be no place without flowers when you
look, and no place without a moon when you muse.*

The rainy season came to an end and good weather ensued, but
it became remarkably hot. The fishmonger woman came at six in
the morning: "How about some today?" or "Don't you need some-
thing?"

The old man from a farmhouse made a rare visit to sell some
mountain pears. The fruit reminded Santoka of the days of his
youth, and his heart was drawn to the fragrance he remembered, but
he had no money to buy and eat one. He was satisfied, however, just
to keenly smell that fragrance.

It must have been gratifying to be able to feel thanks for his
poverty. This was not actually praising poverty, but for a long time
while he was experiencing [the Zen Buddhist principle of] "not one
thing" (無一物), he became accustomed to not worrying too much
about having no money or being inconvenienced. Even with food,
it got so that no matter what was put in front of him or where, he
put his palms together in gratitude and was able to eat with a sense
that this food was delicious, and this from the bottom of his heart.

And much more, regardless of whether it was a fish head, the root of a vegetable, or leftovers from what someone else had eaten, he was able to humbly receive and eat everything without leaving a trace. This was absolutely due to his poverty, and he was unable *not* to feel thanks to that poverty.

The volunteers at the Kawatana hermitage and the caretakers of the temple would have been in a good bit of trouble if, taking care of a begging priest with no income like him, he were to fall sick and die. Noting this, it seems they did not do a lot for him concerning land [for him to rent]. Only Old Man Kinoshita at the lodging house had faith in him, gave him assistance regardless of the matter, and kindly said that he would be Santoka's guarantor.

On July 5, *Hachinoko* [The Begging Bowl], his very first collection of poems that he had waited and waited for, was published. Thanks to Kitaro Uchijima in Kyoto, it was printed on yellow washi paper and bound like a Buddhist sutra. He had to be thankful for Kitaro's kindness, but there were many typographical errors, and the collection somehow did not fit his own feelings.

It began to rain again. Coming down in torrents. One of his molars had been irritating him, but now it hurt terribly. Unable to bear the pain, he pulled it out. The pain finally subsided but, sadly, now only three teeth remained. In this way, holes opened up in his body, one after another.

ほつくり抜けえた歯を
投げる夕闇

Tossing away
a pried out tooth;
evening dusk.

A clock was kindly sent to him with the goodwill of his haiku friends in Kyushu. Somehow it didn't fit Santoka to be carrying around a table clock, but in the end, when the hermitage was built, his friends assumed that he would in some way need a clock, and their friendship was especially gratifying.

It was Santoka's custom to pick up discarded items in the afternoon, and today he picked up a face-powder compact behind the village. Though he washed it several times over, it still had a woman's scent, so it was not quite in keeping with his room. He finally rubbed it with ashes and decided to keep it as a container for an ink stamp pad. With a look about his room he could see that everything in it had been picked up somewhere. From time to time that made him laugh, but he wondered if, for an unproductive human being like himself, if gathering up what other people had thrown away (in contrast to what they had dropped) was truly a living.

That night he was disgusted at having a wet dream. What a sad fact of reality it must have been. And this despite thinking that he had probably just dried up rather than having abandoned sexual desire. He got out of bed at four o'clock and chanted a sutra before his mother's mortuary tablet.

Translator's Notes

1. This is typical of Buddhist names given to describe a person after their death.
2. *Houttuynia cordata, Saururaceae.* A perennial 6–8 inches (15–30 cm) high with white and yellow flowers. Leaves produce an unpleasant smell when rubbed. The Japanese name means poison (*doku*) and pain (*dami*). Called "chameleon plant" in English.
3. 俳句講座.
4. 大蔵経講座.
5. Sesshu (1420–1506). Famous Japanese landscape painter.
6. I have chosen the word "soul" for the kanji character 魂, which can also be translated as "spirit." It is in contrast to 心, "heart" or "mind."

CHAPTER 5

The Gochu-an at Ogori

Summer advanced without the hermitage being built, and day by day the heat increased. Finally, life came to a standstill. Santoka had no stamps to paste on letters to his friends. When, having no other recourse, he tossed the letters into the mailbox without stamps anyway, the mailman kindly went to the trouble to carry them back and caution him.

"Well, the fact is, I don't have any stamps, you see," he replied, and must have felt his poverty clear to the bone.

After this, he drank water, gazed at the flowers, and read with great appreciation Dogen's Shushogi chant and the poetry of Basho. The former was a man of religion and the latter a haiku poet, but Santoka felt that the works these two men left to the world had one flavor that was mutually permeable in terms of their great dignity and purity, despite the two men being so different. Both Dogen's writings and Basho's haiku contained an austerity which might be expressed as having something of "Japanese aristocracy."

Santoka got up at five o'clock, gulped down a meal of barley and, with a plan for the next four or five days, once again set out on a journey of begging. He begged through Hanyu and Atsuta, and the following day went as far as Ogori where he received the favor of being able to stay at the residence of Tatsuaki Kunimori. He walked out to Daido and Hofu, and in Hofu he went for the first time in a long while to the Taneda burial plot. Santoka's house was in ruins, his people were dead, and everything had utterly perished; but the gravestones stood exactly as they had long ago. He dutifully pulled out the weeds that had flourished there and swept the area. He then took a dried-out piece of rotten bamboo as a flower tube, pulled up some buttercups, inserted them in the bamboo tube, and sat in front of the gravestone alone absorbed in reciting the sutras. During his recitation, tears inevitably welled up and his voice stuck in his throat. When he thought about it, he had not shed tears for a long time. He sat there between the gravestones where no one could see him and cried as his heart led him.

This journey became the seed of the karma that would have Santoka leave Kawatana and turn towards Ogori, which was close to his hometown. After just one night of talking with Santoka, Tatsuaki was completely captivated, formed a support group for this mendicant haiku poet, and decided to invite him—the man so distressed by the hermitage construction in Kawatana—to Ogori.

On August 26 of 1932, Santoka finally decided to leave Kawatana. The negotiations for the land had broken down, and he had lost all hope for the construction of a hermitage. Moreover, although the land was to be rented only temporarily, he passed time aimlessly throughout the summer and completely ate through the expenses set aside for the construction of the hermitage.

In the end, there had been no karmic relation between Santoka and Kawatana. The land was good and the scenery was beautiful, but people's hearts had not been quite so attractive. Nevertheless, it is said that "The departing bird does not foul its former nest." Thus, he donated one yen to the Myoshoji temple for the representatives who had brought the negotiations to an end. He then packed up his scant baggage. Both the father and the children at the Kinoshita Inn were sorry that Santoka was leaving after having become disgusted with Kawatana, and did a number of things to help him out.

Leaving today;
the snake gourd
dangling.[1]

けふはおわかれの
糸瓜がぶらり

In Ogori, for the time being, he settled down in a detached room behind Kenji Takenami's house until the hermitage was finished. Tatsuaki brought sake, Fuyumura brought dried plums and scallions, and each carried along other various items as well.

Even though the Santoka support group was going to create the hermitage that would be named the Gochu-an, this was not going to be a matter of once again looking for land and building a new structure. Outside the village of Ogori, going half a mile through the fields to the northwest, there was a quiet community called Yaashi at the foot of the mountains. This was an old farming village of a little over twenty farmhouses and a stone Jizo bodhisattva, wearing a bib and with a broken-off nose, nestled into the root of an old camellia tree. At the highest place in the village on a slightly elevated spot at the foot of the mountain, there was an abandoned thatched-roof house behind a bamboo thicket. It was said that someone had lived in it formerly, but due to some sort of failure he had been unable to continue living there and had fled under the cover of night. The roof was tattered and the support posts askew, but all around the house were trees bearing summer tangerines, loquats, jujubes, persimmons and yuzu citrus. Moreover, it faced the south and there were neighbors nearby; you could say it was a fitting mansion for a haiku poet (or an abandoned person).[2] Fortunately, the house was owned by the Jinbo family, relatives of Tatsuaki; and as they gave permission for its use, Tatsuaki showed it to Santoka, who was delighted.

At this point, ignoring the intensity of the remaining summer heat, Tatsuaki had his students from the agricultural school help out and, although they were amateurs, they repaired the abandoned house. Trying their hands at mending the thatch on the roof, attaching a toilet, pulling out the weeds and repairing the sliding doors, they somehow built a hermitage in which a person could live.

The rent was only fifty sen a month. The name of the hermitage, the Gochu-an, was one Santoka had thought of quite some time ago on his travels. The Kannon Sutra which he often chanted, that is to say the twenty-fifth chapter of the Lotus Sutra, includes this phrase: "If one among them speaks these words . . ." It was this "one among them" (*gochu*) that he used for the name of his hermitage.[3]

Overjoyed that he would not have to stay on and on at a lodging house, Santoka went to the site and made to help out with the work. The young men, however, who disregarded the summer heat and worked along covered in sweat, kept the older man at a distance. This was because Tatsuaki was the overseer. But as it came close to completion, Santoka could not bear not to help. On September 18, he worked at the site from dawn to dusk.

> Tucked into the foothills of Mount Yamate, its tranquility is perfect. I'd like to express this by saying that it's peaceful, but not lonely. There are a number of camellia trees, and I suspect that the plop, plop[4] of the flowers will beat against my heart. There are also a lot of persimmons, and currently the branches are drooping with fruit. Called Yamate persimmons, they are said to be quite prized.
>
> A great number of spider lilies are also in bloom, so there are clusters of red here and there around the hermitage.
>
> I wonder if I should put up this kind of signboard on the Gochu-an:

> Scallions, Garlic and Sake Welcome [5]
> to Enter This Hermit's Cell
> or
> Those Without Sake Do Not Enter

Santoka made jokes about these things. But his mind was now stimulated, and he took a scrubbing cloth and wiped the pillars, the verandah and the doorsill. No matter how he wiped and wiped, however, the old dirt would not come out. Also, there were old nails still in the wood here and there, and when he went around pulling them out with a nail extractor, he found a long clump of a woman's hair hanging from the sideboard. This made an uncomfortable chill creep over him. He finally pulled it off, took it to the vegetable garden behind the house and buried it deep in the earth. I wonder if this might be called "The Woman's Stupa."

On September 20, he finally moved in. Borrowing a cart from a sake shop, he moved his nine articles of baggage—large and small—by himself. You might think that this was a surplus of baggage for a begging haiku poet, but he had received different things from people and, if he was going to live a life of poverty, he would need each one of these pieces of junk right here and from this moment. In that regard, attachment had now shown itself. He had abandoned that attachment and fled from the Mitori Kannon temple in Higo, but today he was seeking the life of an owner of a hermitage (the life he had abandoned) and he was ready to take up residence. Between these two points in time, however, eight years had flowed like a river. He had walked meandering and aimless over the mountains and rivers of western Japan. That meandering journey now had him yearning, on the contrary, for a hermitage; and it had him wishing for one place to settle down and for his own bed. Was this not a great contradiction? No, it was not. The eight years of time he spent walking and begging was induced of its own accord. He now nodded approval to himself and put his ragged bundle on the old verandah. In the earthen-floored kitchen he set up a portable clay cooking stove, and hung his bamboo hat on the left-hand wall of the entranceway. This was because, from this time on, he would be the master of a hermitage.

He made the shelf above the wall-cupboard his Buddhist altar, and there he enshrined his mother's mortuary tablet. He then installed a woodcarving of the bodhisattva Kannon in the corner. He made an censer out of a small bowl he had picked up, and put some ashes in it. There were two four-and-a-half-mat tatami rooms, one three-mat room, and the kitchen. There was also a bathroom [with a toilet only], and he could crawl into it from the three-mat room. Being old, he was happy to be able to enter it from the inside, and this had been worked out with a special request from Tatsuaki. The inner four-and-a-half-mat room faced the south, and there was an open verandah attached to it. It seemed that he would be able to bask in the sun here from autumn through the winter.

On the very first night of moving into the hermitage, Tatsuaki and some others came along and were kind enough to raise congratulatory cups of sake. But when they all returned home, Santoka sat quietly

alone, listening to the voices of the insects. He was indisputably the "one among them." His mind had truly come to settle down in peace. On the other hand, this just might be the place where he would die. Still, after so long a time, he could not help feeling gratitude for the goodwill of Tatsuaki and the others, friends with understanding.

> *Moving here;*
> *spider lilies* [6]
> *in full bloom.*

うつりきて
彼岸花の
花ざかり

Sleep, sleep. Santoka slept surprisingly well after coming to this hermitage. Probably because he had settled down at the very bottom of his heart. Through the leaves of the trees he could see the lamps of his neighbors' houses below, separated from him by two vegetable fields. But he could hear no human voices. It truly was peaceful. Going out the back door from the kitchen and then about fifteen yards (fourteen meters) there was a jujube tree, and beneath that a small well. It was a shallow well—only three or four feet [one meter] deep—but just enough water bubbled up that would not be insufficient for the life of one person. It was a little white and cloudy, but when he tasted it carefully he found it to be sweet and good.

The most important things for living in a place are water and fire. Getting up in the morning, you draw water and kindle a fire. Sometimes, when he kindled a fire by himself, he wanted to cry from happiness. Kindling a fire is being alive. Even if he was destitute, from this point on Santoka would kindle the fire of the "one among them." He would kindle the fire of life. Then, as long as his own life continued, Santoka would produce haiku from his life in this hermitage. It wasn't true that he would be unable to produce poetry here, for he was blessed with the hermitage he had been seeking. He wanted to die writing poetry—writing poetry as long as his life continued—writing the poetry of life.

On the east side of the Gochu-an there was a vegetable field of about 350 square feet [32 sq. meters]. Santoka, who had finally settled into a hermitage, decided to till this field and grow a variety of vegetables. Thus it became the lot of one who had continued on a long, long meandering journey to settle down here and cultivate the earth. Tatsuaki was kind enough to bring him a mattock, and he even got seeds from the agricultural school. When Santoka had abandoned the world and become a priest in Kumamoto, he received the Buddhist name Koho—"Cultivating Furrows"—from his master. Looking steadily at this word, Koho, he thought that it had meant for him to cultivate the mind, to pull out and throw away the weeds of the mind, and to demonstrate without reserve the strength of the life of his very own essence. But it was not just for him to till his mind; it now became his lot to till the earth at an actual site, and to grow by himself only those vegetables that he needed. This was truly the first time ever for him to be playing with the soil. In this tilling he embraced a new enthusiasm and zest, and was able to forget the loneliness of being all by himself.

The morning glow
and rain;
let's plant daikon!

朝焼雨ふる
大根まかう

Last night's loneliness…
I'll plow the field
again.

ゆうべの
さみしさは
また畑を打つ

He noticed, however, that by plowing the earth, it was necessary to take the lives of various insects. Just stepping along, he killed things like earthworms, chrysalises and mole crickets. He looked to his own conscience for having disturbed the peaceful slumber of the bugs that had been sleeping comfortably in the quiet autumn earth until they were killed.

All things taken together, the first patron of the Gochu-an was Tatsuaki Kunimori. He had been a writer for the magazine *So'un* since long before, and was the secretary for the Ogori agricultural school. As a sake drinker, he was in no way inferior to Santoka. Of course it was because of this man that the Gochu-an was possible, and he came to visit almost every day, not just to console the all-alone Santoka's heart, but to look after his personal comfort in terms of all the food and clothing Santoka lacked in his destitution. He was kind enough to bring rice, to carry up ashes [for the brazier], and one day he even dragged up some miso. And, when the two of them returned to the Gochu-an after drinking together, he always departed after quietly leaving a fifty-sen coin on the tabletop. This would immediately be used to pay for the master of the hermitage's shochu and tofu. Tatsuaki was truly a bodhisattva. There was a deep karmic relationship between the two that went beyond friendship.

With the coming of October, the surroundings of the hermitage became more and more autumnal. Every day the persimmons got fatter right before his eyes. White buds appeared on the tea trees. Persimmons and tea; truly typical of Japan. Surrounded by things so Japanese, he led a solitary destitute life, and from that created the haiku that were his passion. Such a life at the hermitage gradually came to fit him. The fifth of the month was Daruma's Memorial Day. Santoka neither looked nor acted much like a monk, but as someone linked to the line of Zen, he tried to savor something of the teachings of the founder of the sect.

Nevertheless, he got derailed. Due to too much shochu. Drunk, he fell down in the street and was discovered by someone in the neighborhood. Having no money, he downed a cup anyway, then hung his head, charged the drink to credit and returned home. One day, he wrote this sort of self-criticism in his journal:

A human being—at least someone like me—hurries along to his grave repeating the same blunders and the same regrets over and over again. Some time ago a sarcastic friend of mine took a look at my foolishness and said, "You never get tired of it, do you—doing the same old stuff." I, however, did not feel his sarcasm all that much. As a matter of fact, even since I came to Ogori, I'm still the same, and have been unable to strip off this bad habit of sake. Isn't this correct?

Santoka did not have a fixed income and did not hope for one either; he had to carry on his life solely depending on what he had been blessed with. Although he had rice for three or four days, he had no side dishes at all; he had been able to grow vegetables in his garden, but there was no soy sauce so he could hardly cook them to eat. He had tried eating a raw daikon with a dash or two of salt, and the first time it wasn't too bad, but by the second or third time he was having trouble. When he tried emptying his purse, he had only four one-sen copper coins. He had no container, so he looked beneath the flooring, pulled out a small empty can, and went off to town to buy some soy sauce. On the path through the middle of the rice fields, by chance he encountered the shopboy from the soy- sauce shop, and right there on the road had the can filled right up to the top. One *sho* was twenty sen, so the charge came to 1.50 sen. But when Santoka was about to pay, the shopboy said, "I don't need it; consider it alms." "I can't accept that," Santoka replied, and the two of them got into a heated argument right there on the road. In the end, Santoka said he could not receive the goods because the shopboy was not the shop owner, so he had to tentatively pay the 1.50 sen. Nevertheless, he *would* receive one sen from the shopboy as an offering and thus make a compromise, to bring the matter to a conclusion. The shopboy was a young Korean, so this was the second time Santoka had received alms from a Korean.

Once while begging in a certain village in Kyushu, he received a dish of rice from a young housewife. After returning home he cooked up something that might do as a side dish, and tasted it quietly by himself. The direction of the wind, however, was unfavorable and, just on this night, he was clearly able to hear the vendor's voice shouting at the faraway Ogori train station, "Box lunches! Sushi! Beer! Masamune![7] Cider!" He could just imagine a scene of people buying these items from the windows of the clanging train, and eating and drinking with gusto. "Wind! Blow the other way!" were the words that escaped his mouth. But there was no one there listening to him. Santoka was always alone.

Gradually he ate all the rice, and by the following day there was "not one thing" in the hermitage. But there were still some tea leaves. And there was water. Santoka was barely able to kindle a fire and boil up some tea. From the shelf he took down a few salty pickles and because they were so salty he drank more and more of the hot, hot tea. At this point he felt grateful for having a full stomach. Just then the mail he had been waiting for arrived. Moreover there was a letter with "substantial contents": a small money order from a friend. He immediately went out to buy rice, boiled up some gruel and sucked it down. He then wrote up a contribution to the magazine *Sanbaku*:

With a submissive heart,
my rice
steamed away.

御飯がふいた
こころすなほに

In attempting to cook his own rice every day, Santoka gradually came to understand the heart of rice. If his own mind[8] was not truly settled down and submissive, his rice would turn out poorly. He would cook with a plain old pot and rickety pieces of firewood brought home from the mountain, so the condition of his mind was reflected exactly in how well the rice turned out. On autumn mornings, the water for washing rice was cold to his hands. He would wipe his hands, kindle the fire, and watch it intensely. At that time, the hearts of both Santoka and the rice became truly submissive through and through, and the steam spouted forth *butsu butsu*, *fui fui*. In this way he wrote the above haiku.

Santoka also knew that cooked rice would be most delicious if cooked steadfastly to the point where the rice at the bottom of the pot became a little scorched. In the end, you sacrificed a certain part of it, and for the first time the whole would be brought to life. You will truly understand the flavor of rice if, like Santoka, you do not use side dishes, but rather sprinkle it with salt and chew it well.

Only rice
      eaten thoroughly
   is rice.

しみじみ食べる
飯ばかりの
飯である

Humbly received,
   it was quite enough;
  I put down my chopsticks for one.

いただいて
足りて
一人の箸をおく

With the charity from the letter with "substantial contents," Santoka went out shopping in the town of Ogori for the first time in a while. For a man as careless as he was, this was shopping with restraint.

Cash: 7 sen	red miso	100 momme[9]
Cash: 6 sen	soy sauce	2 go
Cash: 20 sen	shochu	2 go
Cash: 7 sen	pot	1
Cash: 7 sen	bush clover	5 momme
Cash: 5 sen	daikon	3
Cash: 9 sen	postcards	6
Cash: 10 sen	soba bunches	2
Cash total: 71 sen		

That day a strange thing happened. A man came up to his hermitage carrying something heavy in a *furoshiki* wrapping cloth. When asked, "What can I do for you?" the man replied, "Would you be kind enough just to take a look at this?" This was a ridiculous conversation, and while the pedlar seemed not to have very good perception, he certainly persevered. Santoka had only one robe to wear, and as the autumn deepened his hermitage grew colder mornings and evenings. He could only laugh from deep inside.

After the pedlar left, Santoka went down into the garden, thinking to take a bunch of wild tea flowers and to make an arrangement before his mother's mortuary tablet. But right beneath the beautiful tea flowers, wasn't that a little snake eating a frog? It was such a little snake to be eating a frog, and was a situation was one he felt he should detest but couldn't. It was a battle of desperation for the snake as it would soon have to hibernate. It, too, had to live, Santoka supposed. By Heaven's command, the frog could do nothing more than to "become a Buddha."[10]

October 16. With dawn, a whispering sad rain beat down and passed through. As the clouds that would bring the rain down were just settling on the mountains, Santoka was already up and kindling a fire by himself. Inside the hermitage, which had no electric lights, it was still dark. As he crouched over in the earthen-floored room breaking the dried branches and putting them in the fire, several insects approached. Little bugs! Are you cold in the morning, too? Looking carefully, he could see that a large cricket had a broken leg. Forgetting its usual agility, a large cockroach steadily came closer to the warm oven, sporting its long mustache.

Cockroach,

    your mustache is growing long, too.

あぶらむし
おまへのひげも
のびている

The dew,
     the fallen leaves, too;
     sweeping them all up.

露も落葉も
みんな
掃きよせる

The pennant points out
     the morning
     autumn wind.

朝の秋風を
吹き抜け
さひておく

In the Zen sect there is the phrase, "Returning home, sitting quietly." [11] Santoka, after his wandering meandering journey, was blessed with a hermitage which, although shabby, was a place where he could settle down and take up residence, and for the present, both body and mind had obtained equilibrium. Moreover, the Gochu-an was a thatched hermitage, truly fitting for a haiku poet like Santoka. He was surrounded by grasses, trees, insects and birds, and the diverse four seasons were rich in poetic sentiment. His verse-writing suddenly developed with exhilaration, he daily wrote a great number of good haiku, and he began publishing them in magazines. I first began corresponding with him after he had moved into his hermitage, and on March 17, 1933, I went from Hiroshima to pay Santoka a visit.

I had previously sent him a postcard, so he was good enough to be waiting for me. When he heard the sound of my footsteps, he opened the sliding white-paper doors and kindly hailed me from where he was. "I'll bet you're Oyama-san!" He was a bit ruddy-faced and wore horn-rimmed glasses for what seemed to be acute nearsightedness. This was the first encounter between Santoka and me. He quickly stepped down from the house barefoot, but hesitated there at the entrance. It seemed that he could not help but be pleased at having a visitor . . . although this was the Santoka who despised human society—or rather, who was unable to fit into society and so became a priest—he truly loved people in his asexual way. In the end, without even a proper greeting, a meal was to follow and he was kind enough to exhort me with, "Let's eat! Let's eat!"

I felt a little awkward, but decided to accept. He put a *chawan* bowl, a plate of condiments and chopsticks directly onto the worn-out tatami, and had neither a tray nor a table. As I had just come from the bright outdoors into the semi-darkness of the hermitage, my eyes had not adjusted and I could not see objects well. I added one of the condiments to the hot just-cooked rice and chewed a mouthful. The condiment was a red pepper boiled in soy sauce. I came understand later that Santoka liked hot things. Especially when he was drinking sake: because he had no money, drinking just a little had to be effective; and to enhance drunkenness, eating red pepper seemed to be the best. Nevertheless, I ate one bowl of that red pepper and hot rice, and tears flowed from my eyes. Santoka sat patiently looking at me without eating. When I said, "What do you think, shall we eat together?" he replied, "Here, you see, in fact I have only one *chawan*. I'm waiting for you to finish." I was surprised at this. But indeed, when I thought about it, Santoka was a traveler who had begged for seven years with "not one thing," and as he had just settled into his hermitage, there was no reason for him to have had something like a *chawan* for a guest. I ate one more bowlful, put my hands together in gratitude and put down my chopsticks. Thereupon Santoka took the bowl in his hand and, without even wiping it out, filled it up with rice straightaway and ate with obvious relish. When he finished, he said, "It's rude to ignore a guest who has come from far away, but I'm going to clean this up, so would you be kind enough to step aside for a moment and read a magazine or something?"

With this, he stepped down into the kitchen and washed up the utensils. He had a warped bucket in which it appeared that he had saved the water used for washing the rice rather than throwing it out. In that he washed the *chawan* and the rest. Having washed, dried and turned the utensils upside down on the shelf, he now took the bucket of water in which the rice and everything else had been washed, and dampened a rag for the inside of the hermitage. He then briskly wiped down the verandah, the pillars and the doorsill. This done, he picked up the bucket, went out the back door, and poured the water over the vegetables. In the Zen sect there are strict regulations concerning water, as exemplified by the phrases, "At the Eiheiji, a half ladle of water," and "At the spring of the Soto sect, a drop of water."[12] With one full bucket of water, Santoka washed the rice, washed the *chawan*, wiped up with a damp cloth, and finally provided nourishment for the vegetables. Ultimately, he put it to use four times.

The two of us completely forgot about the passage of time and talked happily together until evening about haiku, Zen, literature in general, and travel. At that point Tatsuaki, looking a bit flustered, brought up a nice meal. We had the sake I had brought, too, and so had our evening meal all over again.

Here is something I learned after Santoka died. He left me his journal as a posthumous manuscript, and I read the entry for the day I first visited him:

Mr. Oyama came to the hermitage just as he had promised. With one look he was like an old friend, and we were immediately on cordial terms. His character was just as I had anticipated, but he manifested a friendly feeling beyond what I had expected. Above all, I was pleased at there being nothing affected about him at all. He is, at any rate, a mellow man.

Many presents: sake, dried mirin-seasoned fish pickles preserved in soy sauce, and bean-jam buns.

Soon Tatsuaki also came to the hermitage, and was kind enough to bring a lot of chicken and scallions. The master of the house was running around pell-mell.

As a consequence of this first visit, I became more and more fascinated by the man Santoka and his work; I often went to see him and, from time to time, he was kind enough to come visit me. In this way our friendship gradually went on to deepen.

Once, I brought along two bottles of a superior sake from Hiroshima. At that time you could buy one *sho* of Kamotsuru sake for 1.70 or 1.80 yen. After arriving at Ogori Station, I discovered a tofu shop at the side of the road going to the hermitage. I bought twelve

cakes of tofu and carried off the heavy presents in both hands. San-
toka was so happy that his face changed color. As soon as I placed
the one-*sho* bottle of sake at the entrance, he brought out a cup, de-
capitated the bottle, and quickly drained off a cupful in one breath.
"Ah, that's sweet, you know. Have you really given me two bottles
of such good sake? Ah my!"

He was good enough to drink even before saying "Bottoms up!"
What a candid child's mind he had. Thereupon the two of us lei-
surely ate the boiled tofu even though it was the middle of the day.
It seemed that he had no rice, so day and night he made his meals
of tofu alone. As for the sake, I drank no more than one cup, but
during that time Santoka drank nine. Incidentally, when I looked
about the hermitage, like before, there was only one *chawan* bowl.
Despite that, he had sixteen or seventeen sake cups put into a card-
board box. "You're quite a drinker, huh. Isn't that quite a lot of sake
cups?" "Take a better look, Sumita-san. Those could be sake cups,
but they're not." When I picked one up and took a good look at it,
I discovered that it was the lid for one of those little tea bottles they
sold for five sen on the train in those days. "Well, you know, I go
around with my begging bowl and at times cross the railroad tracks.
When I look down at my feet, I see that these have fallen there. It
would be a shame to step on them and break them, so I pick them
up and take them home, and that's what I've collected so far."

The sake was going back and forth, and Santoka continued
talking. "Well, you know, I don't understand the world very well. It
seems that people like you who receive a monthly salary often say
that that monthly salary is not enough. On the other hand, because
such people throw away things that can still be used, I'm busy go-
ing around picking them up. I, who am not employed, who earn
nothing, and who of course have no property, am provided for by
others, and live by no other means than by picking up what others
have thrown away. This pot was thrown away behind a hospital in
Yamaguchi. That portable clay cooking stove was on a rubbish heap
in Ogori."

"That's gross! You fed me off of something that dirty?"

"I figured you people would say something like that, so I washed it really well with ashes and then disinfected it with sunlight. So don't worry."

That wasn't something you could say was either good or bad, but I, who easily became discontent because what was before me was never enough, felt somehow that I had been struck with a good thump! Since the two of us were drunk, we lay down in the autumn grasses that were luxuriantly filling the garden and, thinking up haiku for a little while, listened to the voices of the insects.

If there is one,
  that's enough;
washing the rice in the pot.
                    (self-criticism)

一つあれば
事足る鍋の米を
とぐ

In the early summer of 1932, Santoka stretched his legs to go begging in the neighboring districts and, as he walked along *bota-bota* with his feet directed towards the east, he stepped onto the earth of his old hometown, Hofu. There was no reason for the people walking about the town to know that this begging monk had been the young master of the great Taneda so long ago. But for Santoka, the Tenmangu shrine in Miya'ichi, the Matsuzaki Elementary School below the shrine, and the houses that continued on to Hachioji were all exactly as they had been in the days of his youth that he could not forget. With old memories going through his head, he finally stood at the ruins of the mansion that had been the house of his birth.

No traces left
  of the house where I was born;
fireflies.

うまれた家は
あとかたもない
ほうたる

Come! Come, fireflies!
I've come back
to my hometown.

ほたる
こいこい
ふるさとにきた

In between the houses scattered here and there, fields of ripe barley could be seen in the evening dark. Far in the distance it seemed that some children were chasing fireflies, yelling, "Come, fireflies! Come, fireflies!" He lingered there quietly, laying one hand on an inclining mud wall. At that moment a single firefly shined with a bluish light, skimmed his bamboo hat and flew on.

That evening Santoka walked just two and a half miles [four kilometers] and called in at the house of his younger sister Shizu Machida, in Migita. The house, which he had not seen for a long time, stood in the middle of whitewashed mud walls just as it had long ago, the magnolia and other trees growing thick in the garden.

"Elder Brother? I was wondering who it might be." His younger sister stood there at the door staring hard at the completely transformed figure of her older brother. Santoka had walked all day and his straw sandals had come apart, so he stood there barefoot. Having heard that a strange fellow had come to the village, seven or eight of the children who had been looking for fireflies gathered at Santoka's back.

"Do you think he's a priest?" "No, no. He's a beggar," they said in suppressed whispers.

Shizu silently led her older brother around to the well behind the house, drew water and washed his feet. The master of the house was not there that night. Santoka's younger sister picked *chisha* leaves, prepared a meal of *chishamomi* on the spot,[13] and for the first time in twenty years cheerfully poured him some sake. Thinking of her neighbors, however, she did not tell her children that this strange guest was their only uncle. Santoka did not talk much either, but lay down in his warm bed and, ruminating on his sister's affection, fell into a deep sleep.

Santoka woke up early in the morning and was arranging the previous day's haiku in bed when Shizu came in quietly and said, "Elder Brother, this is inexcusable but, well . . . would you leave before the people in the neighborhood get up? We'll have a hard time of it if they start calling you a beggar, you see. I've already prepared your meal."

He understood his sister's mind well. After quickly washing his face, he picked up chopsticks for one person in the wooden-floored room. Shizu had not forgotten to add a two-*go* bottle filled to the top with morning sake. She was kind enough to accompany Santoka to the gate, and silently put a fifty-sen coin into his beggar's bag. Santoka stepped briskly away without looking back. He did not want to show his little sister his tears.

ふるさとは
ちしやもみが
うまいふるさとにいる

My hometown?
I'm in my hometown
Where the chishamomi is great!

After walking a while, a gentle rain began to fall. His straw hat was a big one, so he didn't get very wet. The sandy earth of this southern area was as pure as a sandy beach; and as it was damp, he was happy to step on it with bare feet.

雨ふるふるさとは
はだしであるく

Rain, raining in my hometown.
I walk
barefoot.

In the autumn of the next year, 1933, Santoka's beloved teacher, Seisensui Ogiwara, visited him from afar. His teacher had come down the Tenryu River appreciating the autumn colors, and then extended his trip to travel west. There was a haiku meeting in Onomichi at Kanta Watari's place. I waited for Seisensui at Hongo Station and showed him around the Buttsuji temple, the important Rinzai Zen sect headquarters. There were at least twenty mendicant monks in the seminary, silently observing the Buddha's teachings. Yakushu Yamazaki Roshi was delighted, and invited us in. In the secluded dormitory settled among the quiet mountains, together we took our evening meal of the vegetarian food made by the mendicant monks, and the two of us enjoyed the entire evening with a conversation about haiku and Zen sharing the same flavor. On the following day we went to Hiroshima, and on the fourteenth, I finally guided him to Ogori.

Santoka knew that his teacher was coming and, beside himself with pleasure, had been knocking down chilled sake since morning. Pleasantly drunk, he greeted us at the station. But it was not just Seisensui. Hakusen Kubo from Tokuyama, Mokko Yokohata from Hiroshima, Motohiro Ishihara from Kumamoto, Keinosuke Chikaki from Chofu—about fourteen or fifteen friends-in-haiku came all at once and from far and near. Seisensui was so deeply moved that he seemed hardly able to wait until after the talk he was to give at the Ogori agricultural school. When the haiku meeting at the Gochu-an finally began, it was a truly autumnal afternoon—the kind about which they say, "Persimmons are ripe and shrikes are crying." Thanks to the planning of Tatsuaki and Keiji, the hermitage master with "not one thing" was ready with matsutake mushrooms, tofu, yuzu citrus and perpetual sake. It was sake more than verses, and the master of the hermitage got so drunk that it was hardly a "haiku meeting" at all. Even so, Santoka sat next to his teacher and cooked up some yuzu miso himself on his broken portable clay stove. That was a wonderful thing, but while his talk was becoming animated he didn't notice that the yuzu was being burned completely black. Ah, Santoka.

Bringing the mushrooms from out back;
on the tatami,
rays of sun.

—Seisensui

裏から
茸とつて来て
日のさしている
畳

Everything so delightful!
The yuzu pot
scorched beyond hope.

—Seisensui

何もかも
うれしくて
柚釜の
こげすぎている

Santoka tried to knock down the last ripe persimmon on the tree with a bamboo pole for his teacher, but he was in a very "buoyant" frame of mind and his attempt did not go well. Then, when I picked it up for him and handed it to the teacher, the teacher picked up a fallen persimmon leaf, placed it on Santoka's desk, and put the ripe persimmon on top of that. He then admired its beauty—so thoroughly ripened and shining red.

A single persimmon
left in the sky;
picked for me.

—Seisensui

柿一つ
空へあづけてあった
とつてくれる

At the end of the party, the teacher took a large brush and wrote "The One Among Them" (其中一人) horizontally in large letters for the master of the hermitage. Santoka seemed to be extraordinarily

pleased with these characters, and drank one cup of sake after an-
other, yelling "The one among them! The one among them!"

> *Just as you'd think:*
> *the Gochu-an blooming*
> *with tea flowers.*
> —Seisensui

なるほど
其中庵の
茶の花で
咲いている

> *With this*
> *there'll be enough tea:*
> *the tea tree.*
> —Seisensui

これで茶は
足りるといふ
茶の木

> *In place of the straw hat*
> *hung on the wall,*
> *tea flowers.*
> —Seisensui

笠は掛ける
ところに
かかり茶の花

> *There's a thicket,*
> *and a neighbor, too:*
> *pale daikons.*
> —Seisensui

藪もある
大根の青い
隣もある

There is no doubt that this one day was Santoka's finest at the
Gochu-an. But when night came, everyone returned home and went
back to the east and west. Suddenly, only Santoka remained, and it
is moving to think about how sad and solitary he must have been.
He was, after all, the "one among them."

After Santoka settled into the Gochu-an, his poetry improved
steadily. He also drank a lot of sake, but he was able to enter into a

perfect state of poetic concentration. The number of his verses increased day by day, and one by one they sent forth his solitary light. These verses tugged at the hearts of his far-flung kindred spirits who then corresponded with him often, bringing comfort to his solitude, and inviting him to come and visit.

Santoka loved traveling. For the present he was enjoying his solitary life at the hermitage, but in the spring of 1934 he headed east with the intention of making a grand journey. This journey, however, would be different from the walking begging trips he had made for the eight years prior to moving into his hermitage. This would be a journey visiting his friends-in-haiku who were kindly waiting for him, and his lodging would be firmly arranged. He would hang a Buddhist bag around his neck, put a straw hat on his head and wear a monk's robe, but this would not be a journey of toilsome begging. He would give himself over to the spring breeze and travel free and easy with a light heart as a mere haiku poet.

He first came to my place in Hiroshima in the middle of April. On the day before, he had walked begging from Ogori to Tokuyama, and had been put up at Hakusen's residence. Given the fare for the train to Hiroshima, he went by rail from Tokushima to Miyajima, and from Miyajima he begged along the railroad tracks on his way. Taking off his straw sandals and cleaning his feet, he first came in wearing his bag, and sat down on the wooden floor in the kitchen. Thereupon, he suddenly took everything out of his bag and spread it out on the wooden floor. Rice: one *sho*, four or five *go* of sake. Mixed in with that were some one-sen copper coins. With a practiced shake of his hand, he skillfully separated one from the other. He put the thirty-four or thirty-five sen of change into his purse and pushed the rice towards my wife.

"This is for my meal, Ma'am."

"You don't have to be concerned about that."

"Today's affairs apply just to today. Tomorrow I'll entrust myself to tomorrow's wind. The rice I'm carrying in this bag won't be coming from tomorrow's begging bowl."

This was the first time Santoka came to visit, and I was astonished at his words and behavior.

After that, he talked over sake:

What you can walk in one day, you can cover by train in one hour. It's a real blessing, isn't it. What gave me some trouble after I had boarded the train, however, was my big straw hat. If I put it on, I was a nuisance to the person next to me. And it was too big to put on the luggage rack. There was nothing else I could do, so I held it in my hand. Today, once again, I'm keenly aware that this outfit was made for walking under the blue sky, just as you'd think.

And then, when I wear my robe like this, I get outrageous privileges in consideration of my position [as a priest]. Today, two old ladies bowed to me courteously and then gave me two copper one-sen coins as alms. I thought that since we were passengers on the same train I wasn't quite qualified to receive anything, but since there was no reason to refuse them either, I meekly accepted what they offered, you know.

There were two of us drinking one *sho* of sake, so there was a little left over. Generally speaking, a person who drinks sake doesn't eat a lot afterwards, but Santoka drank a lot and then ate plenty, too.

The two of us arranged our pillows side by side and then went to sleep. In the middle of the night Santoka got up and rustled around like he was crawling towards the kitchen.

"The lavatory's over this way."

"No, there should be something left over from last night, and if I don't rectify the situation I'll have stiff shoulders and won't be able to sleep."

So saying, he opened up the one-*sho* bottle, turned on the electric light, sat down on the wooden floor, and seemed to drink it all cold in just two cups. The following day he stayed in, resting perhaps, the entire day.

Among Basho's rules for traveling is one stating that if you take lodgings, you should not take the same place a second time unless you have some good reason, and I think that's a good regulation.[14] *When spoiled by the good intentions of others, a traveler like me will stop any number of days and, drowned in the charity of others, the journey will become impossible.*

He said this just before I went off to work. Tying on his straw sandals and putting on his straw hat, he stood in the entryway.

"Well, one for the road." My wife poured out a cup of cold sake and handed it over to him. Santoka gave a little laugh, drank it dry in one swallow, and quickly departed. It was a truly graceful leave-taking: he just walked away without looking back. He had told me he was going as far away as the Shinano Road[15], so I had donated ten yen as travel expenses.

That day he went as far as Ihara in Bitchu, which is my old hometown. There he stayed with the picture framer and lover of haiku, Yamabe Bokuro.

Next he took an excursion to Tamashima. There, Jo Fujiwara from Tamashima Women's High School guided him on a visit to the Entsuji temple, where Ryokan[16] performed Buddhist austerities when he was young, and where Santoka now wept at the remnants of Ryokan's life. Then, in just ten days, he took a tour of Okayama, Kobe, Osaka, Kyoto and Nagoya. At the word that Santoka was coming, many of his coterie would gather to greet him, hold drinking parties, and invite him to haiku gatherings. Then, after leaving a *tanzaku* poem card,[17] he would be sent on to his next lodging. During the period of his travels in Kyushu, he had crossed countless mountains and rivers, had walked on drenched by the rain, and had passed lonely nights in cheap boarding houses. For his journey this time, he was embraced by the warmth of friendship, and it may have been—comparatively speaking—a physically pleasant excursion for which money was not a factor. And this was all the more so because both his haiku and his circumstances in life were generally being given recognition. His happy acceptance of a stomachful of "just sake," however, caused him to neglect his journal.

At Tsushima, outside of the city of Nagoya, he was put up by Gyomindo Ikehara, who was the principal of the women's high school there, and a grand poetry gathering was held. Gyomindo

guided him to the Saya no Suikei burial mound, bought a new
bamboo hat for him, and told him to leave to posterity the tattered
bamboo hat he had worn so carefully.

Some of his poems on that trip were the following:

おわかれの
水鳥がういたり
しずんだり

The waterbird at parting:
now floating,
now diving below.

燕とびかふ
旅から旅へ
わらじを穿く

Swallows in flight:
from journey to journey,
tying on straw sandals.

もう逢えますまい
木の芽のくもり

Not likely will we meet again;
clouds
of budding trees.

飲みたい
水の音
たてていた

The dripping sound
of the water
I wanted to drink.

Deep in the mountains,
    if it's butterbur you want,
  they're blooming.

山ふかく
蕗のとうなら
咲いておる

In the mountains it's quiet,
    so I take off
  my straw hat.

山しづか
なれば
笠をぬく

Two poems upon being sick in Iida:

Truly a moon
    of a mountainous district
  of nothing but mountains.

まこと山国の、
山ばかりなる月の

Tomorrow I'll go home;
    cherry blossoms are falling and falling
  and falling.

明日はかへろう
さくら
ちるちつてくる

From Nagoya, Santoka made his way up onto the Kiso Road.[18] Though it was May, the mountain road through the Kiso was cold. Crossing over on the Seinai Road, he started to descend into the town of Iida in Shinano, but at the top of the pass he sank to his thighs in the remaining snow and got into trouble. Even with his strong legs he had difficulty moving on this snow-covered road. Finally, just as the sun was setting, he tumbled down into the town of Iida. Here, Ado Ota and Jakusui Maeda were waiting for him. They immediately called together a drinking party, and with their companions did everything they could to welcome him. But that night Santoka came down with a fever—a bad one which he described as giving him a tingling pain in the chest. The two men were worried and had him seen by a doctor, who said that he had an acute pneumonia. He was thereupon admitted to the Kawajiri Hospital, and a telegram was sent to me: "Santoka seriously ill."

I stood there with this telegram in my hand, gazing toward the sky of Shinshu[19]—so far from Hiroshima—confused about what I should do. Should I take a leave from my post and hurry to Iida, or should I rely on Ota-san and, if by ill luck Santoka died, then go to retrieve his corpse? I was thinking such things over, but then, six days later, Santoka suddenly appeared, terribly gaunt and dispirited, at my entranceway. When I asked him what in the world had happened, he replied:

> *Ado-san was very accommodating. I had been completely chilled by all that snow, and he poured lots of delicious sake from Ena right into me. I suddenly came down with a fever, was diagnosed with acute pneumonia, and put into a big hospital. That was a blessing, but the trouble was that they only let me drink a bitter medicine in the hospital and wouldn't give me even a little bit of sake. Sake is a wonderful medicine for me, so I thought up a plan. I went to the lavatory and then, with the lavatory sandals still on, absconded. First I went into an oden shop[20] and knocked down two cups of sake—with some tofu. And as a matter of fact, I suddenly got better, felt like the old Santoka again, and came back by train, station by station, shaking and trembling all the way. I thought that if I was going to die, I should die at my Gochu-an. But feeling the way I do now, maybe we can think that I'm not going to die yet.*

This was a truly horrific story. It was a reckless affair that only the sake-man Santoka was capable of, but as he had at least returned alive, there was nothing I could do but think that it had turned out all right. This time he stayed at my house for two nights. While I was away at work, my wife took him to a movie.

Santoka returned to the Gochu-an, and during that summer it appeared that he enjoyed living peacefully at the hermitage. In October he completed the manuscript of his second collection of poems, *Sangyo suigyo* (Traveling the Mountains, Traveling the Rivers), and sent it to me. At the end of the book, he wrote this:

> *The number of poems I have belched forth between July of last year and October of this year is close to two thousand. From among those I have picked out three hundred. Then, making a final selection, I have put together these one hundred and forty-one verses. The pleasure of the person who writes them is that of singing his own truth. What this means is that I want to take pleasure in that pleasure without shame.*

At a glance it would appear that he was a slovenly drunkard who had overstepped his bounds, but as a matter of his own first principle of the Way of Haiku, he was being truly serious and self-communing. Towards that first principle, he was very strict. He did, after all, pick only a hundred and forty haiku from two thousand and threw the rest away. Moreover,

> *I returned, at length, to the world of existence, and had the frame of mind of what I would call "returning home and sitting quietly." I wandered aimlessly for a long time. And it was not only my body that was wandering aimlessly, but my mind was wandering, too. I felt bitter about what should have been, and was afflicted by those things that would not go away. But then, finally I was able to settle down with the "things that are." And it was there that I discovered myself.*

This, to Santoka, was one clear vision. He had become conscious of the figure of his own meek self in existence just as it was. He could see within himself the penetrating vision of the ancients expressed in sayings like "The straightforward mind, this is the dojo,"[21] and "The everyday mind, this is the Way." [22]

The first principle of a person who [expresses something in poetry], is that he absolutely must express that thing. In regard to poetry, I must absolutely manifest myself. This is precisely my task, and at the same time it is my prayer.

With the completion of that selection of poetry, Santoka sat alone in his hermitage and increasingly enjoyed days of complete poetic absorption. But in December of 1935 he yet again was goaded on by a mind to travel, and set out on a distant journey with no particular destination.

In the reflection of the clouds in the water, too,
there is something that will not let me
settle down.

水の雲かげも
おちつかせない
ものがある

Santoka was unable to stay still. To put it shortly, I suspect he was beckoned by "thoughts of a fleeting cloud," to borrow Basho's words. Cutting an unsavory figure, he walked along, begging as he went, and finally got to my house in Hiroshima. He stayed for two or three days, and then one day his son Ken suddenly came to the communications office where I worked.

"My father's illness has given you a lot of trouble," he said. In his hand he had a telegram that said: "Your father is dangerously ill. Come soon. Oyama."

"Santoka is well, and is enjoying himself at my place! This is strange, huh."

"The telegram arrived with your name on it, so I rushed over here from the Iizuka Coal Mine in Fukuoka Prefecture, but I've been fooled by the old man once again."

He then telephoned Santoka, who came over right away.

"Ken? I just *had* to see you, so I sent you that telegram yesterday under Oyama-san's name."

"This gave me a start, Father. It isn't anything particularly important, is it?"

"No, there's nothing here to attend to, but I'm going far away on a journey, so I thought if I just saw you that everything would be all right."

At that point, Santoka's eyes were welling up with tears behind his glasses.

"Well the people at the mining office will be busy after this disturbance, so I'd better get back to the mountain right away."

So saying, Ken left immediately after the three of us drank some *bancha* tea at the office.

Santoka had abandoned his wife and child and become a priest, but he was, after all, a human being. And it would not do to completely abandon being a human being. Perhaps it was the affection of a father for his only child that suddenly gushed up. Furthermore, this time he would go off to the east and wander aimlessly and buoyantly through the winds of December, and for him, who owned "not one thing," it would be a grand journey to which he would abandon himself in earnest. The upshot of this journey might be, for whatever reason, his death. Thinking of such things, he was assailed by the strong emotion of "wanting to see you [Ken] one last time," and so sent the telegram without even warning me. I kept my silence and could do nothing more than look straight at this father and child, and see them as different from the world at large.

The next day I took Santoka to Ikino, an uninhabited island off the coast of Takehara in Hiroshima Prefecture. Ikino Island was a "horse island" where the ancient Asano clan had let its horses out to pasture; but at present, a potter by the name of Muhyo Kado was living there and growing *mikan* oranges. He and his wife had built a kiln and the two of them were sending up smoke by firing cookie jars, tea bowls, flower vases, images of Prince Shotoku[23] and things like that. We went there with a K-san from Takehara, and brought along three *sho* of sake. This isolated island was truly separated from the "floating world," and Kado-san and his wife treated us cordially.

The cordial, warm
withering
of grasses.

あたたかく草の
かれているなり

As described in this verse, it was an island of mild winters, and a place like this caught Santoka's fancy. While he thought that he might stay for about two weeks, I returned home after one night. But three days later, wasn't that Santoka's figure casually wearing his straw hat, at my entranceway?

"You didn't stay there very long, did you. I thought you were going to sit yourself down on that island for a while."

"The fact is, you know, well, there's no sake shop on the island, and when the three bottles we brought along were empty, everywhere I looked there was the sea, and I got lonesome pretty quickly. As for me, you know, it's not that I drink from morning till night, but I can't live in a land with no sake for even a day."

This was a natural fact.

As he said that he wanted to see his friends in Kyushu, I bought him a ticket to Tohata and saw him off. He had a great number of deeply affectionate friends-in-haiku in Fukuoka Prefecture, not the least of whom was Rokubei. In the end, he spent the rest of the year in northern Kyushu, and on New Year's of 1936, he boarded the Baikal Maru, a steamer on the European route, as a third-class passenger. This is not to say that he was going to a foreign country. The Baikal Maru had just returned to Moji from overseas, and almost all of the passengers had gotten off there and quickly returned home to various parts of the country by train. Thus, the inside of the boat was almost empty, and someone who must have been well aware of this bought Santoka a ticket for as far as Kobe, and put his buoyant beggar's figure on the luxurious ship that had traveled to foreign ports.

Even among Santoka's journeys, this was a one-time-only special affair. For the traveler who was not hurrying on ahead, this must have been a carefree pleasurable trip. Now with a cabin boy there to kindly show him the way to the dining room three times a day, Santoka became a free-and-easy passenger on this large ship. When the ship passed Sandajiri, he stood on the deck, looked out at the mountains of his old hometown, and wrote this in his notebook of verses:

My hometown:
the brilliance of the snow
on yonder mountain crests.
(on the Baikal Maru)

ふるさとは
あの山なみの雪の
かがやく

His friends-in-haiku—among them Einosuke Hori, Shigairo Ikeda, and Yajuro Hamaguchi in Kobe; and Sanboku Makiyama in Osaka—treated Santoka very well at his coming. They held either drinking parties or poetry gatherings, or at least showed him beneficence at home after home. Thus he enjoyed his journey of early spring.

One of his friends showed him around Takarazuka, home of the famous theater troupe.[24] The Baikal Maru and then Takarazuka—a rather flashy journey for the "one among them."

How beautiful!
The women;
falling spring snow.

春の雪ふる女は
まことうつくしい

This, I think, is a good verse. It is one in which the elegantly simple haiku poet-monk gazes at the city women going in and out of the theater, forgets himself and stares in rapture at their beauty. A snow whiter than face powder was falling, then disappearing on the fascinating clothes the women wore. That night, he returned again to Osaka and wrote this verse:

あてもない旅の
たもとぐさこんなに
たまり

How the lint [25] *has gathered*
inside my sleeves
on this aimless journey.

This is a rather sad verse, I suppose. Compared to the yang verse before it, this is a verse of yin. The family at the house where Santoka was lodging was on vacation, so he was unable to sleep. As he sat stiffly at the side of the bedding they had spread out for him, he heard the clangor of the slow-moving streetcar in the distance. A neon light faintly reached the glass window. How strange this place was compared to his lonely Gochu-an. Finally he got into his nightclothes, had a smoke, and when he picked at the sleeve of the robe he had taken off, found an accumulation of lint inside. He set it down squarely in the palm of his hand, and gazed at it in his single room as the night deepened.

After that, he stayed at Kitaro Uchijima's residence in Kyoto, attended a poetry meeting, and was taken on an excursion to Uji by Sensuiro, where he prayed at the Byodoin temple.

雲のゆききも
栄華のあとの
水ひかる

The animation of the clouds;
the remains of their splendor:
the shining water.

Opening the doors
   of the spring wind:
Namu Amida Butsu.[26]

春風の
扉ひらけば
南無阿弥陀仏

Let's strike the bell,
   bright
    and clear.

うららかな鐘を
つかうよ

Thanks to the goodwill of Sensuiro, Santoka went as far as Ujiyamada,[27] and was able to visit the Ise Jingu shrine for the first time in a long time.

How august:
   the chicken,
pure white.[28]

とふとさは
ましろなる鶏

From there he directed his steps to the east and, following the blowing of the wind, went from Nagoya, Lake Hamana and Shizuoka to Shitada and Ito.

Izu is warm,
   sleeping outdoors good,
  the sound of waves, too.

伊豆は暖かく
野宿によろしい
波音も

また
一枚ぬぎすてる
旅から旅

Again, one more layer,
clothes cast off
from journey to journey.

Santoka bathed in nice hot springs in Izu and looked at camellia flowers to his heart's content. From Odawara he continued on to Kamakura; then in Tokyo he visited Seisensui and stayed with him one night.

ほっと
月がある
東京に来ている

What a relief!
There's the moon;
entering Tokyo.

Pulling himself from the midst of buildings and streets littered with people, Santoka looked up to the sky, and there was the moon coming up. No matter what was happening on earth, catching sight of the moon vacuously floating above let him breathe more easily. It was gazing at the moon that had first made him realize it was his lot in life to be a traveler rambling along in no-mind.[29]

花が葉になる
東京よ
さようなら

Flowers are now leaves.
Tokyo!
Sayonara.

The traveler who had left his hermitage in the last month of the year saw the changing year and greeted the spring, gazed at the flowers, and when those flowers scattered and the leaves grew thick, put Tokyo behind him, took the Chuo Line train into Yamanashi Prefecture, then traveled north from the east of Hachigaoka and entered the Shinano Road.

行き暮れて
なんとここらの
水のうまさは

Overtaken by night,
how tasty the water
hereabouts!

のんびり
尿する草の
芽だらけ

Peeing at ease;
budding grasses
everywhere.

あるけばかっこう
いそげばかっこう

If I walk, a cuckoo;
if I hurry,
a cuckoo.[30]

Santoka was a country bumpkin. A rustic. Released from the streets of Tokyo, he recouped himself at last. On an empty stomach he deeply tasted the savor of the mountain water that bubbled up at the side of the road, walked on, and then stood there to pee. In Tokyo, the cultured capital, he could not stand and pee as he so loved to do. In the mountains full of green leaves, the cuckoo sang frequently and added to the tranquility. The birds of the field do not forget human beings, and coming down from the branches they were kind enough to sing in loud voices at Santoka's feet. How beautiful their beaks and bills. Beneath the blue sky and in the shade of the green leaves, Santoka walked on, his ears cleansed by the voices of the wild birds.

He then called on the old man, Ehan Sekiguchi, who lived in Iwamurata. Although the old man said he was eighty years old, he talked quite a bit and with no diminution of youth or vigor. He made his own Shinano-style soba noodles, and was kind enough to give some to Santoka. This old man was typical of the Shinano region and, from the time he was young, entered the Itto-en sect,[31] studied Zen, cleared wasteland while loving the Way, and while not engaged in farming, took pleasure in writing haiku and poetry in Chinese. Santoka made a good friend and spent six blessed nights in a fine dwelling. Thus, he deeply savored the happiness of having come far on his journey.

Mount Asama right in front,
I eat my box lunch
on the grass.

浅間をまともの
おべんとうは
草の上にて

One day he was taken to some newly cultivated land, and on the green grass spread out the box lunch that filled his heart. The smoke from Mount Asama casting up billow upon billow, this was the fire at the head of the mountain, this was Santoka.[32]

Translator's Notes

1. This is likely in reference to a Chinese story wherein local people, seeing that a sage was so poor he had to cup his hands to drink water, gave him a gourd to drink from. After a day, the sage became disgusted with the new convenience and walked on, leaving the gourd to dangle from a tree, banging in the wind.

2. The words *haijin* (俳人) haiku poet and *haijin* (廃人) abandoned person are homonyms.

3. The phrase in Chinese is 其中一人作是唱言. This would be pronounced *gochu ichinin saze shogon* in Japanese. The *gochu*, or "among them," might also be pronounced *goju*.

4. Camellia flowers fall with a heavy plop all at once, rather than petal by petal.

5. Scallions, garlic and alcohol were to be avoided by Buddhist monks—the first two because one's breath would offend others; the latter because it would cloud one's mind.

6. Spider lilies are called *higanbana* (彼岸花) in Japanese. *Higan* means "the Other Shore," or Nirvana.

7. Masamune: a brand of sake.

8. In Japanese there is no distinction between heart and mind. Both are written with the kanji character 心, and pronounced *kokoro*. I have translated the word as either heart or mind as it seems to fit the context. The reader should keep in mind, however, that to the Japanese they are the same.

9. One *momme*: 0.1325 oz. (3.75 grams)

10. In other words, to die.

11. 帰家穏座. A Zen phrase that means to come home (back to your original mind) and sit quietly (zazen).

12. 永平半杓の水 and 曾源一滴水 respectively.

13. *Chisha*: A kind of lettuce. *Chishamomi* is presumably a dish made of lettuce.

14. These regulations, seventeen in all, can be found in R. H. Blyth's *Haiku, Vol. 1*.

15. Through the central mountains of Shinano Province.

16. Ryokan (1758–1831). Poet, calligrapher and Zen Buddhist monk, famous for his simplicity and childlike manner.

17. *Tanzaku*: a strip of fancy stiff paper used as a vertical poem card at special events or leave-takings.

18. An ancient road between Kyoto and Tokyo, passing through the central mountains of Japan. Officially opened in 1603 but dating to the eighth century.

19. Shinshu: ancient name of Shinano Province (modern-day Nagano Prefecture), where Santoka now was.

20. Oden is a type of traditional Japanese stew.

21. 直心是道場.

22. 平常心是道.

23. Prince Shotoku (572–621): regent and celebrated politician. He promulgated a code of laws for the government of Japan in which he strongly supported the importation of Buddhism, and built a number of temples.

24. A town famous for its all-female theater troupe who play both female and male roles.

25. *Tamotogusa*: lit. sleeve grass. On the kind of robe Santoka was wearing, there was a large vertical opening on the sleeve a little past midway to the elbow. People used this to carry their cigarettes and other small items, but all that accumulated in Santoka's sleeves was lint. Interestingly, this lint was used to stop bleeding in the old days.

26. *Namu Amida Butsu*: the phrase chanted by Buddhists when concentrating on the Amida Buddha.

27. Ujiyamada is the former name of the city of Ise.

28. Beautiful hens and roosters can be seen roaming free at Ise, and are noted for their elegance.

29. No-mind (無心): a transcendent state of non-attachment.

30. *Kakko: cuculus canoris*, the common cuckoo.

31. Itto-en: Shinto-Buddhist syncretic sect founded by Tenko Nishida (1872–1968. Nishida recognized the universality of all religions, and stressed community action and service.

32. Santoka is written 山頭火 in Japanese; lit. Mountain Head Fire.

CHAPTER 6

To Hiraizumi

After a visit to the Zenkoji temple and stopping in at the remnants of the poet Issa's[1] life at Kashiwara, Santoka left the Shinano Road and entered Echigo Province. First setting his sights on Mount Kugami, where the poet Ryokan had spent so much of his time, he plodded along the road that led through the open fields. On the way he visited Gintei Kobayashi in Nagaoka. Gintei was a quiet haiku poet who for a long time had run a photography shop in this city, and he was pleased from the bottom of his heart with this rare guest coming from so far away. Santoka, who was treated with enough sake to fill his belly, was shown around the studio and had his picture taken for a commemoration. These photographs—one with his straw hat on, the other with his hat off and exposing his drunken cloudy face—truly revealed Santoka's character, and after his death were used as frontispieces in a number of different books.

Mount Kugami was quiet. There was a hermitage at the fifth station upon climbing halfway up the mountain. At the entrance there was a stone monument, moistened by the drops from the green leaves, with this verse:

Enough for kindling:
fallen leaves
brought in by the wind.

焚くほどは
風がもてくる
落葉かな

The calligraphy was by Gyofu Soma[2] it seems. He was Santoka's senior by one year at Waseda University.

The hermitage had burned down once, but after that was reconstructed in the same size, with tile roofing. There was one six-mat room and a three-foot [one-meter] space for a Buddhist altar, so it quite resembled the Gochu-an. By this time, however, no one had lived there for a long time, and on the open verandah there were a great number of bamboo leaves carried in by the wind. Santoka sat down on the verandah and smoked a cigarette alone. Very soon a bush warbler started singing earnestly from a nearby branch. From the green leaves in the distance a cuckoo was calling. It was the very essence of tranquility. How had one man had the nerve to live alone for more than ten years on this mountain where the snow fell to over five feet [one and a half meters] deep in the winter? He was unable to keep from comparing his own Gochu-an with this Gogo-an.[3]

More than that, how stained and muddied Santoka's heart was when he compared it to Ryokan's non-coveting mental state, clear as the moon in autumn, and his completely natural way of life. As Zen monks from the Soto sect, they had the same appearance and lived aloof from the world. But weren't their inner lives as different as Heaven and Earth? Santoka became embarrassed, bowed once and, quitting the hermitage, descended the mountain. He walked as far as Shimazaki, stopped by the place where Ryokan died, and even visited his grave. The green mountain leaves reflected in Santoka's eyes were the same that Ryokan had seen long ago, but were they really the same?

Walking through green leaves;
　　did Master Ryokan
　　　do the same?
　　　　　(at Mount Kugami)

青葉わけゆく
良寛さまも
行かしたろ

こころむなしく
あらなみ
よせてはかへし
　　（the Japan Sea）

With hollow heart
rough waves
coming in, going out.
　　　　　(the Japan Sea)

砂浜に
うづくまり
けふも佐渡は
見えない

Crouching on the sandy beach;
today, too,
Sado cannot be seen.

荒海へ
脚投げだして
旅のあとさき

Stretching out my legs
towards the rough sea;
the journey's beginning and end.

Seeing the island of Sado far out at sea to the north would some-how have given him something to go by, but it was a cloudy ash-colored day, Sado was not visible, and he felt hollow and lonely to his very core. Often, poetry can be made of such loneliness. Basho had walked along that rough sea during his journey of *The Narrow Road to the Deep North,*[4] and went from north to south. Now, how-ever, nothing remains of his footprints along the sandy beach road. There is only the lonely sound of the waves. Looking out at those waves, Santoka took off his straw hat and stretched out his legs—so tired from walking—and consoled his feet.

Clouds at the bottom of the sea, too:
the sky of Michinoku;
early summer rains.

水底の雲も
みちのくの空の
さみだれ

Crossing the Nezumigaseki checkpoint, he entered the old province of Uzen. Soaked by a bitterly falling rain, he stood under the eaves of a poverty-stricken house. The householder offered him alms of rice, but Santoka could hardly understand the words in the thick Zuzu dialect[5] that were kindly spoken to him. He thought that he had come far indeed on this journey.

Akitoshi Wada in Tsurugaoka was having a bit of stomach trouble and did not go to work this particular day; rather, he stayed home all day reading. Akitoshi worked for the magazine *So'un*, and was a top-notch writer. His poet's intuition was uncanny, and just as he mumbled to himself, "On a day like today, it would be wonderful if Santoka came by here on a journey," a straw hat seemed to push its way through the green leaves at his gate and, wasn't that a solitary monk coming up to beg? Both of them shouted at the same time,

"Ah, it's *you*, Santoka!"

"Yes! I'm Santoka. Are you Akitoshi?"

"Hey!"

"Hey!"

Akitoshi forgot all about his illness, and poured a beer for Santoka. The two of them got drunk, happily gave each other a hug, and for two or three days forgot about everything other than feeling completely overjoyed. When it came time to sleep, they even slept on the same bedding together.

Thanks to Akitoshi's charity, Santoka was able to ride on a train out of Tsurugaoka. He visited a friend in Sendai, was even shown around Matsushima, and then hurried straightaway to Hiraizumi in Iwate Prefecture.

Coming this far,
    drinking water,
moving on.
        (in Hiraizumi)

ここまでを
来し水
飲んで去る

Overgrown grasses,
    cornerstones, and here and there,
stagnant water.
        —Basho

草のしげるや
礎石ところどころの
たまり水

This was the northern limit of Basho's journey in *The Narrow Road to the Deep North*. Drawn to Basho, drawn to travel, drawn to the summer grasses, Santoka finally came to this place on his endless journey.

Summer grasses!
    All that remains
of the warriors' dreams.

夏草や
つはものともが
夢のあと

Remembering this poem, Santoka also sat down in the summer grasses and looked out over the current of the Kitagami River.

The country is destroyed,
    but the mountains and rivers remain;
Spring in the castle town,
    grasses and trees grow rank.[6]
        —Tu Fu

Basho was attracted to this poem, and with thoughts similar to Tu Fu's, Santoka saw the dreams of Basho's summer grasses, too.

Here were the remnants of three generations of the Fujiwara clan. In the Golden Hall of the Chusonji temple, the pure gold pillars and coffins amidst the luxuriant green leaves struck his heart; and at the remains of the Motsuji temple, he stepped through the stagnant water at the foundation stones and was flooded by an emotion of nostalgia. The life of the warrior Yoshitsune,[7] and then the last moments of Benkei,[8] who followed his master in loyal death! Their histories could not help but be a source of tears. What is now called the Benkei temple was halfway up the trail as he climbed to the Chusonji. Various items—beginning with the subscription list that Benkei carried as he and his master fled up the Hokuriku Road—are preserved there just as they were: his sword, spear and halberd. Even today, the people of the village have not forgotten the anniversary of the day Benkei achieved his great death, standing motionless at the Koromo River, and Santoka was invited to the magnificent Benkei Festival where he heard the stories intoned of that warrior's virtue of long ago. As the current of time has flowed on, the man whose unfortunate life ended in tragedy was looked up to even more than the world's glorified heroes, and the visitor was made to feel this acutely. Such feelings of nostalgia caused a poet like Basho to create great works that would be left to coming ages; but Santoka looked in the mountains for the delicious water that he loved, drank to his heart's content, at length wrote a poem, and buoyantly started off on his journey again.

Santoka's figure appeared at the great gate of the Eiheiji temple in Echizen around July 4. Beaten down by the heat and tired from his long journey, he had probably become haggard beyond recognition. Furthermore, for some reason, he had neither straw hat nor robe, but wore a simple unlined kimono with an old towel hanging from his waist. With this, he did not look like a mendicant priest; rather, he was nothing more than a mere beggar. Regardless of that, when Santoka satisfactorily explained his circumstances, the monk who acted as a receptionist nodded cheerfully, and he was allowed to stay at the temple for a short while to rest and then leave. He was put up in a small room at the end of the left-hand side of a long corridor.

The fact of the matter is that after Hiraizumi, Santoka had once again been drawn by Akitoshi's pure and simple heart, and found his way back to Tsurugaoka. That much was fine, but making Akitoshi's residence a base of operation, he begged for five or six days both in and outside of the city. With the warm and humane sympathy of the local people, there was not a single family that was stingy to him with their rice or money. That was a disaster. With new self-confidence in his purse, Santoka was badly derailed. Which is to say that he checked into a first-class restaurant-inn, became the Santoka he was before becoming a priest, and spent two or three days on a spree of drinking, singing and carousing. As was expected, he was unable to pay up. He thereupon returned to Akitoshi's residence with the bill collector from the establishment in tow. Even then, Akitoshi was kind enough to pay for Santoka without any regrets at all.

Awakening from his enslavement to sake, Santoka was unable to stay still any longer. As a sign of his repentance at having committed the crime of breaking the Buddhist precepts, he resolutely gave up his priestly attire, and returned to becoming Santoka, a mere human being. Taking off his straw hat and priestly robe, he gave them to Akitoshi, and then burned his beggar's bag to ashes. It is said that even now, Akitoshi carefully preserves that straw hat and robe.

In this way, Santoka was once again blessed with train fare, and made his way to the Eiheiji temple.

The great temple was cool and peaceful. Morning and night he received the same gruel as the monks. Taking the lowest seat during the Buddhist religious services, he calmed his mind, took care of his body, and spent six days in self-examination.

The unending sound of water:
to me,
the Buddha.

水音のたえずして
御佛とあり

てふてふ
ひらひら
いらかをこえた

Butterflies fluttering
over
the tiled roof.

法堂
あけはなつ
明けはなれている

The Dharma Hall [9]
opened wide,
open to all.

I think that these verses, for Santoka, were verses of satori. And he also said as much once. Like the butterflies fluttering over the tiled roof, Santoka, too, transcended one barrier, and his mind was flung open.

Santoka trudged back home from his faraway journey. As might be expected, he was tired. Summer was advancing at the Gochu-an, and the weeds were growing thick and wild. Bamboo shoots that had sprouted up in unimaginable places were lengthening to their hearts' content, and grass was growing on the listing roof. "Master of the House on a Journey." He had written this sign with his own brush and hung it up himself, but now what was left of it had been soaked by the rain and taken on an antique patina. The empty house—or perhaps you could say the abandoned house—was absolutely the same as a lair for foxes and tanuki.[10] When he pushed back the lockless door, it slid open easily; inside the house, nothing had changed since the day he had left on his journey. Both the kettle and the tea urn were sitting in exactly the same places. The plate and *chawan* bowl were also right where they had been put—only a light film of dust had accumulated on them. He had returned to his own nest, so he was undoubtedly pleased; but more than pleasure, the first thing to resonate within him was the loneliness of being by himself. When he took off his split-toed heavy-cloth shoes and stepped into the room, he could see that some sort of creeping vine had crawled under his desk from beneath his bedding, and coiled itself around it. In the three-mat room with the northern exposure, there was a pale-colored bamboo pushing its way up through the tatami. He sat down alone and tried smoking a cigarette, but there was nothing he could do about the loneliness penetrating his heart. Nevertheless, from today on, he would have to send up the faint smoke from his abandoned hut all alone, as meager as it might be.

Returning to my hermitage, July 22.

<table>
<tr><td>

Here, once again:
        the grass, too, growing
    just as it is.

</td><td>

ふたたび
ここに草も
しげるまま

</td></tr>
<tr><td>

Making the sound
        of myself,
    alone.

</td><td>

わたし
ひとりの音
させている

</td></tr>
</table>

While things went on this way, the Sino-Japanese War continued in northern China and became increasingly serious. Young men who up until the day before had labored in the fields, today were called to go out on the front. In their place, the remains of the war dead were presented in white boxes,[11] and were returning home one after another. Those who received those white boxes were the young people who were not yet dead and the old mothers and fathers. Dressed in black ceremonial robes, they gathered throughout the prefecture, their tears flowing. Moreover, as the war advanced deeper into the continent, it became larger and larger with no end in sight.

Santoka watched the results of such tragic conditions at the front every day while having no employment at all, producing nothing, not carrying a gun, yet being able to live by the blessings of exactly those people who did such things. The figure of his own miserable self, living on and making useless haiku, had no way of making an atonement to his country for his existence. And there were days when he thought that perhaps if he just died, he could atone himself to his country, which was fighting so hard.

But wait—killing himself would not be following divine will. In the end, there was nothing more for him to do than to create poetry right up to the end of the days he was given to live, and to live poetry. He would have to have an attitude of putting his life on the line, the same as the brave soldiers going to the battlefield.

While Heaven does not kill me, it will have me write poetry.
While I am alive, I will write poetry.
I will write poetry that is my own personal truth.

He wrote this down, affixed it to his cracked wall, and decided to write poetry about the front. At that time, people who were in favor of the war—including songwriters and haiku poets—all played up to the army and were publishing books one after another in the vein of "We'll attack and never stop!" By nature, Santoka did not like people coming together and shedding blood. Still, at this time, anyone who opposed the war would never be forgiven as a Japanese. So perhaps it would not be futile to at least strive to write poems about the pathos of those who had been wounded on the front, mollifying the spirits of the young men who had gone off to die, and to reveal as poetry the reality of the sad scenery of the front. With these feelings, he produced the series of haiku *Jugo* [On the Front].[12]

In the heat of the day,
one stitch after another:
the "thousand-stitch cloth."[13]

日ざかりの
千人針の
一針づつ

This was the scene in the streets of Ogori. Young wives with tears in their eyes requesting other women to put in one stitch with a red thread for their husbands who were going off to war; and the women of the town silently nodding, "Me, too; me, too." They constantly added their own tears with all their hearts, bravely giving their one stitch.

Autumn deepening
all the more;
our national flag, fluttering.

秋もいよいよ
ふかうなる
日の丸へんぽん

Treading firmly on the ground
they will not likely tread upon again;
to the front.

ふたたびは
踏むまい土を
踏みしめて征く

The young men advanced, firmly step by step, over the earth of their villages, under the fluttering Japanese national flag; and for some, perhaps, these may have been farewell steps to the earth of their hometowns. How heavy and deep the cadence of their steps must have been.

Late autumn rains,
no matter how peaceful,
six hundred and fifty gods.[14]

しぐれつつ
しずかにも
六百五十柱

Greeting the remains:

A silent late autumn rain;
placing the white boxes
out in front.

もくもくとして
しぐるる白い函を
まへに

On a day when a cold autumn rain was falling, a great num
ber—in fact, six hundred and fifty—of boxes containing the ashe
of the deceased came to the Yamaguchi Regiment. Santoka was b
himself, but among the crowd of people who silently greeted them
Each soldier carried the ashes of a comrade-in-arms in a continuin
sad procession. This kind of silent, long procession has existed eve
since Japan began, I suppose.

Moreover, it was getting cold, and the war only becoming mor
and more severe.

Snow falling towards snow;
the battle will soon start,
they say.

雪へ雪ふる
戦ひはこれから
だといふ

How valiant,
how sad:
the white boxes.

いさましくも
かなしくも
白い函

A festival in the streets.
    Have those honored men turned to bones
  and come home?

街はおまつり
お骨となつて
帰られたか

A father returning to his hometown carrying his son's remains:

Sweat trickling,
    dropping down
      on the pure white box.

ぽろぽろ
したたる汗が
ましろな函に

The honored bones,
    voiceless[15]
  flowing over the water.

お骨
声なく水の
うへをゆく

Autumn.
    That fragment turns to the earth
  of its own hometown.

その一片は
ふるさとの
土となる秋

And again the following year:

How they leave for the front!
    The green of the mountains
  greener, greener still.

みんな出て征く
山の青さの
いよいよ青く

馬も召されて
おぢいさん
おばあさん

Their horse was summoned, too;
the old man,
the old woman.

これが最後の
日本の御飯を
食べている、汗

This is the last Japanese rice
he'll eat.
Sweat.

ぢっと
瞳が瞳に
喰ひ入る瞳

Eyes staring steadily
into one another;
the eyes.

How poignant the sweat and pupils of those eyes! In the midst of the confused bustling send-off, hadn't Santoka truly seen what he should have as a poet?

足は手は
支那に残して
ふたたび日本に

Leaving his arms and legs in China,
he has come back
to Japan.

Such a series of haiku as *On the Front* will likely be left to later generations as representative of the works of Santoka. Many of the popular so-called "war haiku" of that time, or even the "war tanka,"[16] when brought out and reviewed today are mostly absurd, and the reader can hardly stand to look at them. But the verses that Santoka created, putting his life on the line as "poetry of his own truth," are such that we want to read and savor again, even in times of peace, I think.

The last time I visited the Gochu-an was November of 1938. I put an account from that time into my book, *Nihon no aji* [A Taste of Japan]:

The Gochu-an, which I had not seen for a long time, was surrounded by tea flowers and weeds, and was quite peaceful. The old man was more vigorous than I would have thought. With only two remaining teeth, the old man talked about this and that in rapid succession in a great loud voice as though in a mood of nostalgia. Ordinarily, you see, other than greeting the mailman with a "Thanks for your trouble!" he would sit silently and truly alone for four or five days, lost in a trance of verse-making, so this was not unreasonable. The old man seemed to address the crickets and praying mantises without realizing it. Well really, it appears that he sometimes even spoke to the lamp and the desk; people get lonely, you know. I guess you could say that the old man was a sort of saint of booze, and the fact is that he loved sake and took great pleasure in it. Was it that sometimes Santoka drank the sake, or that the sake drank Santoka? I really don't know, but my one desire was to at least have the solitary and cold old man drink a stomachful of hot sake. His hermitage was so broken down that one had to look at it as the hermitage of an abandoned person rather than that of a haiku poet, and we talked a number of times about building a small hut. But be that as it may, when he lay down on the verandah, he could peek out at the blue sky, and creeping vines crawled through the cracks in the wall without reserve. He told me that on nights when it rained, he had to move his bedding about from place to place. When I looked seriously at this old man who continually sat all day and all night in his broken-down hermitage where he slept alone trying to restrain his solitary self, I didn't know whether I wanted to laugh or cry.

寒けれど
二人寝る夜ぞ
頼母しき

Though it may be cold,
*   sleeping together at night*
*   will not let you down.*

—Basho

There was no way I could leave the old man here and stay the night at a hot spring in Yuda. When I thought that this might be the last time I would stay over in this broken-down hermitage, even slipping my body in between two thin futons on an autumn night turned out to be one kind of pleasure. Anyway, piling magazines and various other articles on top of me, we were able to warm up a bedding for one person. The old man turned down the lamp as the night wore on and, watching his moving silhouette drinking sake on the old sliding paper door, I fell asleep. Outside, the wind that came and blew through the bamboo forest rustlingly informed the two of us that deep autumn was on its way.

The next morning I evacuated my bowels outdoors while gazing at the dew on the leaves of the grasses beneath the persimmon tree. The sun was just coming up, and even now it is difficult to forget how, spellbound by the beauty of Heaven and Earth, the two of us laughed with radiant faces. Santoka was reluctant to say goodbye, so we walked together as far as the train station in Kagawa. In the village, the persimmons were ripening beautifully and the bush clover was scattered over the ground.

わかれてからの
まいにち
雪ふる

After your leaving,
*   it snows*
*   every day.*

Late autumn rain;
　all the rice that was here
cooked up just right.

しぐるるや
あるだけの
御飯よう
炊けた

Translator's Notes

. Issa Kobayashi (1763–1827): one of the most famous haiku poets. Known for the humanity expressed in his poems.

. Gyofu Soma (1883–1950): a poet and critic from Niigata.

. Gogo (五合) may refer to the fifth station up the mountain, or to the five *go* of rice the previous resident monk had received daily from his temple.

. *The Narrow Road to the Deep North*. Basho's famous travel journal.

. *Zuzuben*: the dialect of the far north and northeast of Japan's main island of Honshu. It cannot be understood by most Japanese outside of this area.

. The opening lines of a famous poem by the Chinese poet Tu Fu (712–770).

. Minamoto no Yoshitsune (1159–1189): Military commander and great hero of the wars between the Minamoto and Taira clans. Eventually turned upon, hunted down and killed by the forces of his elder brother, Yoritomo, who then established the first shogunate of Japan.

. Benkei: Saito Benkei Musashibo. An exceptionally tall and strong warrior-monk who, defeated in combat by Yoshitsune, became the latter's devoted retainer. Said to have stood valiantly in front of Yoshitsune's tent receiving the arrows of the enemy, while Yoshitsune committed seppuku.

. The Dharma Hall: the lecture hall in Zen monasteries.

0. Tanuki: a badger-like animal called a raccoon-dog in English. Folklore has it that like foxes, tanuki can change shape and lead people astray.

1. The ashes of the war dead were put in white boxes and ceremoniously returned to their families.

2. 銃後.

3. The "thousand-stitch cloth" was given to young men going off to war as both good luck and a remembrance of those at home.

4. The final kanji in this haiku is read as *hashira*: the counter for Shinto gods. Presumably the souls of the dead became gods.

5. The phrase I have translated as "voiceless," *koe naku*, could also be read as "voice crying".

6. Tanka: Japan's classical poetry form. Lines are in syllables of 5, 7, 5, 7, 7.

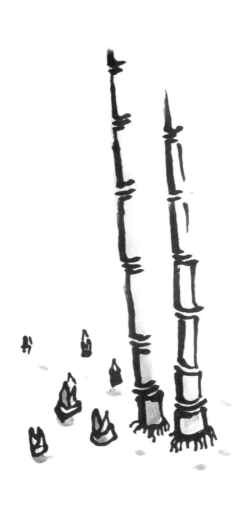

CHAPTER 7

The Furai-kyo at Yuda

At this point, the Gochu-an was already a totally dilapidated house. For the seven years he had lived there since it had been repaired for him, the wind and snow had damaged and passed right through the structure without restraint. In addition, the master of the hermitage loved to go out on journeys, and often did so. The hermitage was often empty for two months or more at a time. When smoke rose up every day and sweeping and cleaning was done inside the place, it somehow had the feeling of a comfortable place to live; but when it was empty for a long time, there was nothing one could do about its going largely to ruin. There were holes here and there in the listing roof, from which you could see the stars. Now a life in which you can see the stars while falling to sleep is very poetic, but when it rained, something cold would spill down and soak the tatami. The walls were also moldering and falling apart, and creeping vines made their way right in.

Walls crumbling;
through them,
creeping vines.

壁がくづれて
そこから鶴草

For the man who wrote this poem down in his notebook of verse, there was nothing to be done about the desolation of the crumbling house and the late autumn that pressed in on him. Santoka lit up a cigarette that somebody had left and, inhaling deeply into his cold body, tried to reflect on the various things that had happened over the seven years he had spent in this hermitage. It wasn't just that the hermitage had gotten old, but Santoka felt that his own body was gradually declining and that his white hair had become pronounced. To say that he was fifty-seven years old meant that his life had stretched six years longer than Basho's, but there were still eight more years to reach Issa's sixty-five. Issa had lost his mother at age three; and Santoka, at age eleven, had seen the figure of his mother who had just committed suicide. This spring on March 6, he had observed in this hermitage the forty-seventh anniversary of his mother's death, performing a lonely reading of the sutras by himself. How had he dared to live on to the forty-seventh anniversary of a body that had been tossed away? During those years, he had taken great care of only one thing: his mother's mortuary tablet, keeping it in the luggage on his back on the days he was traveling, and in a corner of his Buddhist "chapel" when he was in his hermitage. This year, on the day of the death anniversary, bad luck would have it that he possessed not one grain of rice, much less sake. Looking around, he finally found a half-portion of dried udon noodles in the corner of a box in the kitchen, boiled it up, and put it in front of her mortuary tablet as an offering.

Offering udon;
Mother!
I'll have some, too.

うどん供えて、
母よ、わたくしも
いただきます

When he had finished smoking his cigarette, Santoka consolidated what was inside the hermitage. Although we say "luggage," there was really just a little; the troublesome thing was his kitchen equipment. Thinking it sad that it was human nature to be able to forget about everything but eating every day, he wrapped up things like his pot, *chawan* bowl, and soy-sauce bottle in brown paper. Everything else—all the worthless jumbled stuff he had collected in the closet—he took out into the front garden and burned to ashes. Al the things like the postcards and letters he had received from friends were now fed into the glowing fire. What was left over still—empty boxes, worn out clogs—was all the grime of seven years of life.

When it had all burned up, there were only these ashes: the ashes of seven years, left by the smoke that had vanished into the cold, rainy late autumn sky. These meager ashes were blown away by the autumn wind.

With this, he had nicely tidied himself up, both inside and out. He did not even tell his most intimate friend Tatsuaki that he was leaving the hermitage. And of course he did not inform the people in his neighborhood, who had been such a help to him, either. That being so, you might say that he simply fled. But that wasn't right either. He did this because saying goodbye was too sad for him. And because he hated being sent off by people in an exaggerated way. Moreover, if he spoke to Tatsuaki and the others, they would wind up doing something absurd like saying that they would fix up the hermitage or even build a new one. For seven years, people like Tatsuaki, Keibo and Sobo, just to begin with, had been way too indulgent with their goodwill. There were times when Tatsuaki and the others placed more importance in the Gochu-an than in their own homes, and domestic arguments had ensued.

Ah, everything might be summed up in one word: gratitude. There was karma in his coming here, but not in his living here forever. So off he went, leaving silently I suppose. Flowing like water, flying like the clouds—off he went, following the current and the wind.

He wrote, "Master of the hermitage on a journey" on a slip of paper and posted it on the outside of the closed up rain shutters. Then he walked around looking at the vegetable patches around his hermitage, the thicket, and the foothills one more time. How beautiful the withered grass soaked by the late autumn rains. In the center of the thicket, a single camellia with extended branches was blooming in absolute crimson. Santoka snapped off the branch and took it with him.

His baggage he arranged in two pieces and, tying them together with cords, slung them over his shoulder—one hanging in front, one in back. He had forwarded things like his futon from the train station the night before.

Santoka faced his hermitage, placed the palms of his hands together, and said a silent prayer. Not turning to look back, he got as far as the hedge behind the house of the next-door neighbor, Watanabe-san, when he suddenly remembered Kiyoko. She had been a cute little girl who, from time to time, came and peeked into his hermitage, but now she was already a third-year student at a women's school. He quietly opened the window to the room that seemed to be where she studied and, silently placing the camellia branch in the room, said, "Kiyoko-san, sayonara," in his heart.

He had found a four-mat one-room house standing alone just outside the gate of an old temple in the hot-spring village of Yuda, inside the city limits of Yamaguchi. With the help of a Tokushige-san, he had named this the Furai-kyo or "The Home Come in on the Wind," and took it as a temporary place to live. Santoka, with his love of hot springs, had come to Yuda a number of times before this. The truth of the matter was that a man called Wada-san and a number of young poets under the influence of the poet Nakahara Chuya were here. Moreover, Miss Yoneko at the Nishimura Inn was the leader of a street of hot springs establishments and a writer of free haiku for *So'un*. This was out of the ordinary, and such people were kindly waiting for him there.

Here, however, it was quite different from the Gochu-an in Ogori, which was enveloped in the beauty of nature. This was a single structure tinged with the character of squalid back streets where there was the intense smell of human beings. He used the well in common with his neighbors, heard the voices of children fighting, the quarreling words between husbands and wives, and the cries of peddlers; this was an absolutely different universe. Finally settled in, Santoka went out into the alley and, when he looked up at the Furai-kyo, a bird suddenly flew from a pine tree at the temple and came to a quick stop on his tiny roof, neither flying away nor singing.

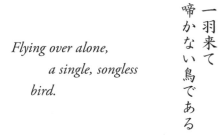

Flying over alone,
a single, songless
bird.

He could not help but think of this single bird as somehow old, flowing from journey to journey, just like his own solitary self.

Well then, receiving the communication from Santoka that he had changed residences, I came to visit and stayed over at the Furai-kyo just once. It was July of 1939. Getting off the train at Yuda Station, I went to the front part of town and, walking along aimlessly, suddenly saw a small hand flag of the Rising Sun raised up on the corner of a narrow alleyway. That day was the day when the bones and ashes of the Yamaguchi Regiment returned home. This flag was a paper hand flag mingling with the many Japanese national flags[1] that fluttered from every house. Beyond all doubt, this has got to be Santoka, I thought. A name plate written with a pen on a scrap of writing pad paper was posted: *Furai-kyo* and *Santoka*. I was standing there smiling and thinking how like Santoka this was when,

"This is it. I'd say you recognized it quite well, you know."

"It's pretty tight, huh."

"What do you mean? It's only half a mat smaller than Vimilakirti's four-and-a-half-mat room."[2]

"Shall we go to a hot spring?"

"Sure."

With this, the two of us went to the Thousand Person Bath, the cheapest in Yuda. An old work of Santoka's was from this hot spring:

Men's privates,
women's, too;
the bubbling overflowing hot water.

ちんぽこも
おそそも
わいてあふれる湯

He had used a rather prickly[3] subject for haiku material, but rather than a distasteful sense, one feels a certain romantic humor of the public bath.

"According to your poem, the Thousand Person Bath seems to be a bath for mixed bathing with men and women."

"No, it's not mixed bathing; it's a scene where a father is bathing his young son and daughter."

So the two of us submerged ourselves in the bubbling overflowing hot water to our hearts' content. It seemed that there was no rice in the Furai-kyo and, as I didn't even for a moment want to trouble the old man to cook, we went momentarily to poke into one of the eating and drinking stalls in the area, and had an afterbath nightcap. You might define it like that, but I had a beer and Santoka had a beer, which we declared was nothing more than the raw material for a pee, so we then had two or three bottles of sake. Sitting there and talking happily, we went on at a leisurely pace. Then we ate. It was a strange little shop, and the rice was served in a box. I remember that Santoka kindly served me the rice himself.

On the way back to the Furai-kyo, we stopped by two houses of colleagues-in-poetry-and-haiku, but neither person was at home. Well, when we returned to his residence, we talked until the night grew late about various things like where he was going, his next poetry collection, and the conditions of living in the present day. We decided that the two of us would sleep on the same bedding, but he had no mosquito net. When I offered to go buy some mosquito coils, he said, "I've got a good technique, so we won't need that. While I make a little smoke, do me the favor of going outside for a moment and hanging around the temple garden."

Santoka fumigated the place by stuffing his portable clay cooking stove with old newspapers, and driving the mosquitoes out with dispatch it seems. When I came back, the smoke was in thick clouds.

"The mosquitoes are all gone. This is just a four-mat house, so it's all right to think of the house itself as a mosquito net, right?

"That's a pretty good idea."

"When you haven't got something, it's better to live without it. When I own a number of different things, they're troublesome when I go off on a journey, so I make a big effort not to have things. It was my plan not to have things even at the Gochu-an, but well, when I tried to consolidate everything there was at the hermitage, I was shocked at the great amount of junk I had. When you settle down to live in one place, junk accumulates, as well as the grime in your mind. Toss that away, then toss away some more, and day by day live as though you were at an inn or on a journey."

As for the futons, I got the thin one and he got the thick one. Even though it was summer, it got chilly in the middle of the night, and in the end I had only a broken sleep. This was the first and last time I stayed over at the Furai-kyo.

Even after he moved to the Furai-kyo, Santoka tried his hand at faraway journeys. Strangely, he did not hold his sake very well after greeting the New Year at the age of fifty-eight. It wasn't that its savor had changed, but he now felt that after three or four cups, his body was filled up. Particularly after getting out of the water of the Thousand Person Bath hot spring, he would get drunk quickly and feel as though he had a slight pain in his heart. Nevertheless, sake was not something he could give up. The only things that would give comfort to his solitude were sake and travel. No, even when he was unable to drink, it was still only sake that was going back and forth in his mind. I suppose that this was a kind of karma after all. Then, when he thought about the fact that his body was gradually getting weaker, he wanted to travel and go as far as he could, and to see the friends that he wanted to be with as long as he was alive. So after moving to the Furai-kyo, he was unable to compose haiku as freely as he had at the Gochu-an. As it was, the Furai-kyo was on a corner of a mishmash of tenement houses on a back street, and he rarely heard the cries of the birds and insects as he had at the Gochu-an. What entered his ears were domestic quarrels, crying children, and the voices of the crowd of housewives meeting at the well. That was an environment that was, on the whole, contrary to Santoka's character. The only thing that gave him pleasure was that Wada-san and other friends-in-poetry often came and talked happily late into the night. There were times when as many as twenty young folks would be packed into his four-mat room, huddled around the burning coals of his portable clay stove and sit up late into the night. Thinking of Vimilakirti's ten-foot [three-meter] square room, he would twist the white hairs on his chin, forget about his age, take on the heart of a very young man, and enjoy their company. This was truly a pleasure.

At last,
　　　　having a household;
　　a new bucket.
　　　　　　(the couple next door)

やっと
世帯が持てて
新しいバケツ

Crows cawing,
　　　　crows flying, no place
　　to settle down.

ないて鳥の、
飛んで鳥の、
おちつく
ところがない

It was not only the crows that could not settle down; the fact was that Santoka had not been truly able to settle down at the Furai-kyo.

After the middle of March, there were days with the warmth of tepid water, and pussy willows were swelling on the banks of the little stream that flowed behind the hot-springs town. The sky cleared to a light green, and clouds like warm cotton floated gently along. As he watched the sky, the clouds, and the flow of the water, he was no longer able to sit still. He quickly thought of a plan, hastily put together the preparations for a trip, left his few domestic implements just as they were, and without either shutting the door or telling his neighbors, suddenly started out on a journey.

He spent one night in Hiroshima at my place. He had had a new robe made for him by Hakusen's wife—again, priestly attire. This was like Santoka: coming like the wind and going like the clouds. From Osaka and Kyoto, he visited a friend-in-haiku and stayed over one night in Nagoya, and from there he walked to Cape Irako.

Coming to visit from far away;
at the tip of the promontory
alone.

はるばる
たづね来て
岩鼻一人

Basho looked up his young disciple Tokoku, who had been banished to Cape Irako, and left this poem:

Sighting a hawk.
How delightful!
Cape Irako.[4]

鷹一つ見つけて
うれし伊良湖岬

Santoka, however, stood alone at the tip of the promontory and looked at the sea off Hekinan.

Santoka mixed with a great number of people whose lives were writing haiku or who were linked to the Way of Haiku, but never had he had someone he might call a disciple. He wrote verses with others or drank with them, but only that—he did not know how to conduct himself as a leader should. Even when his criticism was sought out for others' verses, he would not say much, but only remark, "I like this poem." He therefore dealt with all the young men of his coterie as friends who wrote haiku together. On that point he was quite different from Basho, Issa and the famous haiku poets of both ancient and modern times.

From Cape Irako he entered the mountains and visited the Horaiji temple in Mikawa.

真実不虚
しんしんしづくする
お山

The holy mountain
dripping steadily;
"This is truth, not falsehood."[5]

This he wrote in his haiku notebook.

From there he went on to Mount Akiba, went upstream along the Tenryu River and entered Shinano Province. He toured Ina and, shown around by his friend Jakusui, hiked with staff in hand the remains of Takato Castle, and visited the grave of the beggar Seigetsu [see page 32]. Santoka had gone to Iida from the Kiso area over the Taihei Pass in May of 1934 once before. At that time, he had come down with acute pneumonia the night of his arrival and been admitted to the hospital, but this had not worried him unduly.[6]

He returned to Yuda in May, and there he passed a hot summer during which the war became more and more severe. That summer there was a serious drought that lasted more than sixty days.

涸れて
涸れきつて
石ころごろごろ

Dried up,
completely dried up;
stones rolling, tumbling.

燃ゆる火の、
雨ふらしめと
燃えさかる

The burning fire,
burning ablaze
to send the rain.

炎天のレール
まつすぐ

Under the scorching sun,
the rail,
straight ahead.

In September, when the equinoctial week had passed, both the spider lilies and bush clover were blooming, and the wind became chilly and autumnal. Santoka stayed away from the Furai-kyo more and more, and went off on aimless journeys. Rather than "aimless journeys," they were truly more journeys in search of a place to die. When he reflected on his own conduct and demeanor during this period, it had been simply terrible. He had abandoned the world and taken the tonsure fifteen years ago, so he had the social standing of a priest. But to what purpose had he taken the tonsure, and what kind of shameful life had he led? Only to be drowned in sake and spoiled by the affections of his friends. He had only been able to be meek when it came to women, but this was not a matter of the capability of being human, it was because his sexual desire had dried up completely. No matter how he thought of it, he was just the most foolish of the foolish, the very lowest of the low. That he himself intoned the sutras and wore a priest's robes was just a deception in order to obtain charity from others, and was nothing more than staining the Buddha's greatly virtuous influence. Thinking in this way, he abandoned the priesthood, and came back to being a worldly minded layman. Rather than a Buddhist, begging austerities and holding a Buddhist's begging bowl, he became nothing more than a simple beggar, and so came to conceive of his true form as that of a panhandler.

Back to being a beggar;
one
towel.

もともと
乞食になって
タオルが一枚

In this way, he no longer needed his robe or his begging bowl. In the Zen sect they make a lot of noise about handing down one's robe and bowl to one's disciple, but that was not what this meant. As these were articles he would leave behind when he finally died, off on a journey somewhere, he decided that he would give his begging bowl to Hakusen in Tokuyama and his robe to me in Hiroshima, and with this resolution he hobbled off from Yuda to Tokuyama. He tied a waistband around his slightly stained kimono, put split-toed cloth shoes on his feet, tucked up his kimono from behind, and hung a towel from his waist: this was the dress of a beggar. Nodding to himself, he acknowledged how appropriate a beggar's appearance was to his own inanity.

It was that Santoka who struggled into Hiroshima on September 28. By the time I returned home from work, Santoka had already gotten out of the bath, and was drinking cold sake by himself *chibiri chibiri.*

Well, you see, maybe I've just got one more year. Recently I've felt like my last days are pressing in on me. Dying is more difficult than living, don't you think? If a solitary person like me with "not one thing" falls ill, he causes people a lot of trouble no matter what, you know. But with that said, suicide is unnatural, too.

What do you suppose the birds and rabbits do, Oyama? They die one way or the other, but I've done a lot of traveling on mountain roads and never seen a bird or rabbit die by the roadside. The birds and beasts seem to go away and die so they

won't be seen by anyone, just as though they've disappeared.
Well, me too, you see. I really wonder if I couldn't die like that.
People . . . I mean me . . . I've really become a burden.

He was going on like that, drinking sake as he spoke. Then he told me that he had come today from Iwakuni, not by train, but on foot. Somehow Santoka's hair was much whiter than it had been two or three years before; his teeth, too, had all fallen out; and I couldn't help feeling that his breath was weaker and his color paler.

The next day I took Santoka to Dr. Mihito Ono's place in the village of Tachi within the city limits. Dr. Ono was someone who understood Santoka through what I had told him previously.

"Doctor, Santoka-san says that there's not much left to his life, just about one year."

"I understand. I could see right away that his heart is weakening, just from his breath when he climbed up the stairs. But he's enjoyed his journeys, taken pleasure in his sake, done what he's wanted to do, said what he's wanted to say, has not fooled himself, has mixed with people he liked, written the verses he loved, and had a good life, right? Santoka-san, dying anytime would be all right, wouldn't it? You're a transcendent good child of Buddhist liberation, I'll bet."

"Yes, that's right. I could die anytime at all, but I don't want to be a burden to people. I just want to fall down dead. And I don't want to have anything troublesome like a funeral. I'd just like to quietly disappear from this world."

Doctor Ono laughed, "That's so like you, Santoka, isn't it. I'm envious, you know. People like me are attached to things and pretty much can't go that far, can we. But Santoka-san, dying is not something we do with our own strength. It's something brought about by the Buddha's discretion or by a function of nature, isn't it? It's like in Shakamuni's[7] sermons: things like funerals or the time of death are not up to you, but are left up to random fate, isn't that what we say? Forget about it, and keep drinking your beloved sake in moderation. Drink like Oyama-san."

The doctor talked on like this without even taking Santoka's pulse. As for me, I had come here thinking that he would give Santoka something of an examination, but in the end, we all went to see a movie in Yatchobori. I don't remember what movie it was, but Santoka's eyes glistened from time to time with tears. That evening, we got off the trolley and crossed the bridge over the Ota River.

"Oyama, well, you see, up until now I've walked throughout Japan, and I'm thinking that the old country of Iyo[8] is the best. Its natural features are beautiful and the people there are kind. If I'm going to die anyway, shouldn't I go ahead and cross over to Iyo?"

"I think that would be good; I like Iyo, too."

"My hometown would be fine, too; but for me, who's traveled all my life, making a travel destination my place of dying is probably more like me anyway."

"Going there is fine, but as far as dying goes, it's like Dr. Ono said: it's not up to you, is it."

That night I wrote a long letter of introduction to Hajime Takahashi of Matsuyama Commercial College.

Translator's Notes

1. The *hi no maru*: the red sun on a field of white. Santoka's flag was the Rising Sun flag (*kyokujitsu-ki*), outlawed for some time after the Pacific War.

2. Vimilakirti: main character of the Vimilakirti Sutra (called *Yuima-kyo* in Japanese). He lived in a small ten-foot (three-meter)-square hut, but when visited by a great number of the Buddha's messengers, they miraculously all fit into the room without discomfort.

3. This is not a case of the translator trying to be funny or crude. Oyama uses the word 珍, which would be read as *mezurashii* if written in the ordinary Japanese; but he writes it instead as *chin naru*, the word *chin* being homonymous with the male sexual member.

4. On his visit to Cape Irako, Santoka wrote in his journal for April 20, "Basho sighted a hawk and was pleased, but I was screeched at by a kite and felt nothing more than loneliness."

5. A line from the Heart Sutra that Santoka no doubt chanted every day.

6. This would seem to be a strange way of ending this paragraph, but in Santoka's journal on March 3, he wrote:

   > When I passed by Iida, my heart was filled with deep emotion. "Iida! Iida! Old Ado! Old Ado!" and I pressed my palms together and lifted them in gratitude.

7. Shakamuni is the historical Buddha who lived at some time during the sixth and seventh centuries BC. Buddhist lore and theology is filled with many "Buddhas." The Buddha belonged to the Shaka clan; "muni" means "sage," so Shakamuni is "the sage of the Shaka clan."

8. Now Ehime Prefecture on the island of Shikoku.

CHAPTER 8

The Shikoku Pilgrim

The morning he left for Matsuyama, Santoka put everything together and tied it all up in one large black *furoshiki* cloth, but something wrapped in white paper slipped out of it. He reached both hands out for it as though it was very important.

"What's that?"

"It's my mother's mortuary tablet. When my mother was pulled out of the well, I clung to her cold wet dead body. I didn't think my mother could enter Nirvana dying like that. It was for her sake that I went around visiting temples so conscientiously. I've always tucked it into the bottom of my backpack when I've been on my journeys."

Neither my wife nor I could say anything, but we both shed tears.

In the port of Ujina, a great number of war horses had been assembled to send to the continent.

"Horses have been given their orders, too, huh, Oyama? I'll bet that every one of those horses were treated with affection by the good people who raised them, and the hooves that stepped over the black earth in the countryside are now stepping on the asphalt in the city. Tomorrow they'll be going to the front on the continent, huh. Poor things!"

I bought a ticket to Takahama and pressed it into Santoka's hand along with fifteen yen for spending money. There was a steward whose face I recognized on the ship the Aioi Maru, so after handing him some money for Santoka's blanket and tea, I left. That was the morning of October 1, 1939.

Horses, horses,
> *the faces, faces, faces of the horses*
> *tomorrow going to the front.*

馬馬あすは
征くの馬の
顔顔顔

Buoyantly
> *on to Shikoku;*
> *a perfectly clear sky.*
>> (boarding the ship at Ujina)

ひよいと
四国へ
晴れきっている

Carrying my letter of introduction, Santoka first visited Ichijun Takahashi[1] in the Showa ward of Matsuyama. The two of them quickly became good friends; Ichijun welcomed this vagabond, opened his house to him, and treated him with utmost kindness. He then introduced him to people, one after another, with whom he could get along quite well, like Jun'ichi Murase and Masa'ichi Fujioka. So the old beggar with a single towel quickly became a welcome guest and, as I had anticipated, became intimate right away with the warmhearted affections of the people of Iyo. Then one day he was taken to Yuyama by Tsujita Naotaka, and was caught by Tsujita-san's camera easing his travel weariness by amusing himself next to the mountain stream by the stone dam on the Iwate River.

Making a stone my pillow,
> *tracing the whereabouts,*
> *of the clouds.*

石を枕に
雲の行くへを

This was a haiku from that moment.

After just three days, Santoka proposed that he at last make the pilgrimage journey of Shikoku.[2] Before this—just after he had arrived in Matsuyama—he said that he wanted to visit the grave of the brilliant writer for *So'un*, Shurindo Nomura,[3] but the people in Matsuyama had no idea where the grave might be. Masa'ichi Fujioka first looked for it in the Ishitedera temple, but that night they finally discovered it to be in the middle of a newly established public cemetery in Kawaminami. As soon as Santoka found this out, he went immediately to the gravesite, but by the time he reached it, accompanied by Ichijun and Masa'ichi, the night was totally dark. A cold rain had begun to fall. In the midst of all this, they found the gravestone with the light of a match, and Santoka, seemingly filled with old memories, said, "Ah, is this where Shurindo sleeps?" He caressed the top of the small stone with the palm of his hand, and was unable to leave for a while.

After that, they walked through the town at night, but when the three of them got as far as Matsuyama Station, the last train had already left. The three men spent the night on the bench in the waiting room, and Santoka was sent off the next morning on the very first train. Ichijun skillfully managed to go in the direction of his school and had taken his leave promising to catch up with Santoka at the Koenji temple in Komatsu, where he should wait. Taking along my letter of introduction to Seisui'e, Santoka visited him in Sakurai, was treated to a leisurely drink of sake, made a pilgrimage to the Koenji temple, and met up with Ichijun. A *So'un* poet by the name of Miyuki Kawamura lived close by the temple. There Santoka stayed for four nights and was well taken care of. At that time, a Muso Kimura, who had entered the Itto-en sect in Kyoto, came by Kawamura-san's place and talked about such subjects as the poet Hosai [see page 34]. Muso-san took off the black Itto-en overcoat he was wearing and had Santoka put it on. Santoka had thrown away his priest's robe, and this was quite becoming.

南無観世音
おん手
したたる
水の一すぢ

Namu Kanzeon.
　One line of water
　　drips from her holy hand.

秋の夜の
護摩のほのほの
燃えさかるなり

The autumn night;
　flames of the goma ceremony [4]
　　in full blaze.

あすはお分れの
爪をきりつつ、
秋

Cutting my nails,
　tomorrow I depart;
　　autumn.

　　He left these three haiku, and he and Ichijun happily continued traveling the mountain road beneath the incessantly falling leaves.

落葉
ふみわけほど
よい野糞

Walking through fallen leaves;
　having a proper bowel movement
　　out of doors.

　　　　　　　　　　(to Sumita)

木の葉
ふるふる
野糞する

Leaves fluttering;
　shitting
　　outdoors.

He looked lonely, but was a free-and-easy pilgrim. As he evacuated his bowels outdoors, he remembered me, I suppose.

Where the upper reaches of the Kamo River flow into Nijo, the water reflected Santoka's heart. How steep the mountain must have been. And how beautiful the water.

The steep incline of the mountain;
   the water flowing down,
      bright and clear.

山のけはしさ
流れくる水の
れいろう

Mr. Tessaburo Ishikawa was at the Shijo Women's High School. As a friend of Ichijun's, he was happy to greet the two travelers who had groped their way along until late at night. The next morning, the school principal assembled the entire student body in the auditorium and, against Santoka's wishes, had him give some kind of talk. Santoka felt insecure about this sort of thing. Perhaps this was the first time in his life that he had been thrust into this kind of occasion. He went up to the podium scratching his head. This old man, the very figure of a white mountain goat, fiddled with his beard, said only, "This is Santoka," and beat a hasty retreat down from the podium. The schoolgirls all laughed out loud. After that, Ichijun took up the task and talked for a whole hour.

At Mishima they were allowed to stay at the Koganji temple, and were received warmly by the abbot. From Mishima they went straight to the Sankakuji temple, Ichijun going as far as the Unhenji temple. At the top of the mountain, the two of them waved their walking sticks and went their separate ways, Santoka continuing his journey on the Sanuki Road. He was now alone and plodded on his solitary way chanting, "How many mountains and rivers?" by Bokusui Wakayama.[5]

秋ただふかうなる
今日も旅ゆく

Autumn only deepens;
today, too,
I travel.

From Takamatsu he took a boat and crossed over to the island of Azukijima. He then circumambulated the eighty-eight sites of that island.[6] On the way he visited Kazuji Fuchizaki. Guided by Kazuji, he visited the Nango-an hermitage, rubbing the inscription on the haiku memorial stone to Hosai beneath the large pine, and read:

いれものがない
両手でうける

Having nothing to put it in,
I receive it
with my two hands.

The two of them [Santoka and Hosai] had never met while Hosai was alive, but they quite resembled each other in having received the highest education, in having thrown away everything and staying away from worldly affairs, and in having been absorbed in writing haiku. They were only different in that Santoka's health was sound and that he traveled widely, supporting himself by begging; Hosai, on the other hand, had weak lungs and cooped himself up in a hermitage. Climbing up to the cemetery of the Saikoji temple, which was in a slightly more elevated place than the hermitage, he visited Hosai's grave as well. Thinking ahead of time, Kazuji had brought sake.

Once again,
*　　offering weeds*
*　at this place.*
(before Hosai's grave)

ふたたびここに
雑草供えて

Ceremonial water
*　　at the grave;*
*　I'll sip some, too.*

墓に護摩水を、
わたしも
すすり

The two of them had loved sake, and here they sipped the sake of friendship together.

Santoka returned to Takamatsu. He continued through the autumnal mountains and fields of Kita-to in Ogawa-gun, going around to the temples where they issued amulets to pilgrims, while fall deepened all the more and the mountains were wet with rain.

Raining off and on;
*　　mountain after mountain*
*　after unknown mountain.*

しぐれて
山をまた山を
知らない山

Laying my body down
*　　in the mountains*
*　in late autumn rains.*

からだ
投げだして
しぐるる山

しぐれて
その字が読めない
道しるべ

Late autumn rains;
I can't read that word:
the guidepost.

While pushing through the rainy mountains, Santoka struggled his way up to the eighty-eighth temple, the Okubodera. Then, on the way to the Reisanji temple in Awa, there was no inn so he had to sleep out in the open in the midst of the fallen leaves in the cold mountains.

泊めてくれない
折からの月が
行手に

They won't let me stay;
just then, the moon
straight ahead.

暮れても
宿がない
百舌鳥が
鳴く

Though it's gotten dark,
no inn;
a shrike shrieking.

Another night he slept outdoors by the roadside that followed along the Yoshino River.

まどろめば
ふるさとの夢の、
葦の葉ずれ

Dozing off,
a dream of my hometown;
reed leaves rustling.

Among Santoka's works there are a great number of haiku about his hometown, but this poem about sleeping out in the open is quite touching, the grief of the old man appearing like an apparition. One night, however, he found a small boat tied up at the river and cheerfully jumped in, using it as his lodging; so he had this kind of romantic "sleeping out of doors" as well.

月夜あかるい
舟があり
その中にねる

A bright moonlit night;
there's a boat,
I'll sleep inside.

On October 1, he struggled into Tokushima. He had gone out of his way to visit a small place called Miyajima, and looked around for the vestiges of the life of the samurai Bando Jurobe.[7] In the evening he passed through the town of Tokushima and found an inn. There were two ascetic pilgrims, and a mother and child on a pilgrimage circuit, and so a total of five people slept together like a school of various small fish on hard futons in a squalid room.

ふたたびは
わたらない橋の
ながいながい風

The prolonged breeze
of the bridge I won't cross over
a second time.

誰もいない
落葉掃
きよせてある
昼ふかく

Nobody around,
fallen leaves swept up in heaps;
late afternoon.

Making temple visits to the Onsanji and the Rikkoji, he arrived at the village of Mugi on the third, and noticed later that he had dropped his only hand towel on the hill road between Hiyorisa and Mugi. As he had rather rashly bought and eaten a potato, he did not have enough money for a hand towel. They were kind at the inn in Hiyorisa and went so far as to heat up the bath so that he was able to wipe off the fatigue of three days of travel. Having no hand towel, he thoroughly cleaned his stringed loincloth and used that instead. Sake, however, was one thing he did not do without this night. When he washed his face and then dried it over the flames of the brazier, a woman pilgrim staying at the same inn was kind enough to present him with a new hand towel.

He begged in the rainy streets, went over a number of slopes and passed by a number of beaches. The wind was terrible. His straw hat was blown off, his glasses sent flying, and he had a hard time of it; but he was pleased that an elementary school student who was passing by ran after his hat and picked it up for him. The rain fell down in buckets and he was soaked all the way through to his back. Rather than feeling that he was being struck down by Heaven, he found it extremely delightful. He could not find a place to stay in Shishikui, but as it grew dark, he struggled into Konoura and stayed at the Sanpuku-ya inn on the Tosa Road. On the fifth it was beautiful weather. He woke up at four o'clock and departed at six. He wrote almost poetically in his journal:

The road was wonderful. It was glorious.
> *It was as though I wanted to shout: Mountains! Seas! Sky!*
> *The sound of the waves, the little birds, the water—every-thing was a blessing.*
> *The sun rising from the ocean.*
> *Begging from time to time on the way.*
> *Day by day the number of pilgrims increases. There are good graves, good bridges, good shrines, good rocks and crags.*

*I had my box lunch in a wonderful place. In the shade of
a pine, on top of fallen pine needles, among the flowers of the
rock butterbur, looking down at the broad sea.*

The inn at Sakihama was an amateurishly run family inn called
the Kashio-ya. It was one person to one room and he had the posses-
sion of a lamp, so he was able to edit his haiku and journal. However,
as for the result of his begging:

3rd of the month, cash: 4 sen
rice: 4 go
4th of the month, cash: 2 sen
rice: 5 go

No matter where—even at cheap inns—lodging charges were
thirty sen, and beyond that he could not do without at least five *go*
of rice or twenty sen cash. He deeply felt the difficulty, pain and
wretchedness of begging, but without it he could neither travel nor
live. Encouraging himself, he wrote this in his journal:

*With your actual and present strength, step firmly, step firmly
over the earth and walk on.*

Provisions for his lodging at that time:

Mugi—Naga'o-ya
    Night:
        greens and boiled potato
        salted sardines
        red pepper boiled in soy sauce
    Morning:
        miso soup
        red pepper boiled in soy sauce (x)
        pickled vegetables

Konoura—Sanpuku-ya
  Night:
    boiled greens
    boiled fish
    pickled vegetables
  Morning:
    miso soup
    pickled vegetables (x)

The (x) indicated that he did not eat this item right away, but ate it later as a side dish in his box lunch. On the following day, Santoka stood on the promontory at Cape Muroto, and made a visit to the Toji temple. He looked contemplatively out at the ocean for as long as he liked.

The wave-capped ocean before me;
    but my box lunch,
miserable.

            (at Muroto)

わだつみを
まへに
わがお弁当
まづしけれど

The pines aslant,
    rough waves breaking
just as they are.

松はかたむいて
あら波の
くだけるまま

I, right here and now,
    the blue-green of the ocean
without limit.

われいまここに
海の青さの
かぎりなし

The warmth of the fallen leaves,
the brilliance of the rice
I chew thoroughly.

落葉あたたかく
かみしめる
御飯の光り

Whistling and howling,
they beat on the shore,
they beat on me.

べうべう
うちよせて
われをうつ

Santoka gazed at the expansive scenery at Cape Muroto to his heart's content then made his way to the Toji temple at the top of the mountain. This was number twenty-four of the temples issuing amulets. According to his journal:

There I was unexpectedly bitten by a small dog. It was really nothing, but it seems that the people at the temple were quite concerned. As for me, I hastily descended the mountain. To me, this was karma yet again, and I had to reflect upon myself.

He mentioned this because being bitten by a dog meant that his own Buddha's Mind was insufficient. Hadn't former wise men and ancient sages been befriended by tigers and wolves? To say nothing of small dogs. One imagines that with his self-examination, he urged himself to become "no-mind" or to return to the "child's mind."

At Tsuro he was either refused outright or people pretended not to be at home, and so was unable to take lodging; but when he went as far as the center of Muroto, finally the mistress of one of the establishments there agreed to his request to stay the night. There was not even an electric lamp in the corner of his cold room, so he knocked down a cup in town and, with his improved mood, ended up sleeping soundly.

Nevertheless, about this time Santoka began to lose self-confidence in his begging. With five *go* of rice and twelve or thirteen sen of cash in one day, a man with "not one thing" was in the red, and if this were so, he could not pursue his interests with the disposition of a beggar. More than that, lodging was becoming more difficult between Awa and Tosa.

Going to ruin,
*   bit by bit:*
*   my autumn.*

ほろほろ
ほろび行く
わたくしの秋

A handful of rice:
*   receiving one, then another;*
*   the journey, day after day.*

一握の米を
いただきいただいて
まいにちの旅

Some falling behind,
*   some going ahead;*
*   venerable pilgrims each and all.*

あとになり
さきになり
おへんろさんの
たれから

The short day
coming to an end;
how heavy this pack!

短日暮れかかる
笠のおもさよ

November 7 was a magnificently fine day. The ocean was calm, the weather glorious, and neither his style nor his showing as a beggar were bad. His inn at Hane, the Komatsu-ya, was fine. It was clean and neat, friendly, and the bath was bubbling. As he had checked in early—before three o'clock—he went out to a clear stream and washed his underwear and loincloth. The autumn water was so beautiful that in the end he washed his face, hands and feet as well. Could you not call this a mid-journey ablution? He knocked down a cup and, while enjoying the blessing of "one man, one room, one lamp," wrote down his impressions in his travel journal until late into the night:

Tomorrow, tomorrow's wind will blow.
Today, entrust yourself to today's winds.
It was a good day of happy events.
I am grateful, grateful indeed.

Yesterday I was bitten by a dog, and it made me think.
Today, a dog took kindly to me and I was troubled.
They were both similar small dogs, but . . .
late autumn rain, and I was face to face with dogs!

From there he went on to Nabari. This was the historical landmark mentioned in the *Tosa nikki* [*The Tosa Diary*][8] as the "Overnight at Nawa." The old residence of Yuki Hamaguchi[9] was in Tano. At some point when Santoka had been begging in a mountain village in Bungo, he had seen—in the midst of a cold rain—a newspaper extra about the assassination of Prime Minister Hamaguchi.

From Yasuda he went to Washoku, and stayed in Emisu. This day's earnings were extraordinary—cash: twenty-eight sen; rice: more than nine *go*. Here, too, there was a peaceful, polite, clean and neat inn.

Evening meal:
>   *somen noodles*
>   *plum ginger*

Morning meal:
>   *somen noodle soup*
>   *dried sea slug*
>   *dried plums*

Handed over one sho of uncooked rice; inside, five go of cooked rice. Insufficient funds: thirteen sen.

— When you have money, you don't think about the times when you don't have money; but when you don't have money, you think about the times when you have money. This is something painful for people like me.
— You can understand right away who is a newly married couple. Or, so say the people at my inn. Well, I imagine that's so, you know.

He arrived at the town of Kochi on November 10. He then took up residence, staying at the Yamanishi-ya inn next to the amulet temple until the fifteenth, and begging in the town. In Kochi he first went to the post office and picked up ten letters, receiving news from his friends in other parts of the country for the first time in a long time. But the letter he was waiting for—the one that contained a money order—had not come. He had lost his self-confidence in begging on the way, and had sent postcards to Rokubei and me asking us to send him a little traveling money. On top of that, he had said that he would get to Kochi around 20 November and that we were to please send the money to general delivery. So I had not sent it yet. Santoka's feet had been a little too quick. He shouldn't have had any business staying in Kochi, but every day he peeped in at the post office, then begged in the streets of the city.

Santoka went sightseeing at Kochi Castle, ate his box lunch beneath it, and then picked lice from his clothing. But the results of his begging had not been so good. On the fourteenth there was only one *go* of rice and one *sen* of cash.

In the glaring sunshine,
*   eating all the rice*
I have.

ひなたまぶしく
飯ばかりの飯を

In the bright glare
I don't
*   pick lice.*

まぶしく
しらみを
とりつくせ
ない

On the fifteenth, he was resolved:

Release attachment; do not be particular about things; do not stagnate; flow like water. Isn't this my Way?
*   Move on, move on; tomorrow make whatever departure you will; fasting is good, too; sleeping out in the open is inevitable.*

This he wrote in his journal, and on the sixteenth informed the pilgrim and the young fortuneteller staying at the same inn that he was leaving; he then departed Kochi. He begged through the village of Ina, crossed the bridge over the Niyodo River, arrived at the village of Ochi when night had completely fallen, and was refused at every inn. Slightly intoxicated, he burrowed himself into the storage house of a sawmill and went to sleep. A dog discovered him, however, and barking incessantly, would not let him sleep. A rat also appeared and was able to chew into his bag, so he had a bad time of it. Quite certainly fasting *and* sleeping out in the open could be rather trying.

My hands, my feet,
drawn in, warmly
I sleep.

わが手わが足
われに
あたたかく
寝る

The long night:
barked at by a dog
all night long.

夜の長さ
夜どほし
犬にほられて

Leaving the pilgrim highway, he walked along the Niyodo River to its mouth. In this area the natural scenery was wonderful and the people were kind. It seems also that they were sincere in their faith. The happy results of his begging were fifty-eight sen in cash and 1 *sho* 5 *go* of rice.

Resolved to sleeping out in the open, he hurried to the outskirts of the village of Kawaguchi when a voice called to him from beneath the river embankment. "Venerable pilgrim, won't you sell me some rice?"

When he went down beneath the embankment, there were two huts that perhaps you might have called houses, and the head of the household was weaving a straw basket. Apparently he had seen that the bag hung over Santoka's neck was quite heavy. He bought one *sho* of rice for forty-two sen, and then was kind enough to say, "If you like, please stay here overnight; it's cramped and dirty, but better than sleeping out in the open." Santoka probably thought something like, "When crossing a river, any boat will do," and quickly decided to stay. It was a large family of husband and wife, six children, an old man, a cow, three cats and seven or eight chickens. Simple straw mats had been placed on the wooden planking. There were neither enough *chawan* bowls nor enough futons, so it was pretty wretched. Nevertheless, with the warm solicitude of the husband and wife, he felt an affection just like that of relatives. They all surrounded one large pot and received a bellyful of hot soup.

Santoka was making himself comfortable in warmhearted lodgings for the first time in quite a while. Later, he went off to town and, emptying what little he had in his purse, bought sake for the old man and the husband, and cheap sweets for the wife and children. Tired, drunk, and with the sound of the river shallows not too far away, he fell into a deep sleep.

When the sun came up, the husband said, "Venerable pilgrim, I'm going to teach you something good. About five miles [eight kilometers] into the interior from here, there's a village called Ikegawa. The scenery is beautiful, and I think you will receive many alms. Won't you go and give it a try? Then why don't you come back here and stay one more night?"

Santoka did according to what he had been told, turned off the Matsuyama Highway, and went to Ikegawa. And weren't the elemen-

tary students who crossed his path bowing politely to him one by one? He begged from nine o'clock until noon, the result of which was seventy-nine sen cash and 1 *sho* 3 *go* of rice—more, he felt, than he deserved. And more than that: the beauty of the ravines, the beauty of the mountains and rivers. On the way back to Kawaguchi he leisurely moved his bowels in the fields and then in the mountains, all the while gazing with appreciation at the beauty of nature in late fall to his heart's content.

It was three o'clock in the afternoon when he reached his charitable lodging. Going down to the river, he cleaned both body and mind, and then sucked down a cup. The sun went down behind the mountain ridges early. Tonight the wife went all out and made a delicious vegetarian meal. Santoka pressed his palms together in thanks, and ate up.

> *Evening meal:*
> > *leek fish salad*
> > *ground daikon*
> > *soup with greens*
> > *pickles*
>
> *Morning meal:*
> > *dark miso soup*
> > *boiled beans*
> > *vegetables boiled in soy sauce.*

He slept late and got up at eight o'clock. With that, everyone said farewell. Truly it was "One meeting in one lifetime."[10] The Niyodo River became more and more beautiful. He crossed the Ryokoku Bridge[11] and entered the old province of Iyo. In Nishinotani and Ochide he was refused at every lodging that could be called that name. It was cold, and when he inevitably knocked down a cup in Ochide, the man of the shop felt sorry for him and told him about a small temple called the Taishido at the top of the hill just outside of town. When he went to look, there was a door and matting spread out on the floor, and he decided to spend the night. All throughout the long autumn night he heard the sound of the valley stream.

Water crashing over crags,
    filling a green pool;
    a ceremonial cleansing.

岩ばしる水が
たたへし青さ
みそぎする

Placing the daytime moon,
    there,
    on keen-edged mountains.

山のするどさ
そこに
昼月をおく

Sleeping or waking,
    a long night;
    the sound of the shallows.

寝ても
覚めても
夜がながい
瀬の音

All the streams
    becoming waterfalls;
    deep autumn.

水はみんな
滝となり
秋ふかし

Morning at the Taishido was cold, and a mist covered the entire area. "Tosa was warm, Iyo is cold," he thought. The red leaves of a cherry tree were scattered here and there in front of the temple. When he lit incense, chanted a sutra and said a silent prayer, an old man who seemed to be the caretaker of the temple came up for a visit and asked him a number of things. He said he'd been having trouble with people stealing the donation money, and left.

Santoka headed in the direction of Kuma and started to beg. He received a number of warm steamed potatoes from an old lady

coming from a house by the side of the road. Since, in fact, he had
not eaten breakfast, he sat down on a rock facing the beautiful au-
tumn leaves and the pure scenery of a waterfall, pressed his palms
together in gratitude, and had a truly belly-filling feast. Even with
that, half of the potatoes still remained, so he put them in his bag
for lunch. The landscape in the area of the Gosanto Bridge, with its
huge rocks and blue-green water, was enough to make him imagine
the famous Omogo Ravine farther into the interior.

Rocks, huge rocks,
on all sides;
fall colors on the vines.

岩が大きな岩が
いちめん
蔦紅葉

On November 20, when he straggled into Kuma, the autumn
sun had already gone down all the way.

They cheerfully let him stay at the pilgrims' lodging beneath the
Daihoji temple. There were fourteen or fifteen guests and it was
quite bustling, but there were a lot of rooms, they were clean and
neat, and the middle-aged lady who ran the place was rather kind
and capable. Santoka was able to check into a warm inn for the first
time since he had left Kochi five days before. The bath was bubbling,
too, and he was able to wash off the grime of travel for the first time
in a long time. Sharing the same room with him was a pilgrim who
seemed to be a very serious ascetic practitioner and who offered him
a large piece of mochi rice cake. He chewed it quite heartily and
found it had the taste of back-country mochi.

Santoka handed over the fee of thirty sen and five *go* of rice to the
lady of the establishment, gave a sigh of relief, and with the rest of
his money knocked down two cups of sake in town. He slept quite
soundly until midnight when he suddenly woke up, and so, lying
on his stomach under a dim electric light, continued to write in his
journal.

When he woke up early the next morning, the ascetic pilgrim

once again gave him some mochi. The lady of the house, saying that it was her usual custom, gave Santoka a donation of one sen.

Morning visit to the temple,
myself, alone;
scattered ginkgo nuts.

朝まいりは
わたくし一人の
銀杏ちりしく

He left this poem at the Daihoji, and hurried on the road to Matsuyama. The mist was thick right up to the Misaka Pass. When he walked over the pass and the mist cleared, there was a pilgrim's road with no one on it where the fallen leaves lay scattered, while still more continued blanketing those beneath them. The red leaves were all the more beautiful when a whistling autumn wind blew through. How happy he was to shuffle through the autumn leaves.

Walking,
still walking;
the autumn wind.

秋風
あるいても
あるいても

Until, coming to a certain sunny place, he plopped down on the dry fallen leaves, crossing his legs tailor-style. Ever since morning his back had itched uncomfortably. When he took off his kimono and looked, weren't those lice all over him?

How warm,
the lice
I pick.

なんとあたたかな
しらみをとる

Translator's Notes

1. Ichijun Takahashi is the pen name of Hajime Takashi, first mentioned on page 238.

2. This is a journey set out for believers of the esoteric Shingon sect of Buddhism founded in Japan by Kukai in the early ninth century. The entire distance of the pilgrimage is about seven hundred miles (1126 km), and the pilgrim visits eighty-eight designated temples, from each of which he or she collects an amulet. It is said that about one hundred thousand pilgrims complete this route every year.

3. Shurindo Nomura (1893–1918): born in Matsuyama; began writing tanka and haiku as a high school student. Founded the haiku association, *Izayoi Ginsha*. Died of influenza. Nomura had also participated in the Shikoku pilgrimage. One of his poems:

    > Cold clouds
    >> in every direction
    >> over moonlit fields.

4. A burnt offering of firewood or grain to an esoteric Buddhist deity in order to either stop calamity or increase merit. The fire symbolizes the wisdom that destroys evil passions and ignorance.

5. Bokusui Wakayama (1885–1928): a tanka poet-wanderer who loved to drink and travel. The poem referred to here goes:

    > How many mountains and rivers to cross,
    >> to a country where loneliness ends?
    > Today, again, I travel.

    > (Trans. by Burton Watson,
    > *From the Country of Eight Islands*)

6. A Shikoku pilgrimage in miniature.

7. Famous for allowing himself to be executed for a crime he didn't commit to preserve the reputation of his master.

8. *Tosa nikki* (土佐日記): a diary written in prose and poetry by Ki no Tsurayuki in 935 AD concerning his leave-taking of Tosa Province after serving as governor there. One of the classics of early Japanese literature.

9. Also called Osachi Hamaguchi (1870–1931): Japanese politician; Prime Minister from 1929. Accused by extremists of betraying Japan's military interests and shot at a Tokyo railroad station in November, 1930. Died of his wounds the following year.

10. 一期一会: a saying used in Zen and tea ceremony urging us to see each meeting with others as the only one of its kind at that particular time and place.
11. Ryokoku Bridge (両国の橋): the bridge between the two old provinces of Iyo and Tosa.

CHAPTER 9

The Isso-an at Matsuyama

After making the forty-sixth or forty-seventh temple visit, Santoka arrived at Morimatsu, and from there took a small train to Matsuyama. By the time he returned—sort of tumbling along from Tachibana into his friend Masa'ichi Fujioka's place in Dogo Minami—it was six o'clock.

How warmly he must have been received by the entire Fujioka household. When you think about it, this had been a long journey of over forty days. For a physical body that was now at the age of fifty-eight, a journey of begging must have been trying. In Awa and Tosa he had had bone-splitting thoughts. But the Fujioka family embraced his travel-worn body with great sympathy for the five days up to the twenty-seventh.

Unrestrained, I drank, ate, slept, got up, cleared up, got cloudy, got drunk and sobered up as autumn went on.

During those five days he wrote only this in his journal and composed no haiku. Other than that, it was enough for him to commute every day to the hot springs and recuperate.

From the evening of the twenty-seventh to December 15, they had him stay at the Chikuzen-ya inn in the hot-springs area of Dogo. Ichijun was traveling to Taiwan on school business, and he arranged to pay Santoka's bill on his return. Thus the days passed vaguely with one bath and one cup of sake. He was so free from care that he did not compose very many haiku. But even though he appeared to be simply playing around without a worry, this was the Santoka of strict self-criticism, self-reflection and repentance, and he was not just being spoiled with kindness. He wrote this sort of thing concerning the Chikuzen-ya, praising it as a fine lodging:

> This was truly a fine inn, and a fine lady of the house. In the nearly twenty days I stayed there, I think this inn was the one, of all the pilgrims' lodgings on my religious tour of Shikoku, where I felt most at home. (It is true that the lodging cost forty sen, ten sen higher than other places, but the inns at Dogo were generally like that. Even so, the cost of three meals a day was sixty-five to seventy sen.) The sheets were white and clean, and the living room and lavatory were clean too. The meals, too, were good. The different kinds of fish, the vegetables, the miso soup and the pickles were all prepared with great expertise. The master of the establishment was not particularly good-natured it seemed, but his wife was both well-spoken and skillful with her hands, and was rather a capable person.

During that time, Ichijun and Fujioka-san were looking for a hermitage for Santoka. At first they discovered a perfectly suitable house on the earthen dike along the Ishite River, but the surroundings were no good. They then went around the Johoku neighborhood, inquiring from temple to temple, and at the Miyukidera, the head priest Kuroda said that outside the gate and down to the left there was an outbuilding which they would find suitable for one man's living quarters if they just took a look inside. There was a four-and-a-half-mat tatami room, and farther in, one with six tatami mats, as well as a small cupboard. The small earthen-floored entranceway continued along the six-tatami-mat room to a sort of kitchen, and there was an open verandah on the side facing the east. Going around to the right there were facilities for a lavatory. Ichijun and his friends brought out sweeping and cleaning utensils, swept and wiped down the place, repaired the sliding paper doors, and somehow made it livable for a single person. The rent of 1.50 yen a month, the futon, the desk, the brazier, the pot, the portable stove, the bucket, the *chawan* bowl, the chopsticks and even the rice, soy sauce and salt were kindly provided by Ichijun.

On December 15, 1939, spoiled by the compassion of my friends in Matsuyama and following my karma, it was arranged that I would take up a residence, either for the time being or for the rest of my life. Thanks to the great kindness of Ichijun (from the beginning beyond that of a relative), I will move from the inn in Dogo to a new home at Mount Miyuki. This new home is on elevated ground and is quite tranquil. The mountain is beautiful, the sand pure, the water sweet, and the people not bad, it seems. For an old wanderer like myself, it is a dwelling beyond my portion. It is too good, but I will meekly receive it and go in. The Matsuyama "Furai-kyo" is much more beautiful than the one in Yamaguchi, and is nice and warm.

Settled down,
　　it seems ready to die:
　withered grass.

枯死おちついて
るねるそうな草

Since growing old, he could not help feeling strongly that dying was more difficult than living. Since the previous spring Santoka had felt in both body and mind that the shadow of death was pressing in on him. He wanted himself to be like a wart. He himself could be patient if he became like a cancer or a wen, but he would then be a bother to other people. For him, the very first taboo was becoming a nuisance. Nevertheless, when you think about it, even a wart becomes troublesome for one and all. And if he were to become ill with some drawn-out malignant disease, what then? Wouldn't he be a real nuisance to others? There were days when he wondered if he wouldn't be able to fall down and disappear from the world without anybody knowing it. Still, the solitary Santoka was dogged by the worry that it would not be like that. Thus, when he felt death crowding in, how was it that all things existing in this world appeared to be all the more beautiful?

手にのせて
柿のすがたの
ほれぼれ赤く

Set in my hand,
        the shape of the persimmon:
fascinatingly red.

ゆう焼けの
うつくしさは
老をなげくで
もなく

The beauty of the evening glow;
        lamenting my old age?
    Not even.

一人正月の
餅も酒も
ありそして

All alone,
        I've got New Year's mochi and sake,
    so...

Ten days after the end of New Year's Santoka went on a journey, visiting some very dear old friends, to report on aspects of his Shikoku pilgrimage and his Matsuyama hermitage. He first called on Rokubei in Itoda in Kyushu; then to Shimonoseki to call on Keinosuke Chika-ki; getting off the train at Hofu, he visited the grave of his mother; in Tokuyama he stayed with Hakusen; then he came to my place in Hiroshima. Sitting across from each other at the brazier in the floor well, we drank sake and talked late into the night, but the stories were unending: being struck by the rich warmheartedness of the people of Matsuyama, the beauty of the landscape, the hermitage blessed with a fine location where he was determined to die. Then he asked me to please pick a name for the hermitage. I remembered a line of Santoka's that went, "Twisting a single stalk of grass and changing it into a sixteen-foot Buddha[1] is not bad, but for me, one leaf of grass is sufficient. Sufficiency is where my foolishness sits peacefully," and said, "How about the 'One-Grass Hut?'"[2] The "One-Grass Hut" was all right, but if you thought that it imitated Bodhidharma's one leaf of a reed,[3] it had the stink of Zen. A single leaf at the mouth of a water pipe[4] was also a bit too much. As for the "one leaf," it was reminiscent of the Issoitei, or "One-Grass Mansion" on the Nishi River in Kyoto, so we decided after all on the "One-Grass Hut," the Isso-an.

Our talk went on to a public edition of *Somokuto* (The Pagoda of Grasses and Trees). When I requested Saito-sensei in Tokyo to publish a selection of the haiku from *Hachinoko* [The Begging Bowl] and the seven collections of Santoka's verses written when he was at the Gochu-an, he responded that the publishing house Yagumo Shorin would take on the project. I told Santoka that when he returned to his hermitage, he should write down the haiku of this collection in manuscript form and send it to me, and that I would write a postscript and send it all on to Tokyo. Santoka was happy down to the very bottom of his heart. He then requested me to think up a name, this time for this collection of haiku. We decided that the name of one of the collections within this anthology—*Somokuto*—was splendid, and would be good for the entire work. Seeing that Santoka seemed to feel that death was pressing in on him, I felt gratitude for Saito-sensei's warmheartedness, and was aware of a secret tension in my heart that this affair had to be expedited.

When Santoka returned from Hiroshima, he settled in at the Isso-an all the more in both body and mind.

Tidying up everything around me; 　　*on the ridge of the distant mountains,* *snow.*	身のまわり かたづけて 遠く山なみの雪

Collecting rainwater, 　　*a full bucket today;* 　　*just enough.*	雨をためて バケツ一杯の 今日は事足る

My hermitage crouches down in the foothills of Mount Miyuki, and is embraced by a shrine and a temple. When you get old, it tends to be easy to lose interest in things, and the simplicity of one person, one blade of grass is sufficient. In the end, there is nothing but for my Way to be pierced through with my foolishness.

While the Isso-an was within the temple compound of the Miyukidera, on the east it faced the shrine for the war dead; to the rear of the hut on the west, but set off by a thicket of bamboo, was the Ryutaiji temple. To the south was the undistinguished house of his only neighbors, the elderly mother and younger sister of Daisuke Ito, a well-known movie director. The two women lived there quite peacefully and did various kind things for him as neighboring families might. Quite naturally, the chief priest of the Miyukidera, Abbot Kuroda and his wife were the kind of people who would do things like quietly bring him a plate of boiled spinach. Just north of the hermitage was a huge ginkgo tree which, standing opposite to a large podocarpus tree at the temple entrance, gave a massive sense to the scenery of the compound. The ground of this area was rocks and boulders so that wells were not thoughtlessly dug, and he would have to go about thirty yards (twenty-seven meters) from his gate carrying a bucket to draw water. But for the man who lived as "one man, one blade of grass," there were also days when he could collect a bucketful of rainwater and, if he used it carefully, would not have to draw water at all.

In the past
    and days ahead,
        snow shining.

こしかた
ゆくすえ雪
あかりする

Placing his hands on the small brazier and gazing intently about his hermitage, Santoka smoked a cigarette in a tobacco pipe. At some point he had started the habit of picking up cigarette butts no longer than an inch at the side of the road, and smoking them by stuffing them into the end of his tobacco pipe. In the tiny Buddhist altar was placed a figure of the bodhisattva Kannon as well as his mother's mortuary tablet. On the wall of the four-and-a-half-mat tatami room was affixed a sheet of paper with the two kanji characters for "simplicity" (簡素) written by Toson Shimazaki [5] that I had sent to him. On his desk in a vase for a single flower was a blooming narcissus facing out towards him. It was a lonely one-man, one-grass hut, but how peaceful it must have been, imbued with the feeling of "returning home and sitting quietly." If you thought in detail about the fifteen years since he had left the world and become a priest, there was Ho'onji temple in Kumamoto, the Mitori Kannon temple, the Gochu-an at Ogori, the Furai-kyo at Yuda, and then the Isso-an. And he had also done a good amount of traveling. Now once again he had been blessed by his karma to be the master of a hermitage, and he had gone and come like the flow of water consuming that karma. To the man who had neither wife nor child, the hermitage was by no means a house, but only a temporary dwelling between one long journey and the next. And that was all right. Santoka himself wanly affirmed this and lit up another cigarette.

But where would he drift to this time? He had gone to all the places in Japan he had wished to travel to, and had met all the people he had thought about going to meet. When he thought about it, this One-Grass Hut was the final dwelling at the end of a long journey. There was no other place to go.

In March, I came to Matsuyama on government business for a full week of lectures to a group of male and female communications employees from Ehime and Kagawa provinces; this was at the Taionji temple in Kawagoe, not far from the Isso-an. First I went and took a look for a moment at the Isso-an, then finished my work; after that, two of us—Kochi-san and I—called in at the hermitage. Ichijun, Fujioka, Teikakotsu and others also came, and it was truly one lively evening. Afterwards, everyone went together to a hot spring in Dogo. After drinking, Santoka seemed a little uncomfortable in the hot water, but he was happy because he loved hot springs.

Hot springs and Santoka. They say that solitary people love blazing fires and hot springs, and it was because there were hot springs in those places that his heart was drawn to Ureshino in Saga, and Kawatana in Nagato. Ogori and Yuda were both close to hot springs. The Isso-an, too, was a twenty minute walk to Dogo, and he often went to the cheapest bath there, the Sagi no Yu.

The excellence of a morning bath;
　　　silently I wait
　　my turn.

朝湯のよろしさ
もくもくとして
順番を待つ

I wait my turn
　　　at the overflowing
　　water.

あふれくる
湯へ
順番を待つ

Submerged
　　　in the hot spring,
　　laughing faces.

ずんぶり
温泉のなかの
顔と顔笑ふ

The morning bath bubbling thick and fast.
　　And right in the middle?
　　Me!

朝湯
こんこんあふれる
まんなかのわたし

The loneliness of being by myself
soaked in the hot spring;
an autumn night.

一人のさみしさが
温泉にひたりて
秋の夜

All of these and others were haiku from the Dogo hot springs. Matsuyama was not as convenient as Ogori for trains, and so very few of his friends-in-haiku in other parts of the country came to visit; but as soon as they understood that Santoka had settled down at the Isso-an, a great number of letters and postcards arrived. Packages came with special local products such as pickles from Kyoto, seaweed from Izu Shimoda, and fermented soy beans from Hamamatsu. Then there was his only son Ken, who, after graduating as a specialist in mining in Akita, was employed at a coal mine in northern Kyushu, and then proceeded to faraway Manchuria to be chief engineer at the coal mine in Mishan. During the Ogori period, he used to send Santoka ten yen every month for spending money, but he now increased that to fifteen yen a month. According to the mail, Ken now had a child, and Santoka at last had become a grandfather.

So happy to be born;
closing his hands,
opening his hands.

生まれてうれしく
掌を握ったり
ひらいたり

His poetry collection, *Somokuto* (The Pagoda of Grasses and Trees), was finally published in May. It was a print run of seven hundred copies, and instead of royalties, the publisher, Yagumo Shorin, sent Santoka thirty-five copies. The binding, the printing, the paper—

all were good. It had been printed on pure Japanese handmade paper, was three poems to the page—characteristic of the poetry collections at that time—was elegant and neat, and the thirty-five books were taken by courier to the Isso-an. Santoka presented them to those who deserved a complimentary copy, and sold them to those who would buy them. That was enough to buy sake, but for travel expenses he would again have to cross the sea.

First he brought a copy of *Somokuto* to my place in Hiroshima, although I had already received one sent from Tokyo. Together with Sadao Goto from Bunri University, we dipped into some sake to congratulate this publication and had a good time. I had seen various expressions of Santoka's happiness, but had never seen him so happy right to the bottom of his heart. He expressed his gratitude to Yagumo and Saito-sensei over and over again. If you thought about it and considered the contents, Santoka had sacrificed his entire life just in order to bring this one volume of poems together—this according to Kotaro Takamura's school.[6] And it is a fact that this volume was the most beloved form in which Santoka would appear in the world.

That night, Santoka talked on:

From around February, the haiku gathering called the Persimmon Club was born. The members gather once every month at the Isso-an. It's formed of kindred spirits like Ichijun, Issojo, Teikakotsu, Chiedajo, Musui and Warai. I wake up every day at four o'clock in the morning, clean and sweep the house inside and out, and chant the sutras. Then I make a visit to the shrine for the war dead. For some one as lackadaisical as me, I enjoy a surprisingly reserved life. Abbot Gyokuho at the Ishitedera temple is quite a talker and often comes by, inviting me for sake and conversing for a long time. Goods are cheap on the Iyo Road, spring has come early, and the new green leaves are beautiful. When I entered this hermitage, my very first verse was:

Settled down,
        it seems ready to die:
    withered grass.

おちついて
死ねそうな草
枯るる

and nothing has changed in my mental state. But recently it might be modified to:

Settled down,
        it seems ready to die:
    the sprouting grass.

おちついて
死ねそうな草も
萌ゆる

And he went on like this in his usual toothless quick speech.

In this way he continued on his journey, presenting copies of *Somokuto* from Hiroshima to Tokuyama, and on to Hofu, Ogori, Kawatana, Chofu, Kitakyushu and Itoda. In Hofu he offered one at his mother's grave, and in Kawatana presented a copy to Old Man Kinoshita. Even in such places as these, they were able to feel the passing texture of Santoka's sincerity. It was the same, whether at the Gochu-an, the Isso-an or my place, even just for drinking sake. We never once saw Santoka simply sitting at ease. He would always sit up properly with his back inclined slightly forward, and when he was cold he would bundle up in his vest. He was the true picture of an old man. With age, the goatee on his chin added a luminous patina. As for his teeth, the very last one fell out at the Isso-an, and he chewed everything he ate with his gums. When he stayed at the house of the dentist Futanosuke Shibata, during his journey through Kyushu, he was offered an entire set of false teeth; but for Santoka, it was fine to go on just as nature would have it. He said he would entrust himself to "whatever would be would be," and went on just as he was.

When he returned from Kyushu, the early summer in Matsuyama gradually grew warmer. His hermitage faced due east and was approached only by easterly winds. The north, west and south were walled in, and in the summer the sun burned down from early in the morning and it was hot. This caused him to become a bit run-down. Moreover, the Isso-an was close to a cemetery and was adjacent to a bamboo thicket, so there were a lot of mosquitoes. Even in the afternoon, the mosquitoes from the thicket came inside, so he hung up mosquito netting and there were times when he ate his meals inside the netting. Santoka, principled even when alone, felt that even this was a transgression of the Buddhist precepts.

Silently,
　　inside mosquito netting,
　eating my rice alone.

もくもく
蚊帳のうち
ひとり
飯喰う

The evening glow,
　　right into the mosquito netting;
　I sleep alone.

蚊帳の中まで
夕焼けの
一人寝ている

One night he got falling-down drunk and collapsed right on the Matsuyama Highway. A large number of people gathered, so when his neighbor Ito-san passed by and saw that it was Santoka, he picked him up and returned him home. Santoka admonished himself strictly for such a thing:

In the middle of a war in which the entire country is involved, upright Santoka himself is doing nothing but writing trivial haiku and, even more, drowning himself in sake and being a nuisance to others. Well now, Santoka, get a hold of yourself! Wouldn't that be the right thing to do?

And to this sort of self-condemnation, he began fasting.

The light of the moon
*   deeply penetrating*
* my empty stomach.*

月のひかりの
すき腹ふかく
しみと
ほるなり

Drinking water every day,
*   only water clearing up*
* my body entire.*

まいにち水を飲み
水ばかりの
身ぬち澄みわたる

Should I, should I, should I, should I? [7]
*   At last going out*
* To buy rice.*

かなかな
かなかな
やうやく
米買ひに

Santoka borrowed one yen from Ichijun's wife and then went off to buy rice without much resolution. He had enough money to buy rice at two *sho* of mixed rice for eighty-two sen. The priest's wife at the next-door Miyukidera temple was sent by her husband to buy their allotment of rice and, feeling sorry for Santoka, always asked him to accompany her to pick it up, but on days when he had no money, even that request could not be made.

The women around Santoka at the Isso-an were all gentle and kind to him—his two neighbors, needless to say; and Ichijun's wife; Teikakotsu's wife, Chiedajo Murase; and Fusa Futagami and her mother. They were all somehow worried about this solitary man. Sadao Goto was kind enough to come from Hiroshima during his vacation. He gave Santoka fifteen yen for spending money, they spent three or four days in the city together sightseeing, and then visited a hot spring. After establishing himself at the Isso-an, Santo-ka, strangely enough, became rather affectionate with people. Every time he met with someone, it seems as though he felt that this was a meeting that would never occur again.

On August 3, he again only drank water and tea for the entire day. This was also because he had no food, but basically because Santoka, who was strict with self-criticism, wanted to live with restraint today, all day at least, cleansing his blood and cleansing his mind. One made one's whole life perfect by perfecting each thought, each instant, moment by moment.

As he intently read and savored the *Mumonkan*,[8] he tried to confine himself within his very self and contemplate that self as well.

It was a hot, hot day, but towards evening it rained just a little and cooled off. He forgot about his empty stomach, raised his seemingly transparent body, sat down to his desk, and picked up his pen.

> *I'm troubled by my life day by day. I send off yesterday or greet today either eating or not eating. It will be like this tomorrow, too, perhaps—no, probably until the day I die.*
>
> *But I write haiku every day and every night. Even if I don't drink or eat, I do not neglect writing haiku. To say this in a different way, I'm able to write haiku even if my stomach is empty. The poems in my heart bubble up and overflow like a current of water. To me, living is writing haiku. Writing haiku is none other than living.*[9]

There are many people in the world who have an interest in writing haiku to the extent that they can add some charm to their lives. Also, there are many people who are happy with it as a hobby. Again, there are certain people who write haiku in order to eat, and people who sell *tanzaku* poem cards[10] as well. Santoka's haiku quite definitely did not have those secondary and tertiary significances. Writing haiku is living. This is its first significance.

> *Poverty is not something to be proud of, but neither is it so much something for self-deprecation. In the same way that*

*rich people should not be haughty, we should absolutely be
ashamed to think of ourselves as base or disgraceful because of
our poverty.*

*We must be polished and illuminated by our poverty. To
equate poverty with stupidity is characteristic of small-minded
people.*

Santoka's poverty was an honorable poverty.

*The destitute life:
    the flow
    of water.*

とぼしいくらしの、
水のながるる

*It's better to throw things away than to become attached to
them. It is worse to say too much than not to say enough. Rat-
tling on is above all something to avoid. "Many words means
little content" is a wise saying.*

While brushing away a mosquito, he sat down properly and con-
tinued to write:

I have two wishes.

*One is that I can accomplish writing haiku that are truly my
own. The other, then, is that I die a sudden death. Not to suffer
for a long time even when sick, or to trouble anyone with this
or that, would be to accomplish a blessed death. I believe that
I will pass away without difficulty, either from a heart attack or
a cerebral hemorrhage.*

This is recorded in his journal, and he spoke of the same thing
to people often, but I have reaffirmed it here.

For me, dying any time is all right. I continually have the frame of mind that I could die at any time without regret.

It is regretful, however, that I have not made arrangements for this.

No talent and incompetent, small-minded and self-indulgent, a procrastinator yet honest. I am ashamed to harbor every possible inconsistency, but suppose I could not have been otherwise.

Return to that fundamental foolishness and protect it.

Thoughtfully planting *the seed of a tree* *that will someday die.*	いつ死ねる 木の実は 捲いておく

August 8 is the beginning of fall. By four-thirty he had already visited the shrine for the war dead and returned home. He had gone without breakfast, and just sipped a cup of salty plum tea. He felt that both body and mind were spotless. He had no more than one serving of foreign rice. He divided that—all that he had—for the afternoon and evening, and ate it then.

He stayed shut up in his hermitage all day long, appreciating the *Mumonkan*[8] and writing haiku, and his joy at concentrating on the single track of his inability and talentlessness allowed him to forget his empty stomach.

Before dawn on the following day he heard the clear-toned cicadas for the first time that year. He loved those cicadas whose *kana kana kana kana* resonated to the bottom of his heart. Today, too, he fasted and sipped a cup of salty plum tea. He peered at the *Mumonkan* with the frame of mind that he could die any time, that life and death were the same. After a while he stood up from where he sat alone in introspection, shut up inside of himself. He was free of obstacles and wandering without restraint. He whimsically went to town, stopped in at the Donguri Hermitage, but the master of the place, Ichijun, was not there. He was given an offering of somen noodles from Issojo. Excellent! Excellent![11] He noisily slurped up a second bowl as though it were quite delicious. And how delicious it was!

He then stepped out to visit Teikakotsu Murase's residence, but here too, the master was not at home, and only Chiedajo was there alone. He accepted a delicious lunch without hesitation and, when he by chance looked at the desk, hadn't some colored Tanabata festival[12] *tanzaku* poem cards been placed on it? Santoka was reminded of the days of his youth and, just in that frame of mind, picked up a brush and easily wrote down improvised haiku that just floated up to his mind.

The whispering of the rice plant leaves, too,
the sound of water
of the Land of Abundant Rice.[13]

稲の葉ずれも
瑞穂の国の
水の音

If there is nothing to eat,
the calm,
cool water.

食べるものが
なければ
ないで
涼しい水

Tanabata's
pitiful rain
falling.

七夕の
いぢらしい
雨ふる

Gazing up,
it looks like it's going to clear:
the Tanabata sky.

仰いで
晴れさうな
七夕の空

Tanabata.

Is rain falling
from the Milky Way?

七夕の
天の川より
降るか

He returned to his hermitage feeling good, but when he thought it over again, there were haiku he felt just wouldn't do the way they were. He quickly sent a postcard to Chiedajo with the revised haiku.

Looking up with a "Hey! Clear up!"
It seems like it's going to clear:
the Tanabata sky.

晴れよと
仰げば
晴れさうな
七夕の空

From Tanabata's
Milky Way,
scattered rain?

七夕の
天の川より
こぼるる雨
か

August 14. He got up at four o'clock and sat alone. Today he had only two *go* of barley. This would have to be one day's provisions. The war had become severe, and matches were all sold out no matter what shop he went to. Recently there were very few people who threw away cigarette butts. Just when he was drinking his salty plum tea and boiling up the barley, Ichijun came by after some absence. He said that he had taken a trip from the San'in area to Tokyo; said that in Tokyo he had visited the writer Genjiro Yoshida. He didn't bring a souvenir, so he left him some money as compensation. Santoka speedily went off to the hot springs at Dogo that evening, then had one bath and one cup of sake, and that would have been just fine. But then there was another cup, and again and again another, so that it turned out badly: he got sloppily and totteringly drunk.

In any event, he went to the Han'ya bath for the first time in a long time, but after that got drunker still and everything started to spin around quickly. In the hot weather he fell right down on the ridge between the rice paddies, something for which he berated himself.

The next day, two hundred volumes of his haiku collection, *Kara-su* [Crows],[14] that I had prepared, arrived. The book was in the style of a sutra folding book, and made up so that Santoka's *Karasu* was on the face side while Rokubei's *Suzume* [Sparrows][15] was on the back. Included in a letter was five yen for postage to send them around.

With the five yen, he paid back the money he had borrowed from the priest at the Miyukidera temple, and then went shopping.

82 sen: 2 sho of mixed rice
5 sen: stamps
7 sen: 1 go of soy sauce
5 sen: 1 cucumber
10 sen: a little bit of dried sea slug.

As he returned home, he was aware of the remaining one sen in his purse, and how beautiful the moon was shining over the shrine precincts on the twelfth day of the old Bon festival.[16]

On the evening of the sixteenth, he went to a meeting of the Persimmon Club at Teikakotsu's residence. There were eight of them: Ichijun, Teikakotsu, Warai, Gesson, Ryujo, Chiedajo and Fusa. The haiku that came out of this meeting were not very good, but Santoka was pleased at their earnestness.

Santoka's Obon inside the Isso-an:

A tomato in the palm of my hand;
to the Buddha,
to my father and mother.

トマトを掌に、
みほとけのまへに
ちちははのまへに

Like here,
like elsewhere:
a moonlit night of Obon.

うちのような
よそのような
お盆の月夜

After the moonlit night of Obon
deepens,
coming footsteps.

盆の月夜の
更けてから
まいる足音

Obon's rice
cooked
soft and plump.

お盆の御飯
ふっくら
炊けた

A solitary person's Obon is lonely, huh, he thought.

During this time he thought a lot about poverty. Poverty is painful, but borrowing money doubles that pain. Poverty is not necessarily something one should be ashamed about, but it is shameful if your poverty goes all the way to your heart. For Santoka, in the midst of poverty it was important not to lose one's standards, not to borrow money, not to be attached to the past, and to have no hopes for the future. Then to feel gratitude for having been given life one day after another, then to enjoy life—these he determined to be the secrets of living in the Isso-an. As to his religious outlook, he himself did not believe in the next world. He had completely let go of the past, and so believed intently in the present. The present moment—he would use up his entire body and entire mind that were made to complete the eternal now. Moreover, he believed in the universal spirit but denied the individual soul. The individual became separated from the whole, but then once again was united with it. Life was a summoning, death was a return. To such thoughts he nodded his head in approval.

In September, morning and night became autumnal.

Potato gruel—
　　its heat and savor, too;
autumn has come.

芋粥の
あつさ
うまさも
秋となった

No sake;
　　gazing intently
　　at the moon.

酒はない
月しみじみ
観ており

For breakfast,
　　cool potatoes,
three or four.

朝げは
すずしい
ぢやが芋
三つ四つ

No money,
　　no possessions, no teeth,
alone.

銭がない
物がない
歯がない 一人

He visited the Gyokuto temple on Mount Nishi, visited Hekigo-do's grave, went on to the next mountain and visited the army cemetery. Then he took the road between the rice fields and visited the stone monument engraved with a haiku to the poet Shiki in Yodo.

Bush clover,
　　beginning to bloom intimately
　　at the engraved stone.

句碑へ
したしく萩の
咲き染めている

The flowers of the bush clover were blooming in the foothills around the Miyukidera temple, and the spider lilies were in abundance, as might be expected of spider lilies.[17] Santoka got up early and his back was cold. He took out his old vest and put it on. The priest's wife put an equinox dumpling on a plate and brought it to him. The friendship and savor of the goodwill of one's neighbors, the compassion of people, pierced him through.

Since the money order for the haiku collection had come the day before, he went to town for the first time in a long while and knocked down one cup, then two, no, three. He soaked himself in a hot spring, then even got a haircut and started to feel good. He visited Masa'ichi and Ichijun as he hadn't for a while, and also talked leisurely with Musui and Warai. Then he returned money to various people and went shopping. As he rarely went shopping, he wrote the items down one by one in his journal.

> *2 yen: repayment to the abbot*
> *8 sen: ginger*
> *20 sen: bread*
> *2 yen: rice*
> *20 sen: mochi rice cake*
> *2.40 yen: payment for the newspaper*
> *2.40 yen: sake*
> *15 sen: miso*
> *30 sen: tobacco*
> *10 sen soap*
> *42 sen: udon noodles*
> *52 sen: pressed barley*
> *8 sen: matches*
> *24 sen: soy sauce*

Translator's Notes

1. Short for *ichijo rokushaku* (一丈六尺), a measurement of about 16 ft. (5 m). The standard size of a transformed Buddha (*Dictionary of Japanese Buddhism*). The word "transformed" refers to Buddha's earthly mode.

2. In Japanese, *isso-an* (一草庵).

3. Bodhidharma (Daruma in Japanese) is said to have left the Chinese court, and crossed the Yangtse River on one leaf of a reed.

4. Presumably a common literary or Zen reference. The whole point of this conversation is to somehow give Santoka's hut a Zen or poetic name while still avoiding the "stink of Zen."

5. Toson Shimazaki (1872–1943): famous writer of novels, including *Yoake-mae* (*Before the Dawn*, 1935), some of which were set to film.

6. Kotaro Takamura (1883–1956): poet and sculptor. After studying in France, applied Western aesthetics to Japanese poetry and sculpture. His poetry was almost all in free verse.

7. In Japanese "*Kana, kana, kana, kana.*" The particle *kana* can indicate hesitation or indecision, but the word *kanakana* also means *higurashi*, or green-colored cicada, and no doubt imitates its constant cry. Was Santoka listening to a cicada as he pondered buying rice?

8. *Mumonkan* (無門関): *The Gateless Gate*, a thirteenth century book of Zen koans written in China.

9. "Writing haiku is none other than living" (句作即生活) is a sort of paraphrase of the Heart Sutra.

10. *Tanzaku*: a strip of fancy stiff paper used as a vertical poem card at special events or leave-takings.

11. The Buddha's response to appropriate questions in the sutras.

12. Tanabata: July 7, the Star Festival. The one day of the year when the shepherd boy star can meet with the weaver maid (represented by two stars). If the weather is cloudy or it rains, they must wait another year.

13. An ancient and poetical name for Japan.

14. 鴉.

15. 雀.

16. The Festival of Lanterns according to the old lunar calendar.

17. Called *higanbana* (彼岸花) in Japanese. *Higan* means "the Other Shore," i.e., Nirvana, so very appropriate for the time of the Obon festival.

CHAPTER 10

An Easy Death

The last time I went to visit Santoka was September 25. From Hiroshima I went to the Nyohoji temple in Osu, and after three days and two nights of a training course, got together with Togeda—who is so good at classical poetry recitation—on the road back home. We brought two bottles of Kumenoi sake as a souvenir; Ichijun, Teikakotsu and Masa'ichi came along as well; and that night may have been the liveliest happiest gathering there ever was at the Isso-an. The master of the hermitage said that he wanted to feed me, and with a skill sharpened over many years, cooked me some rice. My stomach was already bloated with tofu, however, so I didn't eat but one bowl of that delicious rice. Later that night we all walked the road to the hot springs at Dogo together. Being drunk, Santoka's steps tended to be disordered. Since there was no bedding at the Isso-an, we all stayed over at Ichijun's place.

The next day when I went to check in at the Isso-an, I found Santoka fast asleep at the entranceway, the soles of his feet in plain sight. He said something to the effect that he remembered being suddenly unable to stand the loneliness after separating from everyone at Dogo, knocking down some shochu, and staggering back to the hermitage. Even though there was no bedding, I thought that I should have slept there with him. Emptying my purse and leaving just enough for travel expenses back to Hiroshima, I squeezed the rest into Santoka's hand. I told him to please go to a hot spring he liked, and added that while it would be like him to go to the cheapest one, the Sagi no Yu, he should go to the Kami no Yu. At our parting, the consummate Santoka said that he was all right now, came with me to see me off as far as Takahama, and stood unmoving at the wharf until my ship was out of sight.

The flies
　　still alive
　　　　remember me.

生き残る蝿が
わたしを
おぼえている

As the insects cry,
　　their lives
　　　　thin out.

鳴けつれて
虫のいのちの
ほそりゆく

As much as I sweep,
　　as much as they fall,
　　　　autumn deepens.

掃くほどに
散るほどに
秋ふかく

In this way, his solitary fall deepened day by day. The sky and waters cleared beautifully.

Things that move are beautiful.
Look at the water.
Look at the clouds.
　　　　x
An attitude of life that does not ask.
An attitude of life that does not reject.
I would like my attitude of life to be empty and elegantly simple.
Step over and transcend yourself!

Empty and elegantly simple. That was the mental state Santoka longed for. Not to seek, not to reject, but to affirm things as they are.

In this there would be no poverty, no wealth, no losing, no winning, no life and death.

As he listened to the voices of October, the autumn colors deepened around his hermitage. The leaves on the huge ginkgo tree had not yet turned yellow, but on windy mornings great numbers of the perfectly round nuts were falling all over.

At the temple
I pick up
tranquil ginkgo nuts.

お寺は
しずかな
ぎんなん拾う

Leaves are falling.
After this, the water
becomes tasty.

落葉する
これから水が
うまくなる

He was pleased more than anything by the taste of the water becoming more delicious. Sake and water. Santoka loved them both unbearably, but he loved water more than sake, and eight years before had prayed that he might write haiku like water rather than haiku like sake. But to Santoka, both drinking sake and writing haiku were a part of his karma, and he was rather unable to enter an environment where both body and mind were as light as water.

The autumn rains were bleak and cold. He was happy to gaze at that rain by himself. Alone inside the Isso-an, it was a joy to listen to the rain, to gaze at the rain, and to shut himself up in solitude.

On the second, he suddenly felt like seeing his friend Shi-suikei-san, or better said, he wanted to be cheerfully indulged by someone who loved sake. Borrowing train fare from Ichijun's wife, he went to Imabari. The two of them drank heavily at the F-Shop, even though the town was highly active with an air defense drill.

Late that night on his way home, a white dog joined him out of nowhere. When he looked, he could see that the dog had a large piece of soft mochi rice cake between its teeth. Whatever the dog was thinking, when it got to the entrance of the hermitage, it put down the mochi and disappeared into the dark. When Santoka took a good look, he could see that it was a large piece of mochi about five inches [twelve centimeters] in diameter with a little bit missing. He suddenly felt that his stomach was empty and ate half of it raw, but having no teeth, it was a bone-breaking dinner. Just at that point, a cat with glittering eyes approached him. When he tossed the remaining mochi to the cat, the cat took it in its mouth and ran off. Being treated by a dog and then giving alms to a cat! Both the hermitage and the mountain were quiet when he returned, and the autumn late night was profound.

The Matsuyama autumn festival was on the fifth, sixth and seventh; and the big festival at the shrine for the war dead continued on until the tenth.

"Mr. Santoka. If you don't have enough spending money for the festival, I have a little bit on hand, so don't be shy."

The abbot next door came over specially to state this. What warmth of feeling he must have had. But he didn't specifically state when Santoka might pick it up, so he just dished out good intentions, and the money was never borrowed. Alone in his hermitage, there was neither Obon nor a festival, but that, too, was all right. In an unguarded moment he had fed a cat the cold rice from the very bottom of his coffers. He made a tea–rice gruel out of what had not been eaten, finished up his festival breakfast, and went out to the town. He walked around and became a guest at friendly households like those of Ichijun, Masa'ichi and Teikakotsu, and was treated quite often to a drink every day.

On the evening of the tenth, the wife of the priest at the Miyukidera was passing by the front of the hermitage, but drawn by a strange feeling in her heart, went inside to take a look and found Santoka collapsed in pain at the entranceway. She approached him and asked, "Sensei, what's the matter?" but there was no answer. She at first thought that he had perhaps gotten drunk and fallen down as usual, but this was different. He had thrown up something with the smell of sake, and soiled the front of his neck and the tatami; his robe was in disarray and he was naked in front, so she pulled the hems of his kimono together, hoisted him into the back room, and settled him down. She then cleaned up the mess, placed some washing utensils next to his pillow, covered him with a quilt for the present and returned home. Still, she was somehow worried. When she informed the priest of the matter, he said, "That's worrisome. But there's a poetry gathering tonight, so Ichijun and the others will be coming soon. Since that's the case, you won't have to bother any further, I suppose," and decided to go take a look at the situation later on.

Not long after, six or seven of his coterie came to the hermitage, but they figured that he had just gotten drunk and collapsed as usual. So they held their haiku meeting until past eleven o'clock as always. From time to time they would peek into the next room and say something like, "Hey, Sensei! Haven't you sobered up yet? You sure sleep a lot, huh!" But that sleep was considerably different from his usual sleep. Everyone was sympathetic, but they returned home leaving Santoka alone at the hermitage.

On the contrary, the wife of the priest at the Miyukidera was strangely concerned about Santoka and did not sleep well. As an uneasy night turned into dawn, she went over to the hermitage to take a look, but it was already too late. Santoka's chest was still a little warm, but he had stopped breathing. She went quickly to inform Ichijun, then ran for the doctor, but everything after that was like a dream, and it's said that she remembers nothing of it.

Thus, according to the doctor, Santoka's death is estimated to have occurred on October 11, 1940, at four o'clock in the morning. He was fifty-nine years old.

Santoka, who had appointed himself "the one among them," and who was the self-styled "one blade of grass, one man," died alone inside the Isso-an. Along with being resolved to die at any time, he had achieved the great easy death that he had predicted a year before and for which he had habitually prayed. Moreover, he had drunk his beloved sake right up to the day of his death, and a meeting for haiku—which had been his life—had been carried on near the very pillow which death was stealing near.

From about that time, the tide of war worsened for Japan, and rice and sake for those who did no work disappeared altogether.

一草庵日記

Diary of the One-Grass Hut

August 3, 1940
Clear weather.

Fasting. I have got to start fasting. And not just because I don't have any food. It will purify both body and mind. At least just one day—today—I want to live humbly and properly. We go on perfecting ourselves, one day after another, and so perfect our entire lives.

Quietly reading books. I confine myself indoors and give myself to introspection. When tired, I sip unrefined tea.

Once again this afternoon there were scattered showers. It turned noticeably cooler, and at dawn my body felt the cold.

August 4
Cloudy, then clear.

Today I fasted again, and felt myself wobbling a little. "I guess I'm getting old," I thought, and forced a smile. With an empty stomach, I went outside. I stopped at the Donguri Hermitage—the master was away—and borrowed the expenses necessary to live from his kind wife. I was able to bring home a little more than two *sho* of rice mixed with barley I bought with eighty-two sen. Ah, the blessing of the savory taste of cooked rice. It's been a while! I tasted the bright light of each grain, one after another, but first offered some at the Buddhist altar, placing my palms together and repenting my sins. I curse my good health. I'm too healthy, and then get derailed because of that.

A message to a friend:

As usual, I've huddled myself into a corner and am continuing on with a life uncertain of its very existence. That life has now been reduced to its last extremity. It's gotten to the point where I must turn a corner one way or another. Will I sink or swim? I'm formulating my new life and organization with all of my body and mind.

August 5
Clear, then cloudy.

I got up early, thinking about myself. I've *got* to establish a moderate way of living. I've *got* to get rid of my selfishness and live with proper discipline. I've been too self indulgent and willful. There's been too much unevenness in my life. A life of reflection without shame, an obliging life without being disgraced before Heaven and Earth, a life that leaves no seeds of future trouble—such a life would be truly spiritually peaceful and quiet.

I go out to the post box for a moment and buy some vegetables on the way. Two large eggplants for five sen, one large cucumber for five sen. The daikon was expensive, so I didn't buy it—one for twenty sen, they said.

The magnolia![1] You can make a flower arrangement with just a single branch. It's my hope to exist just like this tree. Its flower is quite manly, wouldn't you say?

The blowing wind foretells the autumn with certainty. It is the very heart of renewal.

I'm offensive. Contrary to the usual, I want to be foolish. My thoughts are that I'd like to go back to being foolish, to abide by that foolishness, and to pierce it through and through.

Old Ichijun gave Sumita the honorific title of "Abbot Donko." Then Abbot Donko gave Ichijun the nickname "Abbot Donguri."

Certainly, "donguri" seemed pretty good. When I asked if he would give *me* that name, he said, "Go ahead and use it, but think about it: Abbot Santoka is always flying around aimlessly like a dragonfly. *Don* and *ton* are really the same in the end, so 'Abbott Tonbo' is really better." In this way, the three "Abbot Fools" were created.[2] At some point we all vowed together to remain blockheads and fools from then on, and I remember those feelings with nostalgia.

August 6
Clear.

I got up, unable to wait for the east to grow light. Very soon the large drum at the shrine for the war dead was beating out one boom after another. The days have grown considerably shorter. It must be close to five o'clock.

Body and mind are possessed by melancholy. To cheer myself up, I go out, having just received a complimentary ticket to the film *Miyamoto Musashi*.[3] I enjoyed it quite a bit, and it made me think over a number of things. The sword is the man. And isn't this Way of the sword and mind being one path my own path as well? I feel so ashamed that I have no willpower. Ah, no willpower at all.

Literature is the man. Poetry is his soul. If the soul is not polished, how will the poetry shine? The brilliance of the verse *is* the brilliance of the soul. This is the light of man.

The more I think about it, the more I feel keenly that my existence has no value. I, who am totally unproductive, cannot help feeling this. Especially concerning the present state of my existence, which is continually pressing, both externally and internally.

What makes me think this way? At present, I have no margin at all. Neither do I have any self-confidence. Being the kind of beggar that I am, I'm continually unpossessing of even the *passive* value that would sanction a man who had consistent zeal concerning haiku and patriotism.

I think I do not want to live. Quite often I think I would like to die. If you say that this is simply because I do not have the willpower for existence, that would certainly be valid; but with the charm of alcohol, my weak character has the ability to deceive both myself and others. How weak! How fragile! How absurd!

A change of course while on the same road! Right now, this is my last resort. Buck up, Santoka!

August 7
Clear, cloudy, then rain.

I get out of bed with the sound of the drum at the shrine for the war dead.

I run around doing a number of things. At the same time, I went over some verses. My daily penitence has done me the favor of abating a little. "Those things we bear will be redeemed," so calm down, calm down. By calming down you can put up with it, you can bear it.

No money—and this is because I'm so slovenly so often—but I'm not lacking in gratitude. I've done a good number of things I'm sorry for, and even today I had no excuse for the man who came to collect payment for the electric bill. I'm sorry. I'm sorry.

It seems that a good bit of tobacco has arrived at the tobacco shop. With something as simple as this, the human heart feels more comfortable—you feel as though you have the leeway to float above the world.

Recently I can't help feeling acutely ashamed of my big stomach. How despicable!

Blessed with a nice little rain. It gets cooler as the days go on. During the day, it's summer; at night, it's fall.

Today I was able to write a number of verses—a rare occurrence. Thirty poems in one day is too many, but it doesn't happen very often.

Don't be attached to the past. Throw away the ego. Release your obstinacy. Tonight, inebriation was calling me from close by, but I stayed stock still. Be good! Be good! That's the way! That's the way!

It's said that if you live a long time, you'll have a lot to be ashamed of. Ah, I've lived too long. I've been a disgrace too often. One life with a multitude of disgraces. Happily, I haven't lost my sense of shame.

Unable to sleep. It's close to dawn, and I've been unable to sleep. I read the *Mumonkan*.

August 8
Cloudy, occasional light rain.
The beginning of autumn.

Got up early and went to pray at the shrine for the war dead. It's truly autumn. I went without breakfast and had one cup of plum tea. I'm a little depressed. That's because I'm so engrossed in myself, I suppose. Or is it because of the way I infuse alcohol into myself? Either way, there's no mistake that I'm a weakling. Today I made do with the remainder of the imported rice I had—one serving—there was nothing else to be done.

It's because I'm without talent or genius that I've been able to single-mindedly devote myself to my one thread of a road—the path of making verses. I've been incapable of doing anything else. The problem is in whether I will actually do it or not. I concentrate all of my body and all of my strength into achieving my own things. Yesterday, today, and tomorrow, too.

What is unnatural is shameful. That I can't sleep at night is retribution for the unnatural.

August 9
Cloudy, then rain.

Got up at four-thirty. This morning I could hear the cicadas quite clearly. Their cries have a lovely resonance. One I'm quite fond of.

I fasted and had plum tea. I'm prepared to die at any time. I have the attitude that life and death are of one kind. To see both life and death clearly is the karma of Buddhism's great purpose, the sphere where life and death are transcended, where egolessness brings a state of "no-mind" and love moves us to a place where there are no obstacles. This is the place I must set out for. Somehow.

I go out and am bathed lightly by the morning sun. At the Donguri Hermitage I call on the woman of the house, and gratefully receive two bowls of somen noodles. How wonderful! How wonderful! It was quite delicious. Ichijun's wife said she wasn't sure what time he would be back. What an easygoing old man. A vagabond unpained by the bitterness of things. Donguri-sensei. I can just see his round figure tumbling along towards Tokyo, stepped on by others, but without a worry in the world.

Master Teika [4] lives around here. He is like a quick-witted jumping fish, and you could call him Donguri-sensei's pupil. When I stopped in at the Teika residence, here, too, the master was out and his wife was home alone. And from here I received a nice lunch. Wherever I go, I'm always putting people out.

For the first time in many years, I was able to write some Tanabata-festival poem cards. With a gentle nostalgia, it was going back to the country of a child's mind. I longed terribly for my own child in Manchuria.

August 13
Clear, then cloudy.
Third anniversary of the Shanghai Incident.

Rubbing my hands and feet, I felt that I've gotten fat. Well, whether you get fat or thin, peace of body and mind is desirable above all.

Looking around absentmindedly, I caught sight of the abbot out on a begging round. I immediately felt bad as I knew I had to pay back some money I'd borrowed from him right away. Maybe I should go out—the first time in a while—and beg a bit too.

Yesterday, the evening glories were beautiful; and this morning, the bindweeds[5] weren't bad either. I made them into a flower arrangement and enjoyed them thoroughly.

I'm a little disappointed—I was stood up again today. The person who was supposed to come, didn't. So live through it, and live through it properly. I am a Japanese who must survive.

It's just before the Bon festival, so there are lots of people visiting graves. I've been assigned to clean the grave of someone who died, apparently without relatives. Will I end up the same?

All day today, the skies were full of leaden clouds, and it was hot and muggy. To borrow Ryokan's way of speaking, it's good that the summer is hot. That way it seems as though the crickets are chirping up close to you.

The *Mumonkan*, Case 7: Chao-chou's Washing the Bowl.[6] In Japan, of course, we have a deep veneration for Dogen Zenji.[7] Among the great monks of China, Chao-chou[8] is loved and respected.

August 14
Cloudy, then clear.

When my eyes opened, I just lay there without getting up. The clock next door struck four.

With this kind of cloudy leaden sky and hot muggy weather, one worries about blight on the rice plants. Clear up! Clear up! I keep praying that the weather will clear and the sun will shine.

Recently, no matter what shop I go to, they're all out of matches. I can rarely even pick up cigarette butts anymore. Sort of sad.

I received one branch of magnolia, came home and stuck it in a corner of the garden. Please send down some roots . . . like the *raichikutou*[9] that budded. At least, at the very least, by the time I write my final poem . . . I'll settle down and wait.

Today, I cooked up all the barley I had. Then, *just* as I was thinking that this would have to sustain me for the rest of the day, in a rare appearance old Ichijun came to my hermitage. It had been a month since we had talked together, and I was happy to see him. He told me all sorts of things about his trip, and I heard about his failures on the road. He came back having been stepped on all over by people, but now he seemed not even to notice and talked as though he hadn't a care in the world. Don-sensei's[10] unique style of travel dialectic is truly his optimistic child's heart. Saying that he had brought me no souvenir, he gave me the money a souvenir would have cost him instead. Thank you. Thank you so much.

In the afternoon we went to the hot springs at Dogo. A bath and then a cup of sake. And then one more cup. This sent things awry. With one more cup and then another, I was in big trouble. I was, in fact, reduced to jelly. Ah, ah.

The wretchedness of humankind. And my weakness. Lying down just as I had fallen and gazing up at the sky, I denounced and incriminated myself endlessly.

August 15
Clear.

I got up while it was still dark and straightened up the house. Reflection and humiliation. Self-discipline and self-control. The twelfth day of the old Bon festival. There's no end to the people visiting graves.

I go out to buy rice, to buy soy sauce—the morning sun shines warmly down on me. I walk along with the feeling that I can't help feeling grateful to Heaven and Earth.

The seventh collection of haiku is at hand. The sparrows and crows have fluffed up their feathers and come. With a deep interior bow, I sent my thanks to both Empei and Sumita.

There is a saying that goes, "Sake should be drunk peacefully." You should sip sake, but gulp down beer. When you crave sake and gulp it down, unhappiness follows. Gradually but firmly—today a little, tomorrow a little—I'm breaking away from shochu. I'm going to sip my sake peacefully, taste it and enjoy it.

In the heat of the day, I went to the post box and tossed in my collection of haiku, plippy plop.

Stopped by to visit Ichijun and Teika, but neither one was at home. I left my haiku collections and went home. I also did a little shopping.

There's a beautiful moon tonight. I look at it from my bed. What a waste.

Today's shopping list:

> 82 sen – 2 *sho* of mixed rice.
> 5 sen – postage stamps
> 7 sen – 1 *go* of soy sauce
> 5 sen – 1 cucumber
> 10 sen – *iriko*[11]

Money left over was exactly 1 sen.

August 16

Just past four o'clock, the large drum at the To'un shrine begins to sound; close to five o'clock, the drum at the shrine for the war dead does the same. I always get out of bed somewhere in between. It was the same today as well.

I was praying that the thing I hoped to come would indeed come—when it doesn't, I'm always in the position of having no excuses—and in the end, it didn't come again this morning.

I'm alive. Or better said, isn't it a fact that the reason I'm not dead is because I borrow money from my close friends in every direction and load them with trouble? It's not that I have such intentions, but isn't it true that I invite such results consistently? Thinking about this makes me uneasy.

Distant thunder. It seemed as though a rain shower was on its way, but it didn't come. There is a thread of connection that runs between that fact and my mood.

In the evening, out on a walk, I stopped by Teika's house. The regular meeting of the Persimmon Club was taking place, and there were eight participants: Ichijun, Teikakotsu, Musui, Warai, Gesson, Ryujo, Senkijo, and Hozajo. No striking verses appeared, but their earnestness was delightful.

August 17

In the morning, clear; in the afternoon, cloudy; during the night, a light rain. Fourteenth day of the Bon festival.

When I spend Bon alone or on the road, it's real lonely.

Mosquitoes, flies, ants, spiders, and even bees have come flying into my hermitage.

Recently, the lingering heat of summer has been severe.

I must reorganize the things around me. No, I must reorganize body and mind. I don't go outside. I reflect on myself and repent. I must take the stance that all the innumerable phenomena are of one mind and one virtue.

After it got dark there was a little rain, and then a beautiful moon.

- Being poor is painful, but borrowing money is twice as painful.
- Being poor is not necessarily something to be ashamed of.
- Being poor in your mind is something to be ashamed of.

The secret of life as far as I'm concerned is in the following three conditions:

- Do not lose a sense of moderation.
- Do not borrow money.
- Do not be attached to the past. Have no hopes for the future.

Appreciate each day, one after the next, and enjoy it all.

I do not believe in the world to come. I release the past. I simply believe in the present, the immediate present, with all my heart. I consume my entire body and mind in the eternal moment—the body and mind that should be made replete.

I believe in the universal spirit, but deny the individual soul. The individual separates from the totality, then joins together with it again. In that sense, life is a sojourning and death is a return.

My table is poor, indeed. I'm frequently lacking vegetables and sometimes have no rice at all, but that does not pain me in the least. What I am always complaining about concerning my meals is the fact that my stomach is big—way too big. And then there's my

craving for alcohol. With the desire for just one cup, an alcoholic voracity is born.

August 18
In the afternoon, a slight shower.

Morning, noon and night, I'm always thinking of haiku. I even make haiku in my dreams. Above and beyond *being* a haiku poet, I am someone whose walking, stopping, sitting and lying down are all thoroughly haiku.

And being this way, it's easy to think about death. The mind that *waits* for death is too weak. I'm a coward! Thus I rebuke myself.

The immediate moment: like this, like this! Seeking after myself, it's unobtainable. It's foundation is selflessness. Emptiness.

The *Mumonkan*, Case 12.[12] Master Gan's calling.

I make preparations for sending off the seventh collection of haiku. I only make preparations. I have no money for stamps.

I received a cucumber, an eggplant and a melon from the abbot at the temple. How kind, how gracious. Goods grown by hand are bright and shining. I'll spend the day eating through the cucumber. Just like a grasshopper.

In the evening I took a walk. A truly beautiful full moon had come up. It was fully autumn. I walked around endlessly and somehow felt lonely. The grief of a loner, the desolation of the wanderer. A fact for which there is no help.

Thought up some verses . . . two or three . . . four.

I thought about the character of haiku:

- Simplification—to be as simple as possible.
- Self-purification—the body and mind are one.
- Regulations of life—inherent regulations—natural regulations.
- The union of self and other—fusion of subject and object:

  > the flow of nature
  > rhythm
  > the sway of life

- Totality and the individual—to grasp eternity by means of the moment. Then to express oneself using the totality and the individual. To express totality through the individual.
- Symbolic expression is impossible without stepping into the symbolic world.

August 19
Clear.
Sixteenth day of Old Bon. Apprentices' Holiday.

My Bon festival has been absolutely as it is in the original meaning of *urabon*.[13] I have no rice, no tobacco and no matches. Today, too, I will eat cucumber, drink water, and endure my hunger.

When night fell, I finally couldn't stand it any more and borrowed the money for the electric light bill. Which is to say that I had put the bill money in this bag and hung it by the door so that I could pay it even if I were not at home. With that 70 sen, I bought several things: 40 sen – mixed rice; 12 sen – tofu; 2 sen – matches; 9 sen – stamps; 6 sen – postcards.

On the side of the road I saw two or three stalks of the miscanthus I like so much, and so made them into a flower arrangement on a pot on my table.

- The body and mind are one. Practice and understand this doctrine, then comply with it. "Your own mind and your own nature falling away; your original face right before your eyes." —Dogen Zenji.
- If you don't understand the virtue of weeds, you will not understand the mind of nature. Weeds grasp their own essence and express its truth.

I eat my meal slowly inside the mosquito net. Then I submissively plop down on my back with arms and legs akimbo. A happiness that was much too happy.

August 20
Clear.

This morning's sky was unspeakably beautiful.

- I must penetrate my solitude and destitution. It's the only road left to me.
- The environment immediately around me. The matters immediately at hand. Things exactly as they are. My mind exactly as it is. This is the way it must be.
- Regarding my attitude to writing poetry:
  - retreat from greed.
  - body and mind are of one kind.
  - be docile, be strong . . . pay attention to details.
- Yesterday, yesterday's wind was blowing. Tomorrow, tomorrow's wind will blow, won't it? Give life to the now of today. Live through it honestly.
- "You've already drunk three cups of wine from the finest winemakers around, and you still say that you have not moistened your lips." *Mumonkan*, Case 10.[14] The problem of Seizei's Solitary Destitution.

It came, it came! Yes, indeed! Thank you S-san. Your friendship permeates my flesh and bones.

I was immediately off to town, to the offices here and there, paid only what I could pay, bought only what I could buy. Only what I wanted to pay, I didn't; only what I wanted to buy, I didn't. Going that far is best, I think.

A haircut. A bath. A walk. Ah, I feel great!

Sake is sweet. So sweet. Shochu is no good. I went briefly back to the house. After that to Musui's place and a pleasant chat in front of the store. And then off to Warai's place. And then, and then, to the Donguri Hermitage—invited to dinner and I talked too much.

August 21
Clear.

Got up out of bed at four o'clock. Soon the beat of the drum resounded in the distance: Get up! Get up! The twinkling of the morning star at dawn. The reverberation of the first street car. People's footsteps. The sound of drawing water. Heaven and Earth at dawn are both exalted and beautiful.

My mind is at peace and my body is at ease.

I write notes to a number of people. I feel thankful and have deep feelings for my friends. I go out as far as the post box.

I pickle some greens. Tomorrow morning I'll have some fresh-pickled radishes!

The sacredness, purity and peace of salt.

In the evening, to Kami-ichiman. I drop in at the Donguri Hermitage, and we talk for a while about haiku. We discuss going somewhere in the evening of the next month's full moon. He treats me to dinner. The taste of the somen noodles was delightful. Thanks to him, my Bon festival really felt like one.

It was a gentle, reserved day.

August 23
Clear.

I rose early, much too early. And how, then, was the beauty of the dawn at the foot of the mountains?

Finally, I left the house. I was invited to Musui's place for some delicious sake, and after that things didn't go well. Eventually, we overdid it and, drunk, I borrowed a little money from the old man and went off to the hot springs at Dogo—and one more cup; at an *oden* shop, yet another cup, two cups, three cups—and, absolutely soused, I was at the point of falling down at the side of the road when, luckily, a woman from the neighborhood who was passing by kindly accompanied me home. It's wrong. It's just wrong. There's no end to my shame. The fact that I myself don't remember this clearly—doesn't that make it worse?

I'm such a fool! Wasn't it just the other night when I was in trouble at the police box and, there, too, I was lucky enough to have old Ichijun pass by and take me home? Idiot! How about if a man advanced in years started to act like one? Isn't this wartime? Let's straighten up, Santoka. A life without self-confidence is no good. A man without confidence in himself is pitiful. And am I not just like that?

August 24
Clear, then cloudy. In the afternoon, light showers.

Thinking about the disgraceful state of affairs last night gives me an unbearable feeling. I tilt the sake bottle and take a little swig. With that fortification, I pay a visit next door, and thank them for their kindness. I give them a collection of verses and talk for a little while.

Old Ichijun comes to my hermitage. I confess my drunken raving condition of the night before. I feel a little better, as though it were over and done with. Ichijun pulls a copy of old Sumita's recent work out of his big pocket and, holding it up in both hands once in respect, puts it on the desk. The title, *Nihon no aji* [A Taste of

Japan]. It's really a taste of Sumita. The settled sweetness of Abbot Donko. A very touching taste.

Night. Musui comes to the hermitage. I loan him the September issue of *Haiku kenkyu* [Haiku Studies].[15]

— In every man, there is some sort of vice. Mine is the vice of alcohol. If I could just have a taste of sake, all would be well, but . . .
— Leave the grasses growing just as they are. They make a nice home for the bugs, don't they?

August 27
Clear, cloudy now and then. Second day of air-raid practice.

The clock has struck five, but it's still dark. My skin is cold.

With body and mind quiet, I study. I'm going to change my last will and write it down.

In the afternoon, I go to buy tofu. I'll make it last by cutting into cubes. It's a poor meal, but the flowering plant I stuck in the jar adds some elegance. Yesterday and today, two or three stalks of miscanthus.

A refreshing wind is blowing, cleansing the inside of the room. Let it chase away my filthy cravings! The nobility of an open sky without a trace of clouds!

In the evening, Musui came by. And soon after that, Ichijun. We discussed the September regular meeting.

I broke my clogs today, so I could not go out for a walk. Truly wonderful bell-ring bugs[16] are kindly chirping. Their voices clarify the surroundings.

Sound sleep. One of my blessings.

August 28
Autumnal clarity, then cloudy. Light rain at night.

Got up before four o'clock. With the moon at dawn was a fresh cool breeze. A little while later, the siren sounding a warning for air-raid practice. Then the peaceful night turned to bright dawn.

During the morning it was slightly cold, so much so that I put on a bathrobe over my other clothes. I didn't have the money to buy clogs, so I didn't go outdoors. Repairing my indoor sandals, I saved myself from having to go barefoot. In the evening hours I crept under the mosquito netting and read under a precarious light. A taste of old Sumita's *Nihon no aji* [A Taste of Japan]. The chapter "Rice balls" tasted particularly good. Literature is man. Man is literature. Old Sumita's writing is exactly old Sumita, the man. Sumita has a character like pure cotton. It's not mixed with another fiber. A modest, great man. A warm, calm, religious man.

I flattened a cockroach that had been crawling around inside the mosquito netting. Later, I felt totally cheerless. Hey! Old cockroach! Where did you come sneaking out from? Your friends aren't around here, you know.

Sake is my koan. Solving the riddle of sake—being able to truly taste sake will be my final certificate of enlightenment, my attainment of satori.

August 29
Cloudy.

Thank you, thank you! How happy I am. The thing that was coming, came.

I go out to the post office—barefoot—first I buy some clogs. Then, some tobacco; then, of course, two or three cups . . .

It's been five days, I guess. During that time, bean-jam buns, *chikuwa* fish cake, etc.

In the afternoon, I go unannounced to Musui's place and we talk for a long time without getting up. On the way home, I wander around the streets looking at the pleasure quarters, and relax at a carefree movie.

After sunset I take another walk. Spoiled by old Ichijun's wife, I borrow a little money for a drink. Total darkness, and the sirens for the air-raid drill sound with an uneasy wail.

I scurry into the usual *oden* shop. Two or three regular customers are chatting along mindlessly, words like raindrops on a roof. About ten o'clock I return to my hermitage without incident, and fall into a deep sleep just as I am. At the time when the prime minister's "New System" is being promulgated, my behavior tonight is too happy-go-lucky. But this is my only consolation, my only luxury. If you compare this to my usual frugality and indigence, I would hope to receive some forgiveness.

The sake today was delicious. And it follows that the way I felt and acted was good from the beginning, too. I didn't fall apart, I didn't fall down, and I didn't talk too much.

September 1
Cloudy, light rain.
Two hundred and ten days. The first anniversary of the Asian Development Public Service. The anniversary of the Kanto Earthquake.

I walk barefoot around the neighborhood, prepared only to go step by step, changing direction anywhere. Going around on my own, not ashamed of myself. Sleeping alone, not ashamed of my bedding.

A Vow

I swear to carry out the will of our Sovereign Lord, to turn away from my own desires, not to be attached to the past, not to be caught up in every situation, to be cooperative and in accord, and to put all my strength into the New System.

September 1, early dawn
Respectfully recorded, Santoka

September 2
Clear, periodically cloudy.

Down in the lower vegetable fields, they've fashioned some clappers and have set them clacking since early morning. When I hear that sound, the dreams of my youth come right back.

School starts today, and the young boys and girls who are registering are all about. I, too, will study human life again with the mind of a young student from the first grade on.

Release attachment, release attachment. Turn away from indulgence, crush the mind of covetousness. I have an early lunch, not having had breakfast.

There is now a ticket system for rice, and the priest on duty kindly picked up my portion and brought it to me. The abbot advanced me the money for the rice—my apologies, deep apologies.

Recently it's been hot and humid. We really want long spells of sunshine for the rice.

For life during wartime, we should be austere and cheerful.

At night, the sound of a hundred feet caught my attention. Somehow it makes you think.

September 5
Cloudy, then clear.

I went out as far as the post office in Kami-ichiman. Naturally, I visited the Donguri Hermitage.

I hear old Sumita is coming by soon. Dear old Sumita-san. I'm happy, really happy.

I've been invited for dumpling soup and . . . ah . . . I feel so . . . ah.

No money. No possessions. No teeth. Alone.

What kind of person is an individual like this? For shame, shame. You should beat your own body down to the ground.

September 8
Cloudy, then clear.

I gloomily examine myself.

Where am I going? What am I doing? What *should* I do? What *must* I do? Let's examine this right to the very bottom.

I climb up Mount Nishi to pray at the Gyokuto temple, and visit the grave of the haiku poet, Hekigodo. I visit the army cemetery at Mount Asahi.

I gaze at the haiku chiseled on the grave marker of the poet, Shiki.

> *Intimate with the grave marker,*
> *bush clover*
> *beginning to bloom.*

September 11
Clear, then cloudy.

I go in the morning to pray at the shrine for the war dead. The shrine at dawn is especially refreshing and mysterious. Somehow I feel a sense of gratitude—an attitude of self-restraint bubbling up. Gratitude is fidelity. It is the heart of sincerity.

Gratitude to the Imperial House, to the nation. To the people who have given their all for the country, and to those who are continuing to do so. Gratitude to my mother. Gratitude to my child. Gratitude to my good friends. To the Universal Spirit, to the great love of the Buddha—gratitude.

The way of life of repentance, gratitude and devotion that old Ichijun had had preached to him so thoroughly by the master Kukaku Shoni is quite ordinary, but I think that it is most certainly man's fundamental path, the true path that purifies our sins. These three paths are, in the end, one. If you have repentance, you will necessarily have gratitude; and if you have devotion, you will necessarily have gratitude, I suppose. Gratitude is the daughter of repentance and devotion. I must move along, bringing up this daughter of the soul.

Art is fidelity, it is the heart of sincerity. The highest peak of that thing which is fidelity—and the heart of sincerity—is gratitude. And if haiku is not born from the heart of gratitude, it will not truly have the universal character . . . and it will not likely be able to move the heart of man.

If you have the heart of gratitude, you should always be immersed in happiness and calm repose. I would like to be always in the center of the wealth of such a heart. I will live by the heart that worships, and die by the heart that worships. And so I suspect that the world of infinite life and light will kindly carry me along. That is because the heart of pilgrimage ought to have been the native home of my own heart.

The One-Grass Hut—here is the warm room I was led to by old Ichijun, and which was kindly given its beloved name by old Sumita. Though it is but one tree and one grass, I receive the life of the universe, and continue living with intense gratitude. And it was probably in Sumita's mind that I should know this life of thanks.

September 12
Clear.

Unable to bear the loneliness, I stop in at old Ichijun's. After that, I visit Fusa.

At night, Ichijun comes to my hut, says he came out because of the beautiful moon. We talked together until late. It seems as though my humor lightened up quite a bit. The insects softly chirped while the moon shone on their bed of grass. I gaze at the moon from my bed.

September 15
Clear.

I get up early, somehow depressed. Both body and mind feel phlegmatic.

I boil up what's left of the barley and Irish potatoes. Eating this, I am myself an Irish potato.

Somehow or other, it's a day when I feel like getting angry. It's a day when it seems as though I may be defeated by the seduction of death.

To make use of the fallow land, the abbot, his child and wife are all cultivating it cheerfully. Only I am lonely.

The condition of my stomach is not so good. Hanging the mosquito netting early, I sit inside of it and think. A perfectly round moon shines into my room. The Heaven at the bottom of Hell?

The moon is now covered with clouds, now open to view. I, too, am now sad, now smiling. At some point or another, I fall asleep.

September 16
Cloudy – wind – clear.
August 15 by the old lunar calendar. The full moon of mid-autumn.

Today my mental state has cleared up a little.

They've been able to make a vegetable garden out of the fallow land in the garden in front of the temple. I'll try to make a garden in front of my hut, too.

I sold some wastepaper scraps. Recently, the prices are down, but even then I made seventy sen. I got a big profit.

I had planned on going to the hot springs at Dogo, but turned back at the post office. Two small cucumbers – 3 sen. One large daikon – 4 sen. There's a breeze today, and it's cool.

Today, once again, the abbot did me the favor of picking up my ration of rice for me. I'm obliged to him.

Reminiscences and longing for the old days are hard to bear. Outdated and weak with age, huh. Defying man, defying society, defying even myself, I guess.

They want you to be this way, they have you become that way. Just the way you are—that's the law of nature.

Cooked rice, cooked rice. It's been a long time since I've received a bellyful of white rice. This was something I was truly grateful for.

The middle of the autumn and no money. The truth is that's even more lonely than there being no moon. That sounds like a real lie, doesn't it . . .

The aggressive mosquitoes in the autumn wind are biting, so I got inside the mosquito net early and gazed at the moon, read books, thought things over and felt lonely all night.

No one did me the favor of dropping by, even with such a fine moonlit night as this. What's the matter, old Ichijun?

I can't help recalling the monk Hosai's verse:

> *Such a fine moon;*
> > *gazing at it alone,*
> *going to bed.*

I, also, have two or three verses of self-scorn:

	酒はない
No sake;	月しみじみ
quite keenly	観て居り
I watch the moon.	

	蚊帳の中の
The moon shines	私にまで
through the mosquito net	月の明るく
all the way—to me!	

Through the open door,
gazing at the moon;
going to bed.

あけはなち
月をながめつつ
寝る

I'd sure like to have a cup. This is natural. It's my truth.

Gazing at the moon; infinite deep emotions. Thinking of the front lines of battle, I reflect on being at the home front. Far, near; intimate, estranged; surviving relatives, no surviving relatives. *Namu Amida Butsu* . . .

It gets late and, unable to bear the abstraction and seclusion, I take off and walk here and there. I go pray at the shrine for the war dead in the moonlit night. The silhouettes of people now and again. From house to house, people happily gazing at the moon together.

Is it travel weariness? Is it homesickness? Whatever it is, I—tonight's Santoka—was lonely. I ate a potato. A potato is a potato, but this was an Irish potato.

Unable to sleep at all—the neighbor's clock told me it was one o'clock, but for some reason I still couldn't sleep, so I continued reading *Oku no hosomichi* [*The Narrow Road to the Deep North*].[17]

Finally at dawn I dozed off and had a strange dream. I was visiting my dead younger brother and his new bride . . .

At any rate, on towards temperance, on towards simplicity, and then on towards elegant simplicity—in these are the life of true taste.

September 17
Clear.

When I get up, the neighbor's clock strikes five. The moon that falls behind the mountains is beautiful. I've regained tranquility of body and mind. I have self-confidence and congratulate myself that day by day, moment by moment, I will continue on with this clarification.

Tattered and threadbare,
        cold rice, tattered and threadbare;
the autumn cold.

秋冷ぼ
寒飯ろ
　ぼぼ
　ろろ
　ぼ
　ろ

These are my true feelings this morning, and you can't dissemble your true feelings. Because it's right there that the nobility of one's verses exist . . . No mail coming again this morning? Ah, ah. Santoka is lonely.

If—only if—I could stop drinking, how tranquil I would be. First, I would be saved in concrete terms. I would be rescued from the daily life of never knowing whether I would be able to eat or not eat. The distress of being in the red and the suffocation of borrowing money would fade away, and all my petty difficulties would disappear. But I don't feel confident that I'll be quitting sake. Because to me, drinking sake is the charm of being alive!

The signs of alcohol poisoning are appearing thick and fast. Ah, I'm going to the post box for a minute.

On the way, I make up some verses, pick up some cigarette butts, and do some shopping.

> 26 sen – 1 *sho* of barley.
> 10 sen – some pinks[18]
> 6 sen – 1 cake of tofu
> 4 sen – stamps

As I cooked up the rice, I thought of various and sundry things. Concerning haiku:

	spirit – the scent of Japan – truth
Haiku-like things	nature – the scent of the seasons – quiet
	clarity – strength
	expression – the scent of time – fluidity

Works reflecting themselves—complete
Works reflecting the author—incomplete

There is a beautiful moon again tonight; I read and meditated peacefully alone, and went to bed.

September 18
Cloudy.
Tenth Anniversary of the Manchurian Incident. Official Mourning for His Highness Prince Kitashirakawa, Eternal Lord.

At some point I felt like wanting to prepare the brazier. Its appearance is one of the things you can say is at the heart of autumn.

The commands and the sounds of handclapping at the shrine for the war dead are endless. Bending my ear intently to this activity, I am struck by the lamentation for his late Highness and the enthusiasm for the establishment of the New East Asian Order.

Old Ichijun stopped by for the first time in a while—apparently he dropped by the other day, but I was not here. We talk about the New System, we talk about haiku . . .

He's in accord with Prime Minister Konoe's earnest petition, and I'm attracted to the idea of "One hundred million people, one mind," too.

Higan[19] starts today. "Whether it's hot or cold, one makes it to the Other Shore," it is said, and this is truly so.

I had a dream, an indecent dream. When I think about it, it was a shameful dream. Not a sage's dream. I'd prefer not to have dreams like this.

September 19
Autumnal clarity.

I slept this morning, and got up close to six o'clock. Went without breakfast and had one cup of tea.

I air out my clothes and things—all worn out, moldy and dusty, smelly and odiferous.

The autumn mosquitoes are attacking more and more ferociously.

I eat an early lunch of potato and barley mixed with rice. Quite good, indeed, and I am thankful for it.

Trouble has improved people. Being thoughtless, life is often frittered away. Because of its being simple, life is wasted. Rather, then, the will of Heaven should be considered a blessing.

I fully realize that in the perfection of a country, the highest state of national defense and the guarantee of a minimum standard of living are inseparable.

- There are situations where, even though one takes steps, there are no results—for the individual or the nation— but you should absolutely never turn back.
- The amalgamation of the natural and the unnatural—I can find this in my own self. In my solitude, for example.
- A true haiku is not a haiku that seems like one. It is the haiku within the haiku.

In the evening I went to the Shoshuji temple and visited Shiki's grave, this being his death anniversary. On the way back, I called in at Teika's house and then went on to Ichijun's place. I was not in a very good mood, however, and so I had two bowls of udon noodles at the Kameya and went home. After not having been there for ten days, I went to the town, but felt that it was a bit noisy.

At dawn I was surprised by the chaotic ringing of the fire alarm, and it seems as though the elementary school in Aratamamachi burned to the ground. I thought the children were to be pitied more than anyone.

It was a beautiful moonlit night tonight. I slept soundly.

September 20
Autumnal clarity. The rising sun was majestic.

When I opened my eyes, it was dawn. The roosters crowing, the sound of the drum, the echo of the temple bell. A tranquil and awe-inspiring coming of the light. I pressed my palms together and prayed silently.

The morning cold. How good it felt to make a fire again. For breakfast, I steamed and ate an Irish potato.

Both body and mind feel clear. I'm glad I'm able to sleep well these days.

A shrike came close by and shrieked energetically.

The mail—the letter I'm weary of waiting for hasn't come, and I'm somehow dejected. I'm really a weakling, huh. And selfish, too.

The more I calm down, the more my loneliness clears up, and then I'm lonesome again.

Nothing in my purse, and the kitchen is empty. My tasteful appreciation of poverty is not very good. One wants a posture of composed unshakability.

Turning from three meals a day and a dead drunk to two meals a day and slight inebriation.

The misery of an empty stomach that gets hungry easily—such is not without humor.

Robust health. An excess of robust health. So much robust health that I don't know what to do with it.

What kind of reform is self-reform that can't be achieved?

I'd better get myself out of this scatterbrained mood!

Went to visit Musui. He wasn't there. I borrowed some dried udon noodles. Dropped in on the Warai residence. Borrowed some pocket money.

> 70 sen – 2 *sho* of foreign rice.
> 17 sen – half a glass of cheap wine.
> 6 sen – 1 *go* of soy sauce.

Tobacco I can pick up; rice I cannot.

With either Japanese or foreign rice, when you crush dried udon noodles up a bit and mix the two, it's better to make it sticky. This I have discovered cooking for myself. Isn't it cheaper when you do things simply?

I feel the autumn chill morning and night. It's fully autumn. I think about travel.

September 21
Cloudy, a little rain, then clear.

Got up early. Recently it seems that I've been able to sleep well, so mornings are especially pleasant. I made a flower arrangement with some spider lilies. This flower is one symbol of the feeling of Equinox Week.

Recently, I've been reserved; I've been living too much of a reserved life. That's because I've been restricted in the inside and pressed on from the outside. But no matter what, I've had self-discipline and self-control.

From now on, I think I'll keep living more like myself, living the life of the fundamental me. The only thing I'll have to be careful about is not being excessive. Being excessive is unnatural. Being unnatural is not something that continues long, nor is it something to continue with.

I confess my sins before Heaven, Earth and mankind.

Asked to pay up the bill for the newspaper, I was struck dumb. It was not unreasonable. After all, I'm four months behind.

I rarely do, but I went to bed early. I had a number of dreams. Every once in a while I woke up and my lonely thoughts became clear. Urged on by their bodies, insects are chirping, *chinchirorin*. They must be lonely, too.

September 22
Autumnal clarity, pleasant beyond description. Cloudy in the afternoon.

Up before dawn. For a moment I reflected on myself, and was awakened to my mistakes.

The mail came—I was notified of Hoko's obituary. I was, in fact, surprised, but this sad report was not unexpected. Ah, Hoko-kun.[20]

You were a man like a daffodil. As a friend, you were too much separated from me by youth and distance, but I will not forget the many memories of going to Sendai once and visiting you. The sorrow and loneliness that fills me becomes one verse and then another, like overflowing water, Hoko-kun. How glad we are that you graced us with your life until just now. You battled your illness how many decades? That pain, that perseverance, and that concentration. A common man like myself would never be able to accomplish such things. Once again, I bow my head before you. Ah, those who pass away do so indeed, and Hoko, too, passed completely from us, as well. Ah. Alone, I peacefully burned incense and intoned a sutra.

Shoyo Yamano. Sympathetic memories of him are endless. So many verses fluttered down.

Body and mind are tranquil. *Mumonkan*, Cases 11 and 12.[21]

More and more I keenly feel the gravity of the times. A council before the Imperial Presence was held on the nineteenth.

In the afternoon I went to pray at the shrine for the war dead. From morning on, the number of worshippers was endless.

Poverty makes your stomach big. This is a clever understanding from my own personal experience.

This evening was extraordinarily lonely.

Somehow it looks like it will rain tomorrow. On such a festive day, it would be better if it didn't. Not for my sake, but for the sake of others.

Finally I put together five sen, so I can go out and look for some pinks to buy.

I tried sleeping without the mosquito netting, but a swarm of mosquitoes attacked me now and again, so I hung the netting one more time. I hate mosquito netting.

I polished up my verses almost all night

I killed four again tonight. It made me feel bad. It can't be helped, but . . .

September 23
Cloudy, clear from time to time.
Autumnal All Imperial Ancestors' Day. The middle of equinox week.

The perfect weather for an excursion out of doors. I started to get up, but it was too early and dawn did not come for a long time.

I should make a complete confession of my sins, past and present.

Foreign rice is pretty good, too. Without complaints, I am meekly discreet. Holiday people out on a holiday. This is the way it should be; the way it should be.

How delightful! Mail from Ken [his son]. What kind of curse would it be to be discontented and think that it was not the amount of money I had hoped for?

I go to town. It's been almost two weeks since I've walked the streets. I was able to exchange a money order for currency at the Y-Shop. Today is a festival, so I bought only what I was able to buy. Before that, I paid off only what I was able to pay off.

It's been a month since I really knocked a few down. One cup, two cups, three cups . . . I got a little sloppy, but not really falling-down drunk. For me, that was not so bad.

Talked a bit at the Donguri Hermitage. For the first time in a long time I dropped in at Shoichi's residence, gave my respects to his wife, and then went to the hot springs at Dogo. Then, after a lapse of ten days, I took a bath and washed away the dirt and filth. I got a haircut, too! How refreshing that is!

Today I talked a lot. I talked with the abbot; I talked with old Ichijun, too. And I talked with Musui-kun and Warai-kun, as well. *And* I talked with the owner of the *oden* shop and the old man at the chophouse, too . . . Talk about the black market, talk about the violations of drinking establishments and chophouses, talk about heavy drinkers, and on and on.

- Sake is delicious. Truly delicious. Too delicious.
- Giving money to a cat[22] demonstrates the foolishness of the person who gave the money more than the ignorance of the cat to which it was given.

September 24
Rain – a gentle autumn rain.

Got out of bed about three o'clock. I drank and ate what was left over from yesterday.

Yesterday I received some dumplings from the temple, and I was able to buy some myself, so that it has somehow come to seem like Equinox Week.

It is certainly "autumn," and most certainly "purely so." Through and through. Through and through.

First, I've got to pigeonhole the money I borrowed. And for that reason, I'd better be cautious with sake. Even if abstaining from sake altogether is impossible, moderation in drinking it *is* possible.

I should sweep away my slovenly nature and my mood of despair. I should absolutely put these things into action.

Let me record the money I paid back and the shopping I did yesterday:

2 yen	returned to the abbot	2.40 yen	bill for the newspaper
42 sen	bill for udon noodles at Musui	2 yen	rice bill
80 sen	tobacco	2.40 yen	sake bill
10 sen	*hijiki* seaweed	8 sen	incense
10 sen	soap	8 sen	ginger
15 sen	matches	52 sen	pressed barley
20 sen	mochi rice cake	40 sen	flaked bonito
20 sen	bread	15 sen	miso
24 sen	soy sauce		

Curiously enough, my insides don't feel well. Time is naturally catching up with me, I suppose.

This morning I felt a slight chill even with a lined kimono, so I put a sleeveless coat on top of it.

I write three letters. To Hoko-kun, to the Hiiragi-ya shop, to Manchuria—sad letters, shameful letters.

I call unannounced on the abbot and talk about a number of things. It's a lonely day, and I can't stand to be by myself, so . . .

First, I strictly prohibit myself from drinking shochu. Shochu doesn't taste good. You only get drunk. It's damaging both psychologically and physically. Shochu is truly a demon for me.

I have no umbrella, so I borrow one from the temple, go to the post office, and then knock down a cup of sake. Then once again to the post box, then once again noisily knock down another cup of sake. Donguri's cute little son was nice enough to carry over some chestnut rice for me on his bicycle. I ate it immediately. Gratitude, gratitude.

Two bunches of white chestnuts for six sen; I quickly washed and soaked them.

The owner of the K-Shop came to my hut, and I owed him an apology. Leaving the seeds of future trouble with my heavy drinking.

Today I had pure Japanese rice. Yesterday I had pure Chinese rice. And tomorrow . . .

Koshun-kun came to visit this evening. He apparently came to ask me to say a prayer so that his older brother's drinking habit might be straightened out. For me to say a prayer to stop someone's drinking is ironic. I suspect even the abbot would get a smile out of that.

At some point it cleared up and the sky was filled with stars.

Tonight again I slept without the mosquito netting. I slept completely stretched out.

October 1
Cloudy – from time to time a little rain.
Asian Development Public Service Day. National Census Day. The first day of coordinated air defense drills. September 1 by the old lunar calendar.

I get up early and go to pray at the shrine for the war dead. Self-control, self-discipline.

I put the things around me in order so that death can come at any time, calm myself, and read quietly.

At some point I seem to have caught a cold, and am troubled by a dripping nose and coughing.

One year ago today. I'll never forget crossing over the Inland Sea to Matsuyama, and meeting old Ichijun for the first time. How could I ever forget? Already one year has passed. It was a *flurried* rather than a fast passage of time.

I don't leave the hermitage; I meet with no one; I don't spend a single penny; I devote myself to indoor confinement. I go to bed early because of the feeling my cold gives me. Sleep placidly all through the night.

October 2
Cloudy.

A shrike cries sharply. Somehow it looks like it's going to clear up. I got up early, but my head feels heavy, my chest hurts, and I have no appetite. I'm just sitting vacantly. Rather than what you might expect, for myself, I admire the nature of the illness. In all things, there is nothing that is not good for me.

I went out for a moment to the post box and, on the way back, I knocked down my usual, customary cup of sake at the sake shop. Then two cups, then three, and finally, borrowing the money for the bill from old Ichijun's wife, had yet another. I suddenly had the desire to see S-kun and, once again borrowing enough money from Ichijun's wife for the train fare, flew off to Imabari.

I made a phone call, and S-kun kindly juggled his job responsibilities and came to see me. He treated me to a meal and we drank quite a bit. There were friendly feelings at the restaurant in the F-Inn, but because of the air-raid drills, you know, everyone was busy, and no one could settle down to enjoy themselves. So, saying we'd meet again on another day, we went our separate ways on the ten o'clock train, S-kun going one way, and I, the other. It was so dark on the way home that all I could do was to step into the gloom and follow a frazzled path back. Once again, I was made to feel disgust at the wretchedness of alcoholism.

I thank you, S-san, I truly thank you. Not just for the pocket money I received from you, but for the souvenir you gave me.

It was close to two o'clock when I returned to my hermitage. By the time I tidied things up, ate some mochi rice cake, and got into bed, it must have been around four.

That mochi . . .

Tonight, a dog just came out of nowhere, carrying a large piece of mochi in its mouth. I meekly received the mochi from the dog and had my meal. Thank you, Lord Bow-Wow. Lord White Bow-Wow.

I offered what was left to a cat that had also come out of nowhere. Charity from the first to the last! Receiving it from a dog!

> Mochi from the mochi shop.
> Diameter about 5 inches [12 cm]
> The color, slightly black,
> A little missing.

October 3
Rain, then cloudy.

Slept late, rather tired. Feel like I still have a cold. When I think about my meeting with S-san yesterday, there is both pleasure and embarrassment. Humiliation and shame. Gratitude, gratitude.

I return money to the abbot, pay the rice bill, repay some money to old Ichijun's wife, and buy some barley. Then I gulp down two or three cups. I got perfectly drunk, but not dead drunk. I went to bed in the early hours of the evening, but did not put out the lights sufficiently for the blackout, and was scolded by the youthful inspector.

Concerning the character of haiku:

- Symbolism of impression—eternality of the moment— the totality and the individual.
- Crystallization—simplification without constriction.
- Purification of body and mind—transparently clear.
- Kernel, focus, centripedal.

I think my misfortune comes from my being too robust.

October 4
Japanese clarity. Weather that leaves nothing to be desired.

Got out of bed before light. Air-raid warnings have sounded since early this morning. Somehow, I can't calm down. All morning I stay inside and read. In the afternoon, I go to the hot springs at Dogo for the first time in a long while. I cut my hair, shed off the dirt, and feel great. I always go by the creed, "One bath, one cup of sake," but today I only take the "one bath" and defer the "one cup."

The pre-festival scenery is everywhere. Children walking around noisily. The festival in this area will be on the sixth and seventh of this month.

The festival may be a festival, but it's not a festival for me. *My* festivals are the days when I have some pocket money and feel good. On a festival day, the poverty of my table only increases.

Matsutake mushrooms have gotten cheaper. Still, they haven't appeared in profusion.

The inferior ones are forty sen; the superior ones, eighty.

Wouldn't I like some fried matsutake mushrooms and a cup of sake!

In the evening I took a walk and had both keen and somehow bleak feelings. At the Donguri Hermitage, the master was not at home. When I returned home, the rice I had cooked had been eaten by a stray cat.

At night, the air-raid drills ceased, so I was happy to be settled down, but it was warm and a swarm of mosquitoes came in on the attack, and I got the worst of it. Old Ichijun came to visit and, again, I'm grateful. I am grateful—we talked back and forth about haiku until late.

We went out together as far as the shrine for the war dead. The water in the river was gurgling just a little.

As it grew late, the temperature somehow cooled off. The mosquitoes subsided and, alone, I quietly calmed down and was able to read and write.

The evening deepens;
on a hidden tree,
the light of its leaves.

更けて
ひそかなる木の
葉のひかり

October 6
Clear, then cloudy.

The abbot came over specifically with kind words, telling me that if I did not have enough pocket money he had put together a little, so I could borrow some without hesitation. Ah, a warm heart. How kind and gracious. I never plan on taking advantage of people, but I suppose I'll make my request and apologize once again. Ah, ah.

This morning I ate what hadn't been eaten by the cat. Together, with the incident of the dog the other night, I think I should write down a chapter of a literary miscellany called, "A Series of Friends in Hiroshima." I remember one that old Ichijun once wrote, called "The Death of Donko." So no matter what they'd give me for the manuscript, I'd give a treat to Lord Bow-Wow and Lady Meow. I *am* going to treat them, and, of course, I'll have a drink, too.

Dragonflies fly in for just a moment. They fly all around me. Fly while you can. Before long you'll probably fly no more.

Translator's Notes
1. *Taizanboku* (泰山木): *magnolia garndifolia L.*
2. A play on words. Each of the nicknames passed around by the three friends contains the sound *don*, which, if written 鈍, can mean "foolish." *Donko* is a freshwater eel; *donguri*, an acorn. The exception is *tonbo*, which means "dragonfly," but as Abbot Donko points out, there is no real difference: in the Japanese syllabary *to* is written と and *do* is written ど. Although Santoka was an ordained priest, the use of "Abbot" is just a joke.

3. This would be the movie *Miyamoto Musashi*, that came out that year. The director was Hiroshi Inagaki; the character Musashi was played by the great Chiezo Kataoka; and the film was based on the novel of the same name, written by Eiji Yoshikawa.

4. Teikakotsu Murase.

5. *Hirugao* (昼顔): *calystegia japonica*. An evening glory; usually pink.

6. *Mumonkan*, Case 7: A monk said to Chao-chou, "I have entered this monastery. I beg for you instructions." Chao-chou asked, "Have you eaten your gruel?" The monk replied, "I have." Chao-chou said, "Go wash your bowl." The monk gained a deep insight.

7. Dogen Zenji (1200–1253). Brought the Soto school of Zen to Japan from China. Considered to be one of Japan's greatest religious personalities.

8. Chao-chou, (778–897). One one of the greatest Zen (Ch'an) masters of China. There are a number of koans concerning him.

9. 竹桃. Perhaps a kind of peach.

10. Perhaps a reference to the punning in the diary entry for August 5.

11. Written in the katakana syllabary, so could mean either "dried sea cucumber" or "dried sardines."

12. The *Mumonkan*, Case 12. Every day, Abbot Zuigan (Chinese: Jui-yen; referred to here by Santoka as "Master Gan") would call to himself, "Master!" Then he would answer himself, "Yes!" Then he would say, "Wake up, wake up!" At other times he'd say, "Don't be taken in by others," and then respond, "Right! Right!"

13. *Urabon*. This is a play on words. *Ura* could be taken to mean the reverse or wrong side; *bon* to mean tray. In other words, the side of the tray with nothing on it. The original Sanskrit of this word is *avalambana*, which means "to hand upside down." This was a sort of self-inflicted torture to save the dead from the true tortures of Hell. Either way, Santoka's point is well understood.

14. Case 10: A monk, Seizei by name, said to Sozan, "I am a poor destitute monk. I beg you to bestow upon me the alms of salvation." Sozan said, "Master Seizei!" "Yes, sir" replied Seizei. Sozan said, "Someone has drunk three bowls of wine of Haku of Seigen, but asserts that he has not yet moistened his lips." (Translation by R.H. Blyth)

15. 俳句研究.

16. In Japanese, *suzumushi* (鈴虫). *Homoeogryllus japonicas*.

17. Basho's famous travel journal.

18. In Japanese, *nadeshiko*. *Dianthus superbus longicalycinus*.

19. This is a play on words. *Higan* (彼岸) means both the equinox, or autumnal equinox week in this case, and "the Other Shore," or Nirvana. It

can also simply mean "the goal," and it is likely that Santoka had all three meanings in mind here.

20. The suffix "kun" is often used as a familiar form of address between male friends.

21. Case 11: Chao-chou went to a hermit's hut and asked, "Anything here? Anything here?" The hermit lifted up his fist. Chao-chou said, "The water's too shallow for anchorage here," and off he went. Again, he came to the hermit's hut and said, "Anything here? Anything here?" The hermit again lifted up his fist. Chao-chou said, "Freely you give, freely you take away. Freely you kill, freely you give life," and made a deep bow.

Case 12: See note 12 on the facing page.

22. *Neko ni koban*: pearls before swine.

Afterword
by William Scott Wilson

Except for the island of Hokkaido in the far north, Santoka walked the length and breadth of Japan, and his feet probably saw more miles than those of other famous wandering poets such as Saigyo, Basho or Ryokan. With his two small rattan suitcases slung over his chest and back, his begging bowl, straw sandals and bamboo hat, he trudged doggedly through the heat of the summer and snowy mountain passes in the winter. The eleven large volumes that make up his collected works contain, in large part, his journals, letters and poetry written while on the road. Although he did have a few "hermitages" provided for him by his friends and disciples, these were mostly *pieds à terre* where he could rest or return to after more of his "aimless wanderings."

The following are some short sketches of a few of the places where he lived or traveled. Santoka wrote that "haiku is the art of one's state of mind," and his verses reflect each and every step along his way. We start with the place that altered his own state of mind, and set him out on the road for the rest of his life.

Kumamoto.
Only a few minutes after Santoka engaged himself in a near-fatal standoff with an onrushing trolley car in December 1924, a certain Mr. Tokuji Koba gently whisks him through the growing crowd to a small temple not far from Kumamoto Castle. Here, Santoka shares in the upkeep of the temple grounds, practices Zen meditation, chants the sutras, goes out on begging rounds, and generally cleans up his life.

The Ho'onji temple today is in rather sad shape, having suffered extensive damage in the Kumamoto earthquakes in April of 2016. It is a rainy day, and from under my umbrella I can see that the entire inside of the main temple has been gutted down to the ground, and that men are at work with wheelbarrows, stones and concrete, repairing, I suppose, the main foundation. In the cemetery outside, large stone grave markers remain overturned, some in piles, although a number of new, expensive-looking family memorials have been erected here and there. One or two statues of the bodhisattva Jizo and of the "brightness king" divinity Aizen Myo-o have also been placed upright, and in a corner of the yard is a small stone memorial statue of a puppy dog. What has not tumbled over, however, or perhaps was quickly put back up again, is a large, roughly carved stone monument erected in 1942, engraved with Santoka's verse:

> *Today, too, my begging bowl,*
> *flowers in full bloom,*
> *here and there.*

The monument is about ten feet (three meters) high, and stands between the temple gate and the main hall, off to the right. Close by is a tall crepe myrtle with a few remaining pink flowers. Nearer the main hall, whether planted there on purpose or not, is a *fuyou*, a kind of Japanese hibiscus, said to be pale in the morning and red in the evening, not unlike Santoka's face after a day's drinking. This is an urban area, and it is easy to imagine that Santoka may have slipped into a sake bar or two while collecting alms.

This morning there is no evidence of a resident priest and, in the rain, the predominant feeling is one of gray melancholy. But it is here that, the following year, Santoka makes a commitment to Zen Buddhism, has his head shaved by the temple's abbot, and formally enters the priesthood.

In March of 1925, Santoka is made the resident priest at a small temple, the Mitori Kannon, on the outskirts of Kumamoto. Here, he ministers to the local farmers, begs at nearby villages, writes letters and postcards for his uneducated parishioners and establishes a Sunday school and night school that provides the boys and girls of the village with religious education. The temple is up a steep walk and somewhat lonely, and Santoka sometimes walks down the slope at night for a drink.

Today I take the forty-five minute ride out of Kumamoto to the Mitori-mae bus stop, and start up the hill to this small temple. Not too many steps up is a large statue of Santoka in his priestly robes, a broad bamboo hat and staff in hand. Behind him is another large stone monument with his poem:

> *The lowered branches*
> *of the pines,*
> *Namu Kanzeon.*

The low pine branches, now trimmed back, seem to be in prayer, and Santoka follows their example.

Continuing up the old and mossy stone steps, I arrive at the priest's residence, now expanded by quite a bit since Santoka's time. A large stone statue of a wandering priest stands above the house, as ginkgo nuts fall on a tin roof with the sound of gunshots. As it happens, the resident priest is just on his way to town, and we stand and chat for a while. Like many Zen priests, he seems to be a happy man and he chats a bit about the old days. I am disappointed that he won't let me take his photo—he's in layman's garb and says it wouldn't be proper—but he wishes me well, and then drives down the slope for that day's supplies.

I resume climbing the steps up to the temple, which are marked here and there by statues of the bodhisattva Kannon in differing poses and garb. There are some thirty-three of these statues going up the steps and then around the temple at the top, each denoting a different aspect, I suppose, of the bodhisattva. At the peak of the mountain—really a steep hill—is a small, rather unremarkable temple, surrounded by tiny-leaf maples, which, the priest has assured me, are spectacular in the fall. Yellow butterflies flit back and forth here and there in the silence far above the traffic below.

This is the temple where Santoka stays for just a little over a year, ringing the large bell mornings and evenings, and conducting Buddhist services during the equinox weeks and at other seasonal celebrations.

He feels like a fraud. He feels terrible when old folks climb the long steps asking him to pray for a sick child and bringing him rice and vegetables as gifts. When he recites the Kannon Sutra, he reflects that a person of his low caliber has no business doing such a holy thing, and that the results of his recitation will likely be nil. And he is lonely for his friends in haiku. Thus, on April 10, 1926, despite the protests of the villagers, he "shoulders his doubts and leaves on a journey of wandering mendicancy." Now he is free of wife and child, free from taking care of a local temple and its parishioners, and free from anything other than keeping body and soul together. Thus begins his nearly fifteen years of walking, and dedicating himself to becoming nothing other than who he is. He will eventually walk the entire islands of Shikoku and Kyushu, as far north as Hiraizumi on the main island of Honshu, and down through the Kiso Mountains in central Japan.

There are no other visitors to the temple today, the view of the distant surrounding fields is clear and cloudless, and the silence is only broken by the continuing sound of the ginkgo nuts falling on the tin roof below. Like Santoka, I've had enough and walk down the long steps to the main street just in time to catch the bus back into town.

Takeo, Saga Prefecture

The car winds slowly up the mountain, zigzagging through the many switchbacks, until the narrow dirt road finally runs out. I get out, it's summer now—the hottest on record—and just as slowly climb the ancient mossy stone steps, passing by the ancient mossy abutments, up to the Fukusenji temple. The mountain is silent except for the cicadas and Japanese nightingales singing their praise of the

Lotus Sutra: *Hoo-hoke-kyo*! A deep green dominates everything but the gray stone steps.

The Fukusenji is said to have been established 1,140 years ago by the monk Kukai as a Shingon sect temple, and then rededicated in 1260 as a Zen temple, which it remains today. Although it is winter, this is the southwestern island of Kyushu, and, in January 1932, Santoka writes,

> *Today, no doubt, it will be warm and beautiful all day. My plan was to start out early, but with one thing and another, I was delayed, and it was already after eight. I walked two and a half miles [four kilometers] to Taku, begged for an hour, then walked another few miles to Kitagata, then begged another hour, then hurried on to Nishi'e. Today is the day I had an appointment to meet the priest Gesshu for the first time. I had never met him, nor did I know the name of the temple. Asking the people of the area, however, I sought out the families that supported the temple, was told where the road was, and it was already close to five in the evening when I was able to relax in the hall of this mountain temple. I had traveled about ten miles, gave a great cry going up the ninety-four rough-stone steps; gave another at the temple guardian statues—they had been carved over a thousand years ago, it seemed—and a third cry at the maple pillars in the earthen-floored room. I was then warmly greeted by the priest, who completely embraced me. At one look it was like we had known each other forever, and on meeting, we quickly fell into conversation on this and that, both trivial and otherwise . . . it was very much the Zen temple, and he was very much the Rinzai sect priest.*
>
> *Without reserve, I drank, then slept, snoring away.*

The following morning, Santoka drinks a bit of sake, and with that encouragement, crosses the mountain, his breathing lively, and "feels the mountain spirit deeply."

In Santoka's time, the roof of the temple was thatched, but it is now tiled. The main hall is spacious and, although the screen doors have all been opened, is relatively dark inside. The priest—a short stocky man of about fifty years old—kindly comes out to greet me. His head has been shaved but sports about a three-day growth, and he wears a gray informal outfit. After telling me that it was his grandfather who had met Santoka, and speaking a few words about the temple, he invites me to light a stick of incense and to pray for Santoka's soul. This I do, and upon arising, thank the priest for his time in the middle of the day, and see him off to his residence.

The mountain—Mount Iimori—is still quite silent, except for the aforementioned cicadas and nightingales. When Santoka was here, he noted that there were dogs, chickens and cats in the grounds, but none can been seen today. From one vantage point, the view of the valley stretches away. Santoka writes that he is able to see as far away as the sea, but today a mist covers the horizon. Close by the priest's residence is a stone monument inscribed with the poet's verse:

> *Only*
> > *chirped at*
> > *by the crickets.*

On my way down the stone steps to the waiting car, I note a number of empty cicada shells still clinging to the slender branches of the trees.

Kiso, Nagano Prefecture

In May 1939, Santoka walks down the Gonbei Pass to the old village of Narai. A prosperous post town during the Edo period with thirty-three inns to accommodate the many travelers walking the Kiso Road, it is now a "desolate place," according to his journal, with muddy streets, a thin dark wind, but blossoming cherry trees. In former times, Narai had been famous for its *goroku kushi*, beautiful wooden combs bought for ladies waiting at home, but styles had changed and the business had all but collapsed. Transportation patterns had also changed and modernized, and few people walked the Kiso Road as they had for centuries before.

Santoka searches out an inn, one likely none too fancy. The room is dark and cold, and he rejoices when a brazier is brought in and the charcoal lit. Later, he finds a hot spring behind the inn, and happily washes away the day's dust and grime. On the way back, he stops at a sake shop, and is kindly given a plate of winter vegetables as a side dish. "I drank too much tonight," he writes later on, "but was able to sleep well." Travelers are so rare here now, that the proprietor of the sake shop guesses that he is staying over.

> *The stream flows of itself*
> *to the village. I, too,*
> *step through young leaves.*

> *Falling down for a nap*
> *the sky of Shinano*
> *so deep.*

Now, in the twenty-first century, Narai is a very different place. With the awareness that much of traditional Japan was being lost to modernization, the national government began to offer funds for the preservation of a few villages that retained some of the style of former times. Narai was one of the recipients of such governmental largesse, and is now a destination for both Japanese and foreign tourists who would like to get a glimpse of the "real Japan." Although there are far fewer than the thirty-three inns that existed there during the Kiso Road's heyday, there are a still a number of inns, some established hundreds of years ago, with Edo-style architecture and traditional country fare. The one street—the old Kiso Road—is once again lined with shops selling souvenirs and bites to eat, just as it was in the seventeenth, eighteenth and nineteenth centuries. This is a thriving town, but has no sense of something artificially created.

The inn where Santoka puts up that night no longer takes in guests for room and board, but has become a sort of coffee and souvenir shop, remaining in the tradition of serving travelers passing through. An elderly woman minding a small shop that sells woodblock-print postcards enthusiastically accompanies me there,

informing the proprietress that I was hoping to find the poet's lodging place. A two-story wooden edifice of no great proportions, the Marukichi-ya still retains the Edo-period style of open slatted doors across the front and a small balcony bordering the second floor. The rooms upstairs are also open to the street, but are closed by the typical sliding paper doors at night. There is nothing that greatly distinguishes this shop from others on the street, and nothing other than a framed piece of the poet's calligraphy hanging on an inside wall would have indicated that this is the place I have traveled so far to see. There are no customers at the moment, so the proprietress, a woman of about fifty, takes me up a narrow dark wooden stairway to the room where Santoka had likely stayed, and leaves me alone. A few flowers have been placed in a unglazed earthen vase in the corner, but otherwise there are only the straw tatami mats that make up the floor. The room is quiet and still, but has no feeling of loneliness. Looking down on the street at the travelers passing by and warmed by his brazier and his cup of sake, Santoka must have felt some satisfaction at his day's walk and having a good place to rest. After a while, he takes out his pen, writes a number of verses, and goes to sleep. I go downstairs and leave him in peace.

The following day is cloudy and rainy. Santoka moves around slowly, lingers by the brazier, knocks down a cup of sake, but is up

and about by eight o'clock. He walks the fifty yards or so out of the village, noting the bad repair of the old Kiso Road, and starts up the Torii Pass. This is a steep path up over the mountains on the southern border of Narai, punctuated by streams and small trickles of water. As I pass one of these tiny streamlets, almost too small to cup your hands in, I notice that someone has left a small ceramic container for just that purpose. The water is cool and refreshing, and must have helped travelers on their way for many years. The path itself is now composed of dirt or gravel, now of large stones laid down in the seventeenth century to aid the steps of men, horses and other animals of burden. Here and there are scattered the empty husks of horse chestnuts, the edible parts already gleaned by the bears and wild boars that still inhabit the mountains here. Santoka writes:

> *On this road,*
> *how many years?*
> *Huge horse chestnuts blooming.*

> *The sound of flowing currents*
> *falling together here;*
> *wild cherries.*

At the top of the pass there is an old shrine dedicated to the god of Mount Ontake for providing victory in a battle, and a place to view and pray to the mountain for those believers in Ontake-kyo, a sect that combines ancient mountain worship, esoteric Buddhism and the native Shinto religion. Santoka loves this place and writes that "today's path was the best of this journey."

Descending the pass, Santoka reaches the next village of Yabuhara in late morning, knocks down another cup of sake, and continues on. He passes currents of water, monuments to the water god, rare plum blossoms, and clear views of the Komagatake mountain range. I also stop in Yabuhara for a bowl of noodles, and "knock down" a cup of fine sake in fellowship with the poet.

Santoka arrives at the town of Kiso-Fukushima in the evening, and finds a room at the S-ya, a merchant's inn on the bank of the Kiso River. On my own trip, I arrive a bit earlier and, with some research, find that the only S-ya in Kiso Fukushima in 1939 was the Sarashina-ya, the inn where I take lodging every time I'm in the Kiso area. It is currently operated by a friendly and engaging proprietress, as it was in Santoka's time. After dinner, he settles down with a cup of sake, and composes a few more haiku.

> *Lingering for a moment;*
> *the sound of water*
> *without end.*

> *The road where no one*
> *goes, crows*
> *cawing.*

> *The road in bad repair*
> *just as it is;*
> *I totter along.*

> *Deep in the mountains;*
> *little birds,*
> *different songs.*

> *Waters of the Kiso*
> *going south; me, too,*
> *going south.*

In my own room, possibly the same one where Santoka had stayed, and which he described as "excellent," I fall asleep to the sound of the Kiso River rushing by. In the early morning, I look out my window and see the same small birds Santoka heard—Japanese wagtails—chirping and playing along the banks of the river. I have come far in search of this poet, and seem to have discovered him in the same mountain passes, waters, birds, and happy lodgings he found nearly eighty years ago.

After his night at the S-ya, Santoka writes in his journal:

> *Somehow, body and mind are not in harmony; it's raining, so I wanted to stay over and rest, but my pocket book does not agree, so I start off after eight in the morning. I open my umbrella and start to walk. While walking, body and mind seem lighter. For me, walking is a kind of medicine.*

Now he is off, continuing his journey to the southwest, and soon to Matsuyama, where his walking will come to an end.

Matsuyama.

> *Suddenly,*
> *off to Shikoku;*
> *clearing up.*

By the middle of September 1939, Santoka is out of money, and so begins fasting. He tries to sell his raggedy *haori* jacket at a hockshop, but is turned down because of its ratty condition, and in desperation, goes back to his temporary hermitage, drinks water, considers his shameless way of living, and reads.

If there is nothing to eat,
the calm,
cool water.

Suddenly receiving a bit of money from his ex-wife, Sakino, he decides on a road trip, and, watching the evening clouds drifting in the wind, concludes, "It's enough for Santoka to be Santoka; for Santoka to survive as Santoka. That is the True Way."

Five days after receiving the gift from Sakino, Santoka takes a boat from Hiroshima to Shikoku, and spends the months of October and November visiting various temples, visits the grave of Hosai Ozaki in Azukishima, and often stays with friends. Finally, possibly out of desperation, his friends and the abbot of the Miyukidera temple get together and remodel a shed on the temple grounds into a hut which Santoka may use for a hermitage, and which he names the Isso-an. He is delighted.

From this new base, Santoka now takes more trips to visit friends, drops in at the local hot springs, and is able to have poetry readings at his own place.

He also increasingly drinks to excess, once helped home by the local police, another time collapsing in front of a school dormitory.

Finally, on October 10, 1940, he receives a bottle of sacred wine in the morning and becomes happily drunk before noon. Going around to his friends' homes, he announces a poetry reading for the evening, returns to the Isso-an and passes out. Although his friends show up for the reading, he is asleep and snoring loudly. His snoring does not last through the night, however, and Santoka is found dead the following morning, the autopsy declaring heart failure.

Santoka had often expressed his wish to find a place to die, and hoped to pass away quickly so as not to be a bother to his friends. He found such a place and such a time at the Isso-an.

　　　　　　　　　　＞ㅜㄷㄷ　ㄷㄷㅜ＜

The Isso-an, or One-Grass Hut, is a small edifice, made up of a six-tatami-mat room, a two-tatami-mat room, and a small kitchen.

It has, since Santoka's time, been restored, the two-mat room now has a wooden floor, and the kitchen, which likely had a dirt floor at first, has a solid wood floor as well. A tokonoma, or alcove for a scroll or flowers is in the six-mat room. Santoka noted:

> For water, there is a pump sixty feet [eighteen meters] out front, and the water quality is not bad. Firewood I can take freely from the mountain behind. Because the hermitage faces east northeast, the sunrise shines directly into it (although now it inclines a little to the right), and it is perfect for viewing the moon.

Outside the hermitage, there is a single persimmon tree, and on the grounds are three roughly carved stone monuments, each engraved with one of Santoka's verses. The one closest to this little building reads:

Into my begging bowl,
too,
hail.

The morning after Santoka passed away, his disciples and friends cleaned his body, shaved his beard and buried the hair beneath this monument. A few yards away stands another stele that reads:

The spring wind,
one single
begging bowl.

The poem is said to reflect the Zen saying:

> Without one thing, I have unlimited possessions

a phrase Santoka kept close to his heart during his wandering years, and here at the Isso-an.

This morning I am sitting in the six-mat room with Ms Nanae Tamura, the woman who has guided me here, Mr. Yasuhiro Ota, an official of the local Santoka Club, and Mr. Terufusa Fujioka, who met Santoka when he was a child and who retains clear memories of the poet. We will soon be joined by Mr. Tsurugi Takata, a reporter for the regional newspaper. It is an early fall day with clear skies, and although there is a university and houses nearby, the temple grounds, which include the Isso-an, are quiet. We chat for several hours about Santoka, and the various and sometimes conflicting versions of his life. It is a happy and animated conversation, one, no doubt, the old poet would have enjoyed, and into which he would have inserted his own many stories, and somehow managed a cup of sake or two. Who was Santoka, we wonder, and how was he able to write so prodigiously in spite of his hard traveling and sake-bibbling? Oyama's *Haijin Santoka no shogai* (Life of the Haiku Poet Santoka), is, I believe, at least a hint towards an answer to that question.

This is the end of my journey, tracking down just a few of the places important to this man who has fascinated me for years. I light one stick of incense before his mortuary tablet in the tokonoma, bow and pray for his spiritual awakening, and watch as the smoke drifts out through the sliding paper doors, over the wildflowers in the yard, and up towards the open empty sky.

Letting it go, my hands are full.

—Santoka

Bibliography

Works in Japanese

Fujioka, Terufusa. *Hitomoyou*. Matsuyama: Asahi Shimbun shuppan saabisu.

Fukumoto, Ichiro, ed. *Seigetsu kushu*. Tokyo: Iwanami shoten, 2012.

Ikeuchi, Osamu, ed. *Ozaki Hosai kushu*. Tokyo: Iwanami shoten, 2010.

Iriya, Yoshitaka, et alia, eds. *Hekiganroku*, 3 vols. Tokyo: Iwanami shoten, 1992.

Ishi, Kanda. *Santoka*. Tokyo: Bungei shunshu, 1995.

Kurita, Yasushi, ed. *Hekigodo haikushu*. Tokyo: Iwanami shoten, 2011.

Kushidana, Sosoku, ed. *Sawaki Kodo Roshi no kotoba*. Tokyo: Daiho rinkaku, 2009.

Murakami, Mamoru. *Santoka: hyohaku no shogai*. Tokyo: Shun'yodo shoten, 2007.

Murakami, Mamoru. *Santoka: Meishu, kansho*. Tokyo: Shun'yodo shoten, 2018.

Nishimura, Eshin, trans. *Mumonkan*. Tokyo: Iwanami shoten, 2008.

Ogiwara Seisensui. *Seisensui kushu (shinsen)*. Tokyo: Shinchosha, 1943.

Ogiwara, Seisensui; Ito, Kano. *Santoka wo kataru*. Tokyo: Chobunsha, 1998.

Ohashi, Tsuyoshi. *Shogen fukyo no haijin Taneda Santoka*. Tokyo: Horupu Shuppan, 1993.

Oyama, Sumita, ed. *Santoka chosakushu*. 4 vols. Tokyo: Chobunsha, 1971.

Oyama, Sumita. *Haijin Santoka no shogai*. Tokyo: Yayoi shobo, 1984.

Oyama, Sumita. *Nihon no aji*. Tokyo: Kobun shobo, 1944.

Sawaki, Kodo. *Zendan*. Tokyo: Daiho rinkaku, 1997.

Sueyama, Gen. *Genshoku hakubutsu hyakka zukan*. Tokyo: Shuei-sha, 1965.

Taneda, Santoka. *Furaikyo nikki*. Tokyo: Shun'yodo shoten, 1980.

Taneda Santoka. *Santoka: Isso-an nikki/zuihitsu*. Tokyo: Shun'yodo shoten, 2011.

Taneda, Santoka. *Santoka zuihitsushu*. Tokyo: Kodansha, 2002.

Wada, Kinnosuke. *Santoka zenshu*. 11 vols. Tokyo: Shunyodo shoten, 1987.

Watanabe, Hiroshi. *Santoka no shiroi michi*. Tokyo: Kakugawa gakugei shuppan, 2010.

Watanabe, Toshio. *Hosai to Santoka, shi wo ikiru*. Tokyo: Chikuma shoten, 2015.

Works in English

Blyth, R.H. *A History of Haiku*, Vol. 2, *From Issa up to the Present*. Tokyo: The Hokuseido Press, 1964.

Blyth, R.H. *Haiku*, Vol. 1, *Eastern Culture*. Tokyo: The Hokuseido Press, 1949.

Blyth, R.H. *Zen and Zen Classics*, Vol. 4, *Mumonkan*. Tokyo: The Hokuseido Press, 1966.

Japan National Tourist Organization. *Japan, the New Official Guide*. Tokyo: Japan Travel Bureau, Inc., 1966.

Kaneko, Anne & Richards, Betty W. *Japanese Plants*. Tokyo: Shufunotomo Co. Ltd.,1988.

Sonobe, Koichiro, ed. *A Field Guide to the Birds of Japan*. Tokyo: Kodansha International, 1982.

"Books to Span the East and West"

Tuttle Publishing was founded in 1832 in the small New England town of Rutland, Vermont [USA]. Our core values remain as strong today as they were then—to publish best-in-class books which bring people together one page at a time. In 1948, we established a publishing office in Japan—and Tuttle is now a leader in publishing English-language books about the arts, languages and cultures of Asia. The world has become a much smaller place today and Asia's economic and cultural influence has grown. Yet the need for meaningful dialogue and information about this diverse region has never been greater. Over the past seven decades, Tuttle has published thousands of books on subjects ranging from martial arts and paper crafts to language learning and literature—and our talented authors, illustrators, designers and photographers have won many prestigious awards. We welcome you to explore the wealth of information available on Asia at **www.tuttlepublishing.com**.

Published by Tuttle Publishing, an imprint of Periplus Editions (HK) Ltd.

www.tuttlepublishing.com

Original Japanese work *Haijin Santoka no Shogai* by Sumita Oyama © Masakaze Oyama.

English translation © 2021 William Scott Wilson
Illustrations © 2021 Gary Miller Haskins

Cover image *Snow from Momoyogusa: Flowers of a Hundred Generations* by Sekka Kamisaka. Public domain. Digitally enhanced by rawpixel.

Library of Congress Control Number in process.

ISBN 978-4-8053-1655-9

TUTTLE PUBLISHING® is a registered trademark of Tuttle Publishing, a division of Periplus Editions (HK) Ltd.

Distributed by:

North America, Latin America & Europe
Tuttle Publishing
364 Innovation Drive
North Clarendon
VT 05759 9436, USA
Tel: 1(802) 773 8930
Fax: 1(802) 773 6993
info@tuttlepublishing.com
www.tuttlepublishing.com

Asia Pacific
Berkeley Books Pte Ltd
3 Kallang Sector #04-01
Singapore 349278
Tel: (65) 6741-2178
Fax: (65) 6741-2179
inquiries@periplus.com.sg
www.tuttlepublishing.com

Japan
Tuttle Publishing
Yaekari Building, 3rd Floor
5-4-12 Osaki Shinagawa-ku
Tokyo 141 0032 Japan
Tel: 81 (3) 5437 0171
Fax: 81 (3) 5437 0755
sales@tuttle.co.jp
www.tuttle.co.jp

24 23 22 21   7 6 5 4 3   2107TO
Printed in Malaysia